STAYING
HUMAN
THROUGH THE
HOLOCAUST

by Peréz Mázes

STAYING
HUMAN
THROUGH THE
HOLOCAUST

UNIVERSITY OF
CALGARY
PRESS

© 2005 Teréz Mózes
Published by the University of Calgary Press
2500 University Drive NW, Calgary, Alberta, Canada T2N 1N4
www.uofcpress.com

LIBRARY AND ARCHIVES CANADA CATALOGUING IN PUBLICATION

Mózes, Teréz
    Staying human through the Holocaust / Terez Moses ; translated
and edited by Anna Hercz ... [et al.].

Translation of: Bevérzett kötáblak.
ISBN 1-55238-139-0

    1. Mózes, Teréz. 2. Holocaust, Jewish (1939-1945) —Romania—
Oradea—Personal narratives. 3. Jews—Persecutions—Romania—
Oradea. 4. Oradea (Romania)—Ethnic relations. I. Hercz, Anna
Veronica, 1947- II. Title.

DS135.R73M6713 2004   940.53'18'092   C2004-906661-7

We acknowledge the financial support of the Government of Canada
through the Book Publishing Industry Development Program
(BPIDP) for our publishing activities.

Printed and bound in Canada by AGMV Marquis
∞This book is printed on acid-free paper
Cover design, page design and typesetting by Mieka West

Contents

Acknowledgments

Many thanks to my sister Erzsi and fellow survivors who helped me remember. Thanks to Fábian Imre of the Oradea Literator Publishing House for bringing the original Hungarian version, *Beverzett Kötáblák* to the light of print.

I am greatly indebted to all those who worked on the English translation and editing of the book. Maureen Wise of England did the first draft translation free of charge. My daughter Anna verified every word. Audrey Demarsico of Carleton University's College of Humanities did most of the editing. My grandchildren Oren and Amos Hercz read and reviewed innumerable drafts. Thanks to Susan Geroe and Norbert Lempert for their support of the English editing. Thanks to Bill Serson for drafting the map.

My gratitude to director Walter Hildebrandt of the University of Calgary Press for undertaking the publication of the English version. Thanks also to John King, Scott Anderson, Peter Enman and Mieka West of the Press for their work on the book. Thanks to my husband Karcsi for his ongoing encouragement, without whose help and perseverance this book would not have been written. And finally to my daughter Anna Hercz who coordinated it all and made it happen.

Introduction

Donald L. Niewyk, Southern Methodist University

The flowering of interest in the Holocaust in recent years has been nourished by an extraordinary series of important studies of Nazi decision-making, perpetrator motivations, and bystander reactions. Today we know vastly more than we did twenty years ago about how Nazi genocide came about and how ordinary people all over German-dominated Europe were entangled in the mass murder of Jews, Gypsies, and handicapped people.[1] Indispensable to our understanding of these events are survivors' memoirs that assist us in reconstructing history from the standpoint of the victims. Their statements inform us of survival strategies in ghettos and camps and communicate the sheer psychological terror that the prisoners endured. Teréz Mózes' remarkable chronicle of the Nagyvárad (Oradea) ghetto and German slave labour camps in Latvia and Poland reconstructs the experiences of a young woman while enhancing them with the mature reflections of the experienced scholar she is today.

Teréz Mózes' autobiographical account reminds us that surviving the Holocaust depended heavily upon where one lived. German rule was not uniform throughout Europe during World War

II, and some Jewish populations experienced relatively brief German occupation or, in some cases, none at all. Mózes' hometown, Oradea (Nagyvárad in Hungarian), came under German control only in 1944. She would have to endure less than a year of victimization by the Nazis. And yet, had Oradea and its Transylvanian hinterland remained part of Romania, rather than being transferred to Hungary in 1940, she would not have been swept up in the Holocaust at all.

That is not to say that the Romania in which Mózes grew up was free from antisemitism. Like most of the new nations of southeastern Europe, Romania honed its nationalism on friction with the minorities within its borders: Jews, Hungarians, Germans, Russians, and Ukrainians. Together they made up more than one quarter of Romania's post-World War I population. The Jews, numbering 757,000 in 1930 (4.2 per cent of the population), had long been resented for their cultural differences and their over-representation in business, commerce, and the professions. The Jews of Transylvania, in northwestern Romania, were also distrusted for their associations with Hungary.

Transylvania had been part of the Hungarian lands of the old Austro-Hungarian Empire for many decades before World War I. The Hungarian ruling elite had emancipated the Jews of Transylvania, who then became willing allies in promoting the Hungarian language and culture. This won the Jews certain advantages from the Hungarians but no love from the Slavic and Romanian underclasses. In 1918 the "Golden Age" in the history of the Jews of Hungary came to an end with Austria-Hungary's defeat in the World War. Romania, which had declared war on the Central Powers, was generously rewarded with territories that included Transylvania. Although the Jews of the province then became Romanian citizens, they continued to associate themselves with the Hungarians. It was only natural that young Teréz wrote and spoke primarily in her mother tongue, Hungarian, even though she was raised in Romania.

After World War I Romanian antisemitism thrived on the old resentments combined with new fears that the minorities threatened Romanian unity. Rightwing fanatics established the radically anti-Jewish League of National Christian Defence, which found its most devoted followers among Romanian university students. In 1927 those elements chose Oradea, with its non-Romanian majority, to stage violent attacks against Jews and Hungarians. Economic unrest during the 1930s provided fuel for various Romanian fascist and antisemitic movements, the most important of which was the Iron Guard. A rival fascist group, the National Christian party, took power for a short time at the end of 1937. That regime, led by the poet Octavian Goga (the "Goga government" mentioned early in Mózes' memoir), was soon overthrown by King Carol II, who then established a monarchical dictatorship. Both Goga and the king, however, pursued anti-Jewish policies that placed limits on Jewish participation in the economy and stripped a third of the Jews of their citizenship.[2] No wonder, then, that Teréz Mózes prepared herself for life as a seamstress even though she stemmed from a solidly middle class family. Some Jews, like her elder sister Ibi, emigrated, but for others family ties were too strong. Another sister, Magda, who might have left for Cuba, could not make the break. Under the circumstances it was hardly surprising that some Romanian Jews, including Mózes' cousin Pali, turned to communism as a means of building a new society free from antisemitism. An unintended consequence of this, however, was to strengthen the association of Jews and Soviet Communism in the minds of Romanian nationalists.

Romanian antisemitism fell less harshly on the Transylvanian Jews than it did on the mostly unassimilated Jews of Bessarabia in the east of the country, where fearful massacres would occur during the Holocaust.[3] The Jews of Southern Transylvania would remain under Romanian control and experience continuing persecution, but they would survive Hitler's war. But on August 30, 1940, Northern Transylvania, including Oradea, was transferred from Romania to Hungary at Germany's insistence under the terms of the Second Vienna Award. Hungary had threatened to invade Romania for the purpose of regaining Transylvania, and Hitler, who wished to remain on good terms with both countries, arranged the partition of the province. Hungary's acquisition of Northern Transylvania would have disastrous consequences for the nearly 200,000 Jews who lived there.

Transylvanian Jews held little hope for any improvement in their conditions under Hungarian rule. In the years since 1918 indigenous Hungarian antisemitism had been intensified by a Communist revolt led by the Jewish Bolshevik Bela Kun, and Hungary's strongman, Miklós Horthy, had aligned his country with Nazi Germany in hopes of reversing the territorial losses of 1919–20. Hence Hungary had adopted laws restricting Jewish rights that, if anything, were even harsher than those in Romania, and the Jews of Northern Transylvania quickly felt their full force. Soon after Hungary joined Hitler's assault on the Soviet Union in June 1941, Jews who could not prove their Hungarian nationality were rounded up and deported to German-controlled Ukraine. After the war it was learned that eighteen thousand of them had been shot upon arrival. For Jews who were regarded as Hungarian citizens the chief impact of war was the drafting of more than one hundred thousand adult Jewish males into special labour battalions of the Hungarian Army. Before the war Jews had been subjected to the draft as regular soldiers, but now they were no longer trusted to bear arms. As members of these "labour service" battalions they were required to serve Hungarian forces fighting with the Germans in Russia by building fortifications, supplying war material, and clearing minefields. Their treatment was not uniform, but in some cases it was harsh in the extreme. Some units experienced 80 per cent casualties. And yet, most Jews who were members of these battalions were beyond the reach of the deportations that the Germans orchestrated in 1944 and hence were more likely to survive, as was true of Teréz Mózes' future husband, Károly (Karcsi) Mózes.

The Hungarians mistreated their Jews, but they were not yet prepared to cooperate in genocide. Before 1944 most Hungarian Jews were spared the mass exterminations that the Germans had begun in 1941. By 1944 most Holocaust victims were already dead; the Hungarian Jews were the largest population yet untouched. Hitler's occupation of Hungary on March 19, 1944, brought mass tragedy to Hungarian Jewry, but it was prompted by transcending military and diplomatic issues. The German dictator had learned that Hungary was secretly negotiating with the Allies to extricate itself from the war and had decided to intervene with characteristic brutality. Before that time Horthy had put off Hitler's demands to deport the Jews to Poland, preferring more "humane" ways of solving Hungary's Jewish problem. Now he felt entirely at the mercy of the Germans. Adolf Eichmann himself arrived in Budapest to coordinate the deportations of Hungarian Jews and Gypsies and was suitably impressed with the enthusiasm he encountered among pro-Nazi Hungarian officials for the liquidation of the country's minorities. By the end of the first week in July close to 440,000 Jews were deported to Auschwitz, and additional numbers died on forced marches and doing forced labour in Germany. Others were murdered by members of the Arrow Cross party, Hungary's equivalent of the Nazis. In all at least 502,000 of the 725,000 Hungarian Jews and as many as 28,000 of the 100,000 Hungarian Gypsies perished in the Holocaust. The death toll would have been higher still had Horthy not summoned up sufficient courage to suspend the deportations in July 1944. But by then most of the Jews had been deported from the Hungarian provinces, including Northern Transylvania.[4]

As was true throughout Hungary, the ghettoization and deportation of the Jews in Northern Transylvania were characterized by a high degree of cooperation between German and Hungarian officials. In April 1944, Eichmann's SS unit and the Hungarian Ministry of the Interior elaborated a master plan to concentrate, plunder, and deport the Jews, starting with those of the provinces. Budapest's Jews were to go last. Mayors, prefects, and other civil servants were instructed to take orders from dejewification squads of the Hungarian police; officials who objected either resigned or were replaced. At least 131,000 Jews then in Northern Transylvania were ghettoized between May 2 and 10, 1944. The largest provincial ghetto, holding between 20,000 and 27,000 Jews (estimates vary), was in Teréz Mózes' hometown of Nagyvárad. The city held a second ghetto, located at the edge of town, with approximately

8,000 Jews from the surrounding area. The provincial ghettos lasted only a few weeks, just long enough to expropriate the Jews' wealth and make arrangements to deport them to Poland. All the ghettos were liquidated between May 15 and June 9. Several thousand Jews managed to evade ghettoization by fleeing to Southern Transylvania, still under Romanian rule, where they survived with the aid of coreligionists there. Fifteen thousand Jewish males from Northern Transylvania were serving in Labour Battalions of the Hungarian Army on the Eastern Front and hence were not swept up in the deportations. By the middle of June only a handful of labour servicemen and other exempted Jews remained in Northern Transylvania.[5]

In many ways the sharpest passages in Mózes' memoir are those depicting the Nagyvárad ghetto.[6] It was, above all, hideously overcrowded. The town's Jews then made up nearly 25 per cent of the population, but they were packed into only a few square blocks surrounding the Orthodox synagogue. Mózes is generous in her appraisal of the ghetto's Jewish Council, led by Sándor Leitner, which performed the difficult task of organizing Jewish life while attempting to satisfy the Hungarian police and their German partners. She also shows that the Jews of the ghetto were imaginative and resourceful in adapting to conditions of starvation, sickness, and extreme brutality. Especially vivid is her description of the reign of terror imposed by police commander and ghetto boss Jenö Pétterfy, whose men efficiently and systematically expropriated the Jews' property and punished gentiles who attempted to hide valuables for them. She acknowledges the family ties that prevented her and many others from escaping across the border into Romanian-controlled Southern Transylvania. Throughout this description of ghetto life there is no hint that the Jews were conscious of the fate that was being prepared for them. Before ghettoization most had listened to broadcasts from London that contained information about German atrocities, but evidently it had not registered.[7] Ghetto inhabitants were only too ready to believe official stories about plans to relocate them in agricultural districts of Hungary away from the war zone. As a result there was little resistance in the Nagyvárad ghetto and most of the deportees arrived at Auschwitz with no idea of where they were or what was about to happen to them.

Teréz Mózes' experience of Auschwitz was brief, routine, and crucial. Unlike the majority of the twelve to fourteen thousand Hungarian Jews who arrived daily at the extermination centre, she was not gassed but selected for work. Young and strong, she was sent on to Riga, the capital of German-occupied Latvia, arriving there early in June 1944. By then the Riga ghetto had been liquidated and about twelve thousand surviving Jews of both sexes had been assembled at Kaiserwald concentration camp or one of its 465 nearby work sites and satellite camps.[8] Teréz and her sister Erzsi were put to work at the Spilve military airport near Riga and later at the German Army

Apparel Centre at Milgravis. The latter assignment was a stroke of luck since the Wehrmacht always treated slave workers better than did the SS. After about ten weeks the sisters and their coworkers were evacuated westward by sea as the Soviet Army approached Riga. The description of deliberate drowning of those prisoners who were left behind, which Mózes draws from a literary source, probably is not based on fact. The Germans would not have needed to use their overstretched air force to massacre prisoners in barges. And yet, the story contains some element of truth, for German evacuation ships carrying concentration camp prisoners and German refugees were sometimes attacked in the Baltic by Allied planes and submarines, resulting in significant loss of life.[9]

Teri and her sister Erzsi were sent to Stutthof concentration camp along with tens of thousands of other slave labourers from northeastern Poland and the Baltic states. Located at the mouth of the Vistula River about twenty miles east of the German city of Danzig (today Gdansk, Poland), Stutthof had been established in 1939 as an internment camp for Poles and became a concentration camp in 1942. When large numbers of Jews were sent there in 1944 it was greatly expanded and, unusually for a concentration camp in Germany proper, provided with small gas chambers and crematoria to eliminate those too sick to work. Additionally, overwork, malnutrition, exposure, and inadequate medical care resulted in an appalling mortality rate. Of 115,000 prisoners sent to Stutthof, 65,000 died. In the summer of 1944 there were 57,000 prisoners in the main camp and its thirty-nine subcamps. Teréz and Erzsi made it through the selection and immediately were farmed out to subcamps devoted to building tank traps and other defensive fortifications designed to slow the Soviet advance. This backbreaking work, much of it done in conditions of freezing cold, was their gravest test.[10] It was interrupted in January 1945, when a Soviet offensive sent the Germans reeling toward the Oder, taking as many of their slave workers as possible with them. Evidently the SS men guarding the sisters and their comrades panicked and left them alone to await the Russians. Unlike the far larger numbers of prisoners who completed the death marches into Germany, this group would not have to endure three more months of hell.

Growing interest in gender analysis of the Holocaust assures that every female survivor's account will be read for evidence of the particularities of women's experiences.[11] There is much in this memoir to support the view that women came together for mutual support by forming or intensifying close bonds with relatives as well as complete strangers. The sisters Teréz and Erzsi were inseparable, and when Erzsi lost hope, Teréz "forced her to live." Women who had been separated from their relatives bonded with "camp sisters." These in turn joined small groups of friends, many of them made on the

Staying Human through the Holocaust

spot, to form surrogate families in the camps and, later, on the long road home. Mózes also points out, however, that such behaviour by no means characterized all the women in her experience. The extent to which women's group cohesion enhanced chances of survival, and how it may have differed from men's experience of the Holocaust, are likely to remain subjects of debate for some time to come.

More than is true of most Holocaust memoirs, Teréz Mózes' story draws us away from comfortable stereotypes about Nazi genocide and into what another survivor, Primo Levi, has called the "gray zone" of moral ambiguity that was inhabited by perpetrators and victims alike.[12] Mózes shows that the behaviour of gentile neighbours in Nagyvárad and of German guards in the camps was by no means uniform but ranged across of broad spectrum from vicious to helpful. She also registers selfish as well as selfless behaviour among her fellow prisoners, including the theft of food, the most understandable and the least forgivable sin among starving prisoners. The same may be said of her description of the prisoner functionaries in the camps: the Kapos, prisoner doctors, clerks, block seniors, and the like who ran the camps for the Germans in return for privileges that enhanced their chances of survival. Where these administrators felt a sense of solidarity with the rank and file, they were capable of ameliorating punishments and work assignments, but always within limits set by the SS. They, too, displayed a broad range of behaviour, from the best to the worst.

The women's Soviet liberators are, for the most part, sympathetically portrayed in this account, although an instance of rape is forthrightly recorded. It is also abundantly clear, however, that in January 1945, aiding civilian refugees was not a high priority for an army still engaged in desperate struggle with the Germans. Teréz Mózes and her friends would have to secure shelter and transportation on their own. Her critical depiction of Poles as indifferent to the plight of Holocaust survivors is understandable but needs contextualization. The women had been liberated near Neumark (Nowe Miasto) in an area of northern Poland near the border with prewar German East Prussia. Between the wars its mixed German and Polish population had gotten along well enough, but when Nazi Germany annexed the region in 1939, most of the Poles had been expelled. By the time the Soviet Army arrived, most Germans had fled westward, and the Poles encountered by Mózes and her group were newly returned or else refugees themselves. Moreover, the Poles also had experienced enslavement by the Germans and massive loss of life and property; the devastation Mózes encountered in Warsaw was only the most egregious case of what happened over vast stretches of the country during World War II. Hence Poles certainly viewed themselves as no less victims of Nazi atrocities than the women in Mózes' troop, and they may also have believed that former camp prisoners were recipients of special privileges granted by the Soviet authorities.

Now to get home, with Erzsi seriously ill and the transport system in chaos. In Lublin the Red Cross, whose intervention the women had longed for in vain while in the camps, came through with critical assistance.[13] The Soviets, rather than allow the camp survivors to go directly home, held them in displaced persons' camps in the USSR for several months, probably in order to distinguish individuals who had collaborated with the Germans from authentic refugees. As was also true of displaced persons' camps erected at about the same time by the Western powers in conquered Germany, it was troubling for Holocaust survivors to be forced to rub shoulders with people who might have helped exterminate their friends and relatives.

Home was now once more named Oradea, the city having reverted to Romania at the end of the war. The two thousand survivors who returned to the city seemed untroubled by this change; the events of the last years had severed many of the old ties with things Hungarian. Impediments to starting over in what was becoming a communist dictatorship are only hinted at in this memoir. Unmistakable, however, is Mózes' determination to record her wartime experiences, at first for the edification of her family, and later for a wider audience. This must have been reinforced by her impatience with Eastern

European communist regimes that were reluctant to acknowledge the specificity of Nazi policies against the Jews. Following the downfall of communism in the early 1990s and the publication of this and other Holocaust memoirs in Hungarian and Romanian, a slow process of historical clarification has taken place that is only now beginning the bear fruit. In 2003 the President of Romania, Ion Iliescu, announced the formation of the International Commission on the Holocaust in Romania. Headed by Elie Wiesel and comprised of scholars from several countries, it is charged with studying the persecution and destruction of the Jews and Gypsies of Romania and of those under Romanian control during World War II. In 2004 Hungarian dignitaries and foreign guests dedicated a Holocaust Memorial Centre in Budapest, based around a restored synagogue that in 1944 was used as an internment camp. Hence this memoir is more than a valuable document of the Holocaust in Northern Transylvania. It has also helped to change the way history itself is viewed in Romania and Hungary.

NOTES

1   A useful overview is found in Donald Niewyk and
     Francis Nicosia, *The Columbia Guide to the Holocaust*
     (New York: Columbia University Press, 2000).

2 Ezra Mendelsohn, *The Jews of East Central Europe Between the World Wars* (Bloomington: Indiana University Press, 1983) pp. 171–210.

3 A reliable general study is Radu Ioanid, *The Holocaust in Romania* (Chicago: Dee, 2000).

4 Randolph L. Braham, *The Politics of Genocide: The Holocaust in Hungary* (New York: Columbia University Press, 1981), pp. 595–671.

5 Randolph L. Braham, *Genocide and Retribution: The Holocaust in Hungarian-Ruled Northern Transylvania* (Boston: Kluwer-Nijhoff, 1983).

6 Her account is virtually unique. One may also consult the Oradea diary of Eva Heyman, but its value is limited by the extreme youth of its author. Eva Heyman, Judah Marton, and Moshe Kohn, *The Diary of Eva Heyman* (New York: Shapolsky, 1988).

7 George K., a Jew from Szombathely, Hungary, recalled hearing reports about Auschwitz on BBC broadcasts but dismissing them as propaganda. Donald L. Niewyk (ed.), *Fresh Wounds: Early Narratives of Holocaust Survival* (Chapel Hill: University of North Carolina Press, 1998), p. 375. On the problem of obtaining and absorbing reliable information about the Holocaust at the time it was happening, see Walter Laqueur, *The Terrible Secret: Suppression of the Truth about Hitler's Final Solution* (Boston: Little, Brown, 1981).

8 Andrew Ezergailis, *The Holocaust in Latvia, 1941–1944* (Riga: The Historical Institute of Latvia, 1996), pp. 361–370.

9   Christopher Dobson, John Miller, and Ronald
    Payne, *The Cruelest Night* (Boston: Little, Brown,
    1979); Günther Schwarberg, *Angriffsziel Cap Arcona*
    (Göttingen: Steidl, 1998).

10 Cf. Trudi Birger, *A Daughter's Gift of Love: A Holocaust
    Memoir* (Philadelphia: Jewish Publication Society,
    1992).

11 On this somewhat controversial topic, see Judith
    Baumel, *Double Jeopardy: Gender and the Holocaust*
    (Portland: Valentine Mitchell, 1998); Dalia Ofer and
    Lenore Weitzman (eds.), *Women in the Holocaust* (New
    Haven: Yale University Press, 1998); and Nechama Tec,
    Resilience and Courage: Women, Men, and the Holocaust
    (New Haven: Yale University Press, 2003).

12 Primo Levi, *The Drowned and the Saved* (New York,
    Vintage, 1989).

13 A balanced assessment of the International Committee
    of the Red Cross in World War II is Jean-Claude
    Favez, *The Red Cross and the Holocaust* (Cambridge:
    Cambridge University Press, 1999).

Chronology and Place Names

Europe, Transylvania, and the surrounding region underwent tremendous political changes over the twentieth century. To help the reader navigate my journey, I used current place names throughout the book. Exceptions are the name of the concentration camps that have German names.

A simple political geographical chronology of the region is presented below as well as the names of frequently mentioned places under different masters.

Up to 1919	Hungary (all of Transylvania)
1919–1940	Romania (all of Transylvania)
1940–1944	Hungary (only Northern Transylvania)
1944– today	Romania (all of Transylvania)

Place names mentioned in Romania

Romanian name	*Hungarian name*
Oradea	Nagyvárad or Várad
Şimleul Silvaniei	Szilágysomlyó
Cluj	Kolozsvár
Sighetul Marmatiei or Sighet	Máramaros Sziget or Sziget
Baia Mare	Nagybánya
Satu Mare	Szatmár
Dej	Dézs
Arad	Arad
Marghita	Margita

Concentration camps and place names mentioned in Poland

Polish name	German name
Oswiecim	Auschwitz – Birkenau
Nowe Miesto	Neumark
Dorbek	Dörbek
Gutowo	Guttau
Stutowo	Stutthof
Gdánsk	Danzig

Staying Human through the Holocaust

LIFE BEFORE THE HOLOCAUST

*W*hen I look back and try to remember how I was in those far-off times, the picture of a holiday evening comes to mind. It is Passover night, the eve of the eight-day-long holiday when, since ancient times, Jewish people have traditionally commemorated their freedom from slavery in Egypt. For days we too had been preparing for the holiday with great excitement by cleaning house, baking, and cooking. Now, the family is together, enveloped in holiday spirit. We are all sitting around the table, covered with an immaculately white starched damask tablecloth, set according to tradition. A multitude of flickering candlelights are soaring from the shining silver candlesticks. The centrepiece, a large seder plate, is filled with a variety symbolic food, each representing aspects of the once wicked state of bondage. There is also the matzah plate with the traditional three pieces of matzah representing unleavened bread, covered by a matzah cover embroidered with golden thread. In accordance with tradition, my dear father, Ignác Klärmann, is sitting in a comfortable easy chair at the head of the table; on his sides sit respectively my mother, Miriam Szmuk, and their first-born, my brother Dezsö, whom we called Duci. Naturally, we four sisters sit there as well, by age – Ibi, Magda, Erzsi, and I, the youngest, Teri. According to tradition, my father reads aloud the Haggadah, the miraculous story of the exodus from Egypt. Although the story is repeated year after year, we are all listening in awe. It is in this holiday spirit that we arrive at the highlight of the evening.

I am fourteen. According to tradition, I would hand over the *afikoman*, a piece of matzah hidden by an adult to be found by the youngest child, only if my father granted me a wish. This ritual was meant to maintain the attention of even the youngest members of the family during the ceremony. I have not hinted what I might ask for to anyone, and now everyone turns a curious gaze on me.

"Father," I say, "please let me continue my studies at the state high school."

My brother Duci, who was ten years older than I, had gone to the Commercial Academy in Vienna. In our town Oradea, in the 1930s, there was a commercial school with very good reputation. Since my father was a leather merchant, the family had always expected that my interests would be in the same direction. For me, however, high school would be the first step to university studies. In making this request I was expressing my long-term intentions. I saw a warm and playful look dance across my father's eyes for just a second, then he quickly became serious. He gave his consent, with one condition: "You can continue your studies until your first poor marks."

He could not scare me, nor was this his real intention. I felt that with his apparent objection he only wanted to increase my joy.

Some of us children, myself included, were born in Șimleul Silvaniei, a warm, cheerful little town in the northwestern part of Romania. Favoured with splendid geographic location at the foothills of the Magura Mountains and surrounded by vineyards, the town was situated in the valley of a small river, the Crasna. Its main street, bordered on both sides by large single homes, cut straight through town, from the train station to the Zalău highway. Romanians, Hungarians, and Jews lived there. Every third or fourth family owned a few acres of land on the Magura, which provided the population with rich crops, fruits and wine. Downtown, the ruins of the medieval Báthory fortress called to mind historic eras. In the centre of town stood a baroque style Jewish synagogue, a masterpiece of art. I was ten years old when we moved to Oradea (Nagyvárad in Hungarian), a much larger city, which in the common language was called Várad.

Golden Anniversary
of my maternal
grandparents. My
parents are in the
middle of the back row.

OPPOSITE PAGE The
Great Synagogue of
the Oradea Orthodox
Jewish Community.

THIS PAGE The Zion
Synagogue of the
Oradea Neolog Jewish
Community.

The population of Oradea numbered about ninety to one hundred thousand inhabitants, in a mixed composition – Romanians, Hungarians, and around 25 to 30 per cent Jews. Situated at the eastern edge of the Hungarian border, the city enjoyed a very lively commercial life. The Jewish population visibly contributed to the city's economic and cultural progress, and to the development of its cityscape.

My father was a much-admired intelligent man with broad views, known as an extremely honest wholesaler. He purchased animal pelts in bulk throughout the entire country, then brought the merchandise to Oradea for storage in the rented merchandise warehouse, from where he distributed it to various leather-processing factories. He sold great quantities of wild animal pelts to merchants in France, Italy, England, and sometimes even America. He worked with enthusiasm, often providing employment for several relatives. We were comfortable, but not wealthy. My dear mother looked after each person of the seven-member family with a great deal of love and devotion. My brother Duci, after finishing his studies, worked for some time as a bank clerk, then with my father, trying to learn the secrets of the leather industry. Later he joined my father's business as a partner. My sisters Ibi, Magda and Erzsi, after graduating middle school, learned the piano, foreign languages, and a little sewing, to become well-rounded housewives and mothers later on. I, the youngest, aspired to an intellectual career.

Until 1918, the area where my family lived belonged to Hungary. Therefore, within our home Hungarian was spoken as the primary language. According to the educational system of those days, I went to a Jewish denominational school, graduating first from a four-year elementary school, then from a four-year middle school. Under these circumstances, I lived in a totally Jewish environment. My classmates were Jewish, and with few exceptions so were my teachers. The primary language of both classmates and teachers was Hungarian. Yet, the language of instruction within the school system was Romanian, a language we did not speak well and had difficulty understanding. However, this did not prove to be troublesome in that given environment. Later, the situation changed.

After graduating from middle school, I continued my studies at the Oltea Doamna high school, a Romanian state-run school, where I had been accepted after a difficult and highly selective entrance exam. Here they expected us to speak the language of the state flawlessly.

I found myself in a new situation at the high school, and I soon realized that I was different. When I first felt this difference, I presumed that it was due to my inability to speak the Romanian language well, being of Hungarian background. Our new classmates were friendly with us, although they never invited us to their homes. This friendliness increased when people began to discover my skill in mathematics.

They began to seek me out to ask for help. This held in check, to an extent, the feeling of inferiority that was beginning to grow in me.

It was 1934. A year had passed since Hitler had taken power. In Germany, the persecution of Jews was increasing. *The New East*, a Transylvanian Jewish journal edited in Cluj, and *Our People*, the paper of the Jews of Oradea, reported anti-Semitic occurrences as they happened. We read the news with shock, but it was as if these events were taking place on another planet rather than a few hundred kilometres away. We thought they were extremist and transitory events and considered them to be of no real consequence.

Older people reminded us of 1927, a year of fascist student demonstrations. Members of the student congress held in Oradea had broken the windows of shops owned by Jews. They had appeared suddenly in synagogues, breaking and destroying everything around them, and they had defiled the sacred scrolls of the Torah. This vandalism was followed by a few years of latent anti-Semitic activity. Later, the Iron Guard, the most extreme party of the Romanian fascists, gained strength. Articles inciting people to violence began to appear. At first, they appeared in the columns of extreme right-wing magazines such as *Sfarma-Piatra (Stone Crusher)* and *Porunca Vremii (Order of the Day)*. Worried, we spread the frightening news by word of mouth as we felt a growing danger. At the same time, however, we were relieved that our families and friends were untouched.

One day at school, I was playing with a classmate's pencil case when it suddenly popped open. To my surprise, I caught a glimpse of a swastika inside. I was shocked. Later, I saw the same emblem under that girl's lapel. The symbol already inspired terror in me. At that time she was wearing it secretly, not showing it off as she would do later on. My friends and I realized then that the danger had penetrated into our own immediate environment. We became more prudent and circumspect as we grew more vulnerable. It never entered our thoughts that we could do anything to oppose it.

At the end of sixth grade at the secondary school, I had to decide whether to continue my studies in the arts or the sciences. I chose science even though a shortage of applicants meant it was not offered at the Oltea Doamna school. My classmate Magda Lévi and I undertook the study of physics and chemistry on our own and sat the required exams. This took enormous effort, but we chose to do it. We began to prepare during the summer holidays. Another school, a convent called Notre Dame De Sion, had a small science section. Classes were taught in French and the school fees were very high. This school wanted to increase its number of science students, so it offered Magda and me a reduced registration fee. After a few weeks we accepted this offer. Later, when my father could not pay even the reduced amount, the nuns lifted the fee completely because they did not want me to leave the school.

The school was well known for its democratic nature. I did not experience any discrimination in class. Although I was behind in French compared to those who had learned it from childhood, I felt that I was respected for my knowledge of mathematics and physics.

I was in the eighth grade, which would be the equivalent of the twelfth grade in North America, when two family events occupied my attention: both of my older sisters got married. Ibi, the eldest, who was sensitive and very attached to our parents, married a young man from Budapest. Magda, the next oldest, the loveliest and most charming of us all, married an engineer from Bucharest, who was a Cuban citizen. I, who was the fifth and youngest in the family, suddenly acquired a new status. This did not alter my behaviour, though; I remained a conscientious pupil and kept my interest in school.

In 1934 a terrible event of international significance took place. The Austrian chancellor Dollfuss, who had opposed Hitler's occupation of his country, was assassinated. With his death, the path Germany had been preparing was clear. Our worst fears were realized when Germany annexed Austria in March 1938. My father was in Vienna at that very time. Nothing happened to him because he was a foreign citizen, but his business partners and friends became outcasts from one day to the next. Jews were chased out of their homes. They were forced into humiliating jobs such as scrubbing streets, and they were treated brutally. Their savings were confiscated, their properties plundered, their shop windows broken. Many Jews lost their lives. Everyone escaped who could, but the vast majority had nowhere to run, and they were dragged away to concentration camps.

This event, known as the *Anschluss*, brought the borders of Germany nearer to us and to all of eastern and southeastern Europe. Czechoslovakia was in the most immediate danger. We were very disappointed when the League of Nations made no attempt to impose sanctions on Germany. The governments of both England and France were engaged in a policy of compromise. After weak and belated protests, they accepted the annexation of Austria.

My father returned home seriously ill. For days on end, we could not get a word out of him. We were very disturbed by the events. However, we continued our everyday activities. Even today I cannot understand how we did it. Perhaps it was a survival instinct. We analyzed events from a detached perspective. In our naiveté, we repeated again and again, "That could never happen here." And so I continued preparing in earnest for my baccalaureate exam.

A geography lesson is imprinted in my memory. One of my best friends, Hédi Silbermann, was asked to talk about the route of the Danube River. In her answer, she named the six countries through which the Danube passes. She mentioned three capital cities: Budapest, Vienna, and Belgrade. The lay teacher maliciously reminded her that Austria was no longer an independent country, and that Vienna was therefore no longer a capital. Hédi's cousin was a refugee from Vienna who had arrived in Oradea only a few days earlier, after much suffering. At the teacher's reprimand, Hédi broke into tears. We could not calm her, and the order in the class was shattered. Several indignant girls reported the incident to the Mother Superior.

We had a similar reaction when the same teacher advised the Jewish girls of our class that it was a waste of time to prepare for the baccalaureate and that we would do better to choose practical professions. She tried very hard to demoralize us, and that hurt us deeply. Because of her we lost some of our self-confidence and our desire to study. We were pleased when we heard that this teacher was reprimanded. In our naiveté we thought that this would put an end to further insults. This may have been true within the school grounds, but while we continued our studies uninterrupted, the country was racing toward fascism. The first extreme right-wing government, led by Goga, came to power in 1937. Although it was deposed within forty-four days, it influenced the period that followed.

On election day, I accompanied my father to Şimleul Silvaniei, the town of my birth. In the train stations where we stopped, a great commotion was going on. People were singing and dancing. The gypsies were especially happy because they had been granted the right to vote, a right that had been taken away from the Jews. In consequence, the Jews traveling on the train were brutally beaten and thrown out of railway cars moving at full speed. Fortunately, no one recognized my father and me as Jews, but the anxiety of the moment made my father relapse into his illness and he was overcome with intense pain.

After the fall of the Goga government, we were a little relieved. I applied myself to my studies with new enthusiasm, and I took the baccalaureate exam at the end of the school year. My friend Hédi's brother Gyuri Silbermann was studying at a Belgian university, and partly through his influence I was preparing to go there to study textiles. I was attracted to the artistic side of this subject, and I also wanted to make good use of my skills in mathematics. Because of political events, I was forced to change my plans, as did many others. The situation in Czechoslovakia was becoming increasingly dangerous, and there was an imminent possibility that the mountain region of Sudatenland might be overrun. Although the Western Allies had made clear their love of compromise, the outbreak of war now looked inevitable. In such circumstances, my parents would not even consider sending me abroad. And really, there would have been no point. As the political situation deteriorated, so did my prospects of finding a job. Somehow, however, we had to plan to continue to survive.

After careful deliberation, my friend Sári Feldheim and I decided to learn dressmaking. On September 15, 1938, with the streets crowded with returning students, we took our places at the sewing machines. It pained me to change my plans in this way, but once I had made my choice I applied myself diligently to this new profession. I learned to sew in a prestigious fashion house, under an excellent dressmaker. In my spare time, I tutored math to students who were preparing for their baccalaureate exams. And I took English lessons. Every hour of the day was accounted for. This ordered way of life helped to calm the tension that had been building within me.

My calm did not last long, however. That year held another terrible blow for the Jews. Hitler and the Gestapo organized the first great "spontaneous" Jewish pogrom in Germany. On the night of November 9, the windows of thousands of synagogues were smashed. This was *Kristallnacht*, or "crystal night." During that night and the two days that followed, 267 synagogues and prayer houses were set on fire in Germany. Thousands of homes, businesses, and shops were looted. Almost a hundred people died, and a large number were wounded in those few days. Twenty-six thousand people were transported to internment camps. And then the Jews were ordered to rebuild, at their own expense, the shops and buildings that had been destroyed. Even worse, a tax of one billion marks was imposed on the Jews that remained outside the camps. It seemed that the limits of endurance had been reached. But not yet.

Following the annexation of Austria and the *Kristallnacht*, life continued its inevitable course. The division of Czechoslovakia took place. In the spring of 1939, the Germans occupied most of Czechoslovakia without meeting any opposition. On March 15, after President Hacha of the Czech state signed, under duress, that he personally called in the German forces, Hitler marched into Prague and announced in the Hradzin Castle that Czechoslovakia had ceased to exist. Shortly after, they divided Czechoslovakia.

The Czech-Moravian protectorate was created. The Slovakian state had proclaimed its own independence a day earlier. Meanwhile, the Hungarian forces advanced into the sub-Carpathian region.

Mass executions quashed the formidable resistance efforts of the Czech people, and the fate of the Jews in this area was sealed. The Germans confined the Jewish population in ghettos and internment camps. Later, with the outbreak of the Second World War, it was rumoured that Jewish girls from Czechoslovakia had been taken to brothels on the front. We were struck dumb by such news, and we did not know how much to believe. Later, however, many sources confirmed that all the rumours had been true. The Italian writer Malaparte, a war correspondent on the eastern front, has depicted the tragedy of these girls in his book *Kaput*, published after the war. Each group was kept for three months and then exterminated.

And then, in the autumn of 1939, the Germans attacked and occupied Poland in just a few days. On August 23, 1939, a non-aggression pact had been signed in Moscow between Germany and the Soviet Union. According to this pact, the eastern portion of Poland came under Soviet control, along with Finland, Latvia, Estonia, and Bessarabia. On September 1, 1939, German ground forces started their march on the full length of the Polish border. War had started without a declaration of war. A state of war was declared two days later between Great Britain and Germany, as well as between France and Germany. Poland, however, received no help at all, and the German forces overran and occupied the country within four weeks. The real war against the Polish people started only after the achievement of that quick victory. Hitler strove to decimate the Polish people and eradicate its elite leadership, thus creating opportunities for German settlement. Meanwhile, the Germans jammed hundreds of thousands of Polish Jews into ghettos. We only found out about this at the end of the war.

I remember the agitation that filled my dressmaking workshop. Events were transmitted by special announcements, and we kept the radio on at all times. Thousands of Polish refugees crossed the border to take shelter in Romania.

The machinery of war was in motion in Europe. We tried without much success to predict Romania's official position. As for our own situation, we were sure we could expect nothing good. Until then, I had cherished occasional fantasies of studying in France or Belgium, but now it became obvious that I would have to give up all of my hopes. Education was now the least of my worries.

Bad news arrived from Hungary. The first anti-Jewish laws were introduced: Jews were excluded from public life, their activities were limited, and men were conscripted to forced labour. The first anti-Jewish law appeared in 1938 when Kálmán Darányi was governor. He had promised that it would result in a "more effective civic and economic balance." First, the law limited Jewish intellectual activities. It reduced the proportion of Jews employed as doctors, lawyers, engineers, writers, journalists, and office workers in particular professional bodies to 20 per cent of the population. Once the quota was reached, all others were denied the right to practice their profession. Thousands of people lost their incomes. In 1939, the second anti-Jewish law further limited the civic and economic position occupied by Jews. From that time on, racial criteria reduced the proportion of Jewish participation in civic life to 6 per cent.

This sounded even worse than the previous restrictions. It prompted my elder sister Ibi to make a decision that seemed to us very brave. She and her husband had been living in Budapest, and on the advice of a friend who had settled in Ecuador, they decided to move to America. The plan distressed our family a great deal. It had already hurt us to lose Ibi when she married and left for Budapest, and it was difficult to accept the idea that an ocean would separate us. Fortunately, however, my parents did not oppose the newlyweds' resolution. Parting was even harder for Ibi than it was for us. It seemed unfair that, although she was the one most attached to our home, she would be living the farthest away from it. For a while, we continued to write to one another, but as the war escalated, communication became impossible. As the war went on, we thought her new home was a safe haven where she was far from danger and pain, and we comforted ourselves with the thought that at least she and her little family had been spared. Years later, we learned that she had fallen seriously ill and had barely managed to recover, but we had no idea.

While Ibi emigrated, my other sister Magda, who was living in Bucharest, had her own troubles. Her husband's foreign citizenship began to cause him problems. His right to engage in professional activities was restricted, and he was told that he must leave the country within six months. My sister, who was pregnant at the time, returned home from Bucharest with her husband. After the birth of their daughter Anikó, my brother-in-law left for America while Magda remained behind. She had decided not to subject her infant to the risks of wartime travel.

My family in 1938:
My Mom (Mrs. Ignac
Klarmann, nee Maria
Szmuk) and Dad (Ignác
Klärmann). Behind
them, from left to right:
Ibi, Magda, Duci, Erzsi
and myself.

Staying Human through the Holocaust

My home on Spiru
Haret Street. We were
taken to the ghetto
from its second floor
corner apartment.

We, the four sisters: Erzsi,
   Ibi, myself, and Magda.

At the end of the 1930s and the beginning of the 1940s, we lived as secluded a life as possible. My sister Erzsi, my friends and I were all in our twenties. I was twenty-one and Erzsi was twenty-three. We were young adults without hope for the future. We wanted some sort of social activity, and in answer to our many requests the Jewish Women's Union decided to organize a traditional ball at the Jewish hospital. This raised our spirits a little. In the end, however, given the situation, the more practical-minded women decided that our ball would have to be imaginary. The money designated for ball gowns and the revenue from admission tickets were directed towards maintenance of the Jewish hospital and aid for refugees.

In our grey, monotonous lives, participation in presentations or visits to art exhibitions brought a touch of colour. Until the authorities forbade it, we went to a free lecture series on literature and the social sciences and heard poetry recitals at the Open University. Viktor Brassai was often the highlight of these recitals. I remember the artists Ernö Tibór, György Ruzicskay and Alex Leon from that period and the lanky, slightly stooping frame of Alfred Macalik, whose emotive landscapes were still unknown to me then. The drawings of Alex Leon made a powerful impression on me. I felt we were on the same wavelength. The artist sensitively evoked and captured the mood of the society in which we were living. His drawings expressed the fear caused by our uncertainty about the future, and the sense that we as individuals would be lost in the currents of history. He drew prophetic, breath-taking pictures of the racial persecution that had yet to reveal its full force and to which, with a weapon in his hand, he himself would fall victim.

In 1940, events rushed on. Our fears proved to be well founded as Hitler's Germany demonstrated its military skill and strategy. We learned about a new concept: the lightning war or *Blitzkrieg*. By means of surprise attacks, Hitler first terrified then crushed European nations.

In the evenings, after work, we listened to radio broadcasts and talked late into the night, trying to keep pace with the events. In April, we were astonished to learn that German troops had occupied Denmark in just four hours. We hoped that now at last the great allied powers would intervene and that France would lead the way in stopping further expansion. It did not happen. In May 1940, the fascists went around the Maginot Line, brought Holland to its knees, and then forced Belgium's surrender.

Until this time, I had not been interested in politics. In peacetime, I used to feign interest when people reminisced about the First World War. Now my friends and I were constantly studying maps and considering reports about the armed forces. Not a month passed without some important event. In May, Hitler occupied Norway and attacked France. Then the unthinkable happened. On June 14, one month before

Bastille Day, the Germans entered Paris and met no resistance. Nazi boots resounded on the pavement of the city of dreams. Our hearts went out to Paris. But all we could do was to acknowledge that fact, as we had so many others in the past months, and add it to our column of losses. With sinking hearts, we waited to see what would happen next. We tried to predict what the future might hold for Transylvania and its Jewish population. We knew that Hitler was blackmailing Hungary and Romania with territorial disputes. We did not know what was going on behind the scenes.

Although a pro-German government had assumed power in Romania, German forces occupied the territory between the Prut and Nistru rivers. At the time, we were unaware of this because of a secret agreement between Germany and the Soviet Union, as had been the case with the partition of Poland. With the Soviet Union's occupation of Bessarabia and Northern Bukovina, communism had moved nearer to our borders. This misled many people, who thought their only refuge from fascism was in the Soviet Union. There was great turmoil in my family when it became known that my cousin Pali Szmuk had chosen to enter the Soviet Union illegally, like the sports teacher Klári Sonnenvirth and many progressive intellectuals. Young people made spontaneous marriages and left for the East. They naively thought that as sympathizers they would be welcomed with open arms. For a long time we received no news of them, and we hoped that they had escaped the Holocaust. Only a few of them returned home many years after the war. My cousin Pali came back from Arkhangelsk after ten years disillusioned and prematurely aged, a broken man. He travelled as far as Budapest, where he learned of the tragedy of his family, and never returned to Oradea again. He settled in Israel. Many years later, he told us about his ordeal. Stalin, suspicious of foreign subversives, had sent him and thousands of others to do forced labour in the far north of Siberia.

When the second Vienna Award, under which Hungary acquired Northern Transylvania from Romania, was issued in 1940, I was visiting my relatives in Sighet. My mother's parents and their brothers, sisters and children had all lived there at one time. By 1940, Sub-Carpathia belonged to the Soviet Union, and it was feared that Sighet might be annexed as well. I did not want to be separated from my parents, so I left for home immediately. In August, Northern Transylvania was annexed by Hungary. We passed our days full of fear, anxiously expecting the two Jewish laws to be extended to us in Transylvania. Jews who remained on the other side of the border felt the same anguish that we felt when considering the future.

Oradea (now called Nagyvárad) was temporarily placed under a military administration, which was then replaced by a civil administration. We were reassured when Endre Hlatky became Prefect and Dr.

Istvan Soós the mayor, both highly respected in the community. We should have seen what followed as a warning. To prevent their possibly liberal and benevolent approach to governance, three officials from the capital joined them in office, with Dr. László Gyapay as deputy mayor. Later, when draconian measures were to be implemented, he was named mayor with plenipotentiary powers. Our fears proved to be well grounded.

From the very first days of the annexation, the wheels were set in motion for a scheme to oppress the Jews, and an anti-Semitic campaign began in the papers. Directives restricting Jewish rights followed one after another. Regulations affected Jews working in professions and businesses. Over the course of a few days, Jewish shops disappeared from the main streets. Of 120 Jewish lawyers, only twelve received work permits. Most of these were because of special distinctions, such as having received medals in the First World War. As a result of press regulations, five of the eight Hungarian-language newspapers were closed. Only three remained: *Hungarian Pages (Magyar Lapok)*, *Popular Sheets (Néplap)*, and *Liberty (Szabadság)*, the last with its title changed to *Nagyvárad*. These newspapers, of course, published only articles by racially trustworthy writers approved by the Chamber of Journalists. Racially acceptable people, sometimes in the military, were appointed to take over Jewish businesses. Jewish industrialists or merchants needed to find a Christian business partner if they wanted to continue their work, a so-called *strowman* or silent partner who took half the proceeds.

My father and my brother Duci entered into a partnership with a Christian tanner named Varga. I continued to go to my dressmaking workshop, but where my baccalaureate under Romanian rule had exempted me from attending the school for apprentices I found that it had now become obligatory. I also had to stay out of civic life. Despite the restrictions, though, we were all glad that we could still go on working. The struggle to find our daily bread continued, and we were entirely absorbed by it. We had accepted our fate. "Survive!" had become our motto. We had no idea at the time how precarious our chances of survival already were.

In the summer of 1941, at the order of the Office for the Control of Foreigners (KEOKH) in Hungary (including the county of Bihar where Nagyvárad (Oradea) was located), all Austrian, Polish and Czech Jews who did not have Hungarian citizenship were arrested. They numbered more than thirty thousand people. The news spread like wildfire. Among those arrested was Albert Münzer, the son-in-law of Ede Pásztor, the editor-in-chief of a magazine. His wife and daughter followed him in spite of their Hungarian citizenship. The teacher Reb Roth Mosche Csesznye, with his wife and six children, was also arrested. The community tried to obtain their release, but were unsuccessful. Those arrested were crowded into cattle cars in ghastly conditions and taken to Kamyenets-Podilskyy in western Ukraine. There they were handed to the Germans. Their lives ended in a volley of machine-gun fire.

Mr. Rabbinovits, who had been the rabbi of Munkács (today Mukachevo in the Ukraine), was one of the few who escaped this mass butchery. He committed his life to saving those who were being persecuted. My father was at the meeting where Rabbinovits told his story to the town's Jewish citizens. He gave a full account of his horrible experience, and he made an appeal to the Jewish community in Oradea to help the refugees in an organized way. The butchery at Kamyenets-Podilskyy sounded an alarm, and the Jewish community in Oradea opened its purse. Everyone gave, but we stayed where we were. We should have been thinking of a way to save ourselves. Probably many did think about it, but the possibilities were extremely limited. Some had emigrated abroad. We later learned that one of the Ullmann families had taken refuge on a hillside covered with vineyards. This could have been a solution for a few families but not for the entire Jewish population of thirty thousand. It was difficult to get into Palestine then because of British policies. Nevertheless, many undertook the journey.

In Oradea there were two *halutim* camps, where many young people prepared themselves for *aliya*, a future life in the Jewish homeland. The Zionist movement, however, was not supported by the town's three spiritual leaders (the chief Orthodox rabbi, the Neolog rabbi and the rabbi from Wisnicz). Added to all the other problems at this time, this lack of support may have deterred people from emigrating in larger numbers. The situation was worsening daily. Many people were now unemployed. Listening to foreign news broadcasts was forbidden. Many people were sent to prison and later to internment camps because they did not pay minor fines or because of unfounded personal accusations. Spreading alarmist rumours was a punishable offence. We no longer had the courage to speak except in whispers.

My brother Duci ended up in the internment camp at Kistarcsa. Before that, however, the police in Oradea kept him for three weeks for questioning. Then the entire guild of leather merchants was arrested, one man after another. Our days were filled with fear. My poor brother, who was still free at the time, sent me in secret to his partner, Varga the tanner, who was living outside of the town, to warn him about what was happening. My sister-in-law Olga could not cope with the pressure of the countless difficulties and fears, and she fell ill. She was not well enough to spend hour after hour waiting outside the police station, but this now became absolutely essential. We had to get food and warm clothing to him and ask permission to meet with him. While I was waiting outside the prison, I heard many moving stories about the fate of some people. The daily tension of our situation took its toll on me, and I was exhausted.

In the end, the inevitable happened. The first orders arrived for the mobilization of the labour battalions. People had already been taken to work in villages near Oradea. Dr. Sándor Grünwald, a lawyer from Nyiregyháza, came to Oradea in the fall of 1940 to serve as a conscript for a year. He arrived at our house in his splendid sergeant uniform. A few months later, he was stripped of his sergeant's stripes, and then his bayonet was taken from him. He became a simple Hungarian soldier, but he still wore a uniform. Eventually this was taken away too. Being Jewish he was regarded as unreliable and was sent unarmed to do national defence work in a labour service battalion.

Men between the ages of eighteen and forty-five had to do labour service, but this age limit was often disregarded. The first summons took us by surprise and did not affect everybody. Many doctors, lawyers, engineers, journalists, clerks, and civil servants were summoned under the pretext of removing unreliable left-wing sympathizers. The aim was to eliminate the Jewish community's leaders. Personal revenge often played a key role. It was a good time to settle old scores.

Those first summoned were called to Marghita. The first detachments assembled here, unarmed, and were sent immediately to the eastern front in the Ukraine. They were treated with such brutality that most of them perished there. Those who went to the Uz valley in eastern Transylvania received the same treatment. After the first work battalions were organized, a general summons followed. Those who were summoned had to present themselves at Baia Mare or Sein.

My brother Duci, after spending a few months in the internment camp, was sent to Sein and then to Budapest, where he worked in the Western Railway Station. His wife moved back to her parents' home in Satu Mare. Their son Gábor was born there. Neither we nor his father ever knew him because he died of blood poisoning when he was only a few weeks old.

One after another, all of our friends and acquaintances were summoned for labour service. Among them was József Révész, who later became my sister Erzsi's husband. Erzsi returned disappointed from their farewell meeting. She had hoped that they would get engaged. But in Józsi's opinion this would have been an irresponsible move. Given that it was wartime, he felt that he had to consider the possibility that he might become disabled. He did not want Erzsi to be bound to such a promise.

A good friend, Karcsi Mózes, whom I married after the war, was also drafted. In spite of all the legal restrictions limiting the number of Jewish students, Karcsi managed to complete his medical studies because of the goodwill and the sensibilities of the professors of the faculty senate. In 1941 he was one of the best students and graduated as a medical doctor. While working in Budapest at the Jewish hospital on Szabolcs Street, he got his summons. Following a series of hardships, Karcsi ended up in the same battalion as my brother Duci, and he became the battalion's doctor. They were taken to the Ukraine together.

Those in the labour battalions who had been sent to the front could not leave, nor could they send or receive letters except for one standard postcard per month. In spite of this, however, we learned a lot about them. We received news through well-meaning soldiers and from others whom our parents paid upon receipt. The labour battalions' situation was dreadful and we were very worried about them. Their food ration was the minimum necessary for survival. On this diet, they were sent out to do hard physical labour. They dug ditches, built bridges, and raised earth, wooden, and concrete fortifications. Given that it was wartime, this work would not have been shocking in itself, for surely ordinary soldiers did not have an easy time in the trenches. The difference was in their harsh treatment; in the poor food they received; in the deplorable accommodations they were forced to endure; in the discrimination on the grounds of race, nationality and religion; in the endless humiliations and offensive remarks; in the beatings and their defencelessness; and in the fact that they were outside the law. People who a few days before their call-up enjoyed the respect of society and family, had in a few hours become "rotten Jews" and "filthy stinking pigs" whom anyone could insult or kill without consequence.

The members of the labour battalions were also used as mine sweepers. In the areas where manoeuvres took place, Jews from labour battalions were sent ahead of armed troops to walk across suspected minefields. We only learned about this later.

Months passed as we awaited news from the front. We got used to this new way of life as well. My father worked within the much stricter limits imposed by the new regulations. My mother and my two older sisters, Magda and Erzsi, looked after the home. I sewed, studied, and taught other students.

In the summer of 1943, a rather peculiar idea occurred to me. Given the circumstances, even today I cannot understand it. But I was not the only one with this kind of idea, and for that reason I think it is of interest to record. I was now working with my friend Sári Feldheim's younger sister Ági in a prestigious dressmaker's workshop. Ági and I decided to leave for a two-week holiday at Lake Balaton. My father was appalled. He could not understand how I could even think about a holiday when my brother and our friends struggled in labour battalions. My father had never punished any of us children, but we knew by his attitude what was expected of us. He did not forbid me to go, but he did express his disapproval. Until then, I had never disobeyed him, but now a longing to travel and see the world came over me. I left with a bitter taste in my mouth. Perhaps it would be my last chance. At the time, those words were on everybody's lips. Although I did not agree, I too fell into the same trap: to experience what I was still able to do, to see, to live.

A few months later, when we had been dragged off to a concentration camp, I met deported Polish women. They pointed out to me that since 1939 they had been involved in a life and death struggle in ghettos and concentration camps while we Hungarian Jews were still able to move about freely. Instead of thinking about a way to resist, we had only been living for the present. And they were right. Later I thought about it often: where did we go wrong? What could we have done in the circumstances? Could we really have done anything? And why did we do nothing?

It was as if we were deaf. And we were badly informed. Newspapers and radio broadcasts did not mention the tragedy of the Jews in central and eastern Europe. We did not know the truth. We were sure of one thing, however: it could never happen in our country. Perhaps this blind naiveté best explains our passivity.

That same year, in 1943, my sister Magda's husband arrived in Cuba. He returned to his job in the sugar factory, and immediately sent a new passport to his wife and child along with boat tickets for the journey. They had to board a ship in Bilbao, Spain. The date of their departure was fixed. Through the Papal Nuncio's office, we procured the necessary transit visas. Everything was ready for the trip. They would not even have to travel alone, as a neighbour of ours, Dodo Diósi, was leaving on the same ship to marry an American citizen. But our Magda could not bring herself to leave. She was unable to make the break from the warmth and security of her home. She hid the passport, so that she would not get into trouble on account of her foreign citizenship, and she no longer talked to anybody about her intention to leave. As she had kept her original citizenship, she continued to live with us. There was nothing unusual about the fact that she was living with us at the time. With the men gone for labour service, the young women left behind simply returned to their parents' home. Anikó, her daughter, brought colour and warmth into our drab yet certainly not monotonous lives.

German troops entered Hungary on March 19, 1944. It felt like being hit by lightning, but it was not unexpected. I had already purchased a railway ticket to Budapest for March 20. I had been planning to have an operation to correct a deviated nasal septum that gave me a lot of trouble. Right after the occupation, the Germans banned all travel. My father advised me to stay at home, and fortunately I listened to him. Those who were found on trains or in railway stations when the ban was introduced were rounded up and sent off to the internment camps in Sárvár or Kistarcsa. They never returned. They were deported directly to concentration camps.

Sándor Leitner, the president of the Orthodox Jews in Oradea, and Dr. Samu Meer, the president of the Neolog Jewish community, had received special permission to go to Budapest to attend the National Assembly of the Jewish Council, the *Judenrat* called for March 28. This was to be the last general assembly of the Jews in Hungary. I only learned about the details of the conference many years later when Sándor Leitner published *The Tragedy of the Jews of Oradea*. From this it is clear that the unmistakable behaviour of the Gestapo and its insatiable demands on the Jewish community foreshadowed their terrible fate. And still our leaders believed them. Perhaps they simply wanted to believe them. Today it is hard to decide which was the case. The promise made by the SS in the original invitation said that the Jews could rest assured that they would not be harmed in any way. They could continue their religious, cultural, and social activities undisturbed. Yet they should have known that the Nazis were adept at using fraud and deception. This is how the Gestapo was introduced to us. Despite widespread despair, there was still no panic.

At home in Oradea, in spite of the numerous arrests and other adverse indications, we continued to have faith. It was reassuring that Miklós Horthy, the country's regent, did not lose his leadership position. We hoped that Horthy and the newly installed government of Sztójay would protect the Jews and would resolve the Jewish problem by legal means. However, more decrees followed quickly. Bank accounts were closed. Jewish writers were identified and their works were publicly burned. Regulations concerning exempt Jews became more stringent and strictly defined. The Chamber of Advocates in Oradea retained only two Jewish lawyers in its ranks, Dr. Bertalan Stern and Dr. József Berkes. The Chamber of Journalists excluded from their ranks the half-Jew Béla Katona, and Sándor Marot who at one time had been the president of the Association of Journalists and the vice-president of the National Organization of Minority Journalists in Romania. They also excluded István Márton and Elemér Jakobovits. Exceptional status was granted to Nándor Hegedüs, ex-representative of the Hungarian Party and to József Biró, the art historian. The Chamber of Actors excluded Ernö Szabó, one of the best actors of this time, who was half Jewish and had enjoyed a great following.

Our movements were restricted more and more. These were the times when postings on shops, cafes, and the municipal swimming pools forbade entry to "Jews and dogs." Our participation was forbidden everywhere. In order that every Jew could be easily supervised by anyone, at any time, we were ordered to wear a distinctive sign: the yellow star. Suddenly, to produce the yellow star, a new business opportunity was created for those who, with the help of the authorities, benefited from our misfortune. The star was of a set colour, canary yellow, and also a fixed size. Since wearing the yellow star was obligatory, both on the street and at home, we stayed up until late at night sewing this stigmatizing mark onto our clothes and pullovers. It was sewn onto everything

My future husband with his family of whom he was the only survivor: my father-in-law Mózes Izsák; my mother-in-law Mrs. Izsak Mózes born Erzsike Lindenfeld; Karcsi; younger sister Magdus and older sister Lilli.

The same family with
the yellow star.

from the children's tiny dresses to the old peoples' vests. Even the kind of stitching was specified so that it could not be removed easily. Once in a while, someone would be stopped and sent to an internment camp for wearing a star that was too loosely attached. The streets became deserted. We no longer ventured out unless we had no other alternative.

I can remember my first outing wearing the star. Rather than feeling shame or humiliation I felt naked and utterly helpless: "Look at me, this is who I am: I am a Jew. You can do anything you want with me." At the time, there was something heroic about it, although it was not my own wish to wear the symbol proclaiming my Jewishness. Even before this, I had never attempted to conceal my Jewishness, but since my return from the Holocaust I feel a stronger identification with the Jewish community.

When I stepped onto the street for the first time wearing the star on my breast, acquaintances hurried past me. I would like to believe that they were a little ashamed of themselves. One man addressed me, and more than that, he joined me and accompanied me on my way. He was the director of the apprentice's school and was wearing the uniform of a reserve captain. I do not know if talking to a Jew was one of his assignments, as I presumed then since I was unable to trust anyone, or if he wanted to lend me strength as his later behaviour demonstrated.

If, on March 31, 1944, I and many others had listened to the short-wave radio broadcast from

Budapest, perhaps we would have known what was coming. László Endre, who later became Secretary of State to the Home Secretary, revealed that "to date government decrees only served as an introduction to a series of new directives, which within a short time will lead to the final solution of the Jewish problem in Hungary." And yet we still did not comprehend that a final act was being prepared for which all of the measures to date had only been preparatory. We were still blind and continued to hope that the situation would not get worse.

Events followed inexorably. Shops owned by Jews were closed. Radios were confiscated; savings were seized. No one could keep more than 3,000 pengö (sufficient for an average family to live on for a few months). The larger Jewish homes were occupied. People were given one or two hours to evacuate their homes. Everything except a small quantity of groceries, clothes and bed linen had to be left behind. In addition, mass arrests created a nightmarish atmosphere. Those arrested were accused of subversive political activity or of sabotaging the war effort. The authorities arrested the community's leaders and the wealthy, while each day the Gestapo made new demands on the Jewish community: they wanted a fully equipped three-hundred-bed hospital in twenty-four hours; they wanted typewriters and office equipment; they wanted machinery for road construction. Every new directive meant fresh trauma for us. My parents were extremely affected when the

Photo taken of me
before the deportation

oldest synagogue in Oradea, a Baroque style synagogue near the former Jewish hospital, was occupied and transformed into a military barracks.

At the same time, the verification of exemption documents began. The real aim of this measure was to retract as many exemptions as possible. The family of Sándor Katz, a war veteran who was confined to a wheelchair, lived in a house adjoining our courtyard. Mr. Katz, who had a 95 per cent disability status, had died three weeks earlier. Since the disability status could not be changed after his death, the family kept their privileged situation. This meant that they did not have to wear the yellow star. In spite of this, their documents were later destroyed and they were deported. In a town that numbered between twenty-five and thirty thousand Jews, only sixteen families were spared. Among those spared were the repeatedly decorated engineer István Radó, the tobacconist Herman Lefkovits, whose war disability status was 100 per cent, the chemical engineer Miklós Stern, and the engineer Sándor Hevesi.

On April 28, 1944, the Hungarian Council of Ministers accepted two decrees that sealed our fate. The first called for the expropriation of Jewish homes and the identification of new accommodations. The second granted the German request that fifty thousand people be sent for labour service. The decision was made that the families of those in the labour battalions should also be sent to Germany. Those two decrees were the forerunners of the ghettos and deportations.

2

IN THE ORADEA GHETTO

*D*ays full of terror followed. Arrests became routine. From one day to the next, people lost their jobs and livelihoods. The Jewish population was forced to surrender more goods, and was plundered without mercy. And yet that was not all. Bad news spread like wildfire, predicting much worse things to come. Railway workers were saying that in the sub-Carpathian region and in Sighet the villages had been emptied of Jews. They were led away from their homes on foot or by cart, gathered together in larger towns and then loaded into cattle cars and sent to unknown destinations.

But oh, eternal Jewish optimism! We tried to look at this development too from the authorities' perspective, to justify to ourselves what was nothing other than madness: they were on a frontier, an area for military manoeuvres. We worried about our relatives and friends, but we continued to be hopeful for ourselves. We were deluded by the thought that this was the fifth year of war and that time was on our side. The fanatical advocates of the "final solution to the Jewish problem" had also realized that time was short, however. They brought their plans to fruition in record time. László Endre, the Secretary of State who was known as "the butcher of Hungarian Jews," called a meeting on April 30, 1944 at the Oradea town hall. Information had leaked out that a *ghetto* was to be organized. Officially this was denied, but events led us to believe that the authorities were preparing something. On May 1, the SS General Obersturmbannführer Dannecker, who had organized the Warsaw ghetto, arrived in Oradea. On May 2, a larger unit of gendarmes arrived from the other side of the Danube. At the same time, those who had been arrested were unexpectedly allowed to return home. And even these events did not open our eyes. Despite the warning signs, we were shocked by the announcements posted on walls on May 3. I quote a few lines from the abrupt order signed by Dr. László Gyapay, the deputy mayor:

> Jews obliged to wear the yellow star are forbidden to leave their homes from the time that my announcement is made public. Until further orders, Jews may only leave their homes between 9 and 10 in the morning. Therefore outside these hours everyone is obliged to remain at home. By the order of the royal Hungarian government in Nagyvárad

(Oradea), I will place all the Jews obliged to wear a yellow star in the ghetto....

People read the announcement in silence and rushed home. Within hours a wooden fence two metres high was being erected. This fence would surround the ghetto. Our neighbors who still had the right to move freely told us that the area around the big Orthodox Jewish synagogue on the left bank of the Körös (Crișul) River had been designated for the ghetto. This was the poorest and most crowded Jewish quarter. It included the following streets: Mezei Mihály or Kert (Avram Iancu), Capucinus, (Prahovei), south to the Nagy Piac (1st December) Square and Liliom (Crinului), then further on to Váradi Zsigmond (Kogălniceanu) and the group of houses on the eastern edge which used to be a food market, closing with Vámház (Sucevei). The Capuchin monastery was separated from the ghetto with wooden boards. The area around the Kaszárnyatér (Cazarmelor) Square, which also included Köröslaktanya, and was normally reserved for street cleaners, had been earmarked for the Jews from the provinces. There, many of those interned in the ghetto lived in the open air.

The area for the ghetto covered about one fifteenth of the total area of the town. More than a quarter of the population of ninety thousand was to be crowded here. Of the thirty thousand Jews living in Oradea then, five or six thousand were in the labour service at that time. It took six days to shut the Jewish population into the ghetto. Our turn to move came on the

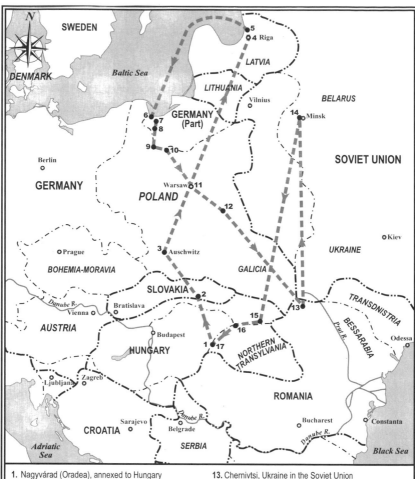

1. Nagyvárad (Oradea), annexed to Hungary
2. Kassa (Ko
3. Auschwitz - Birkenau (near the village of Oœwiecim and the city of Krakow), Poland under German occupation
4. Riga, Latvia under German occupation
5. Kaiserwald (camp near Riga) in Latvia under German occupation
6. Danzig
7. Stutthof
8. Dörbeck
9. Gutowo (Guttau), Poland under German occupation
10. Neumark (Nowe Miesto), Poland under German occupation
11. Warsaw, Poland
12. Lublin, Poland

13. Chernivtsi, Ukraine in the Soviet Union
14. Slutsk (near Minsk), Belarus in the Soviet Union
15. Sighet or Sighetul Marma Sziget), Romania
16. Satu Mare (Szatmár), Romania
17. Oradea (Nagyvárad or Várad), Romania

–·–·– 1938 Borders
■·■·■ 1943-1944 Borders

Source: Base map information from *A Concise Historical Atlas of Eastern Europe,* Dennis P. Hupchick and Harold E. Cox, St. Martin's Press, New York, 1996.

A NAGYVÁRADI GETTÓ TERÜLETE 1944

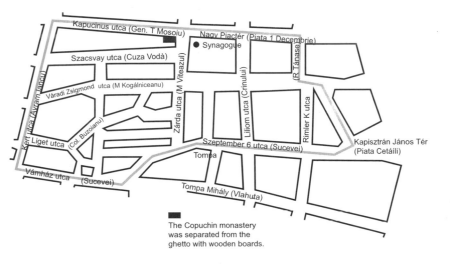

The Copuchin monastery
was separated from the
ghetto with wooden boards.

evening of the third day, on May 6. We were no longer allowed to go out except between nine and ten in the morning, when we tried to buy food.

We spent two days packing. Every now and then we secretly listened to the English news on the BBC at our neighbours' house, as they had been exempted from wearing the yellow star. Our own radio had already been sealed off. At first we filled suitcases, but then, when news arrived that these were being confiscated with all their contents, we began to stuff things into bags – bedding, clothes, groceries, cooking utensils, a small supply of wood and coal. I glanced at the bags. Was this all we had after my father's forty years of work? Although we did not complain or cry, we had tears in our eyes most of the time. It was like a funeral. We were burying our beautiful family life, all the happy years spent together. And as for our home, we felt that even if the situation should ever change, it would be impossible to recapture its former cheerfulness.

From time to time we looked out the window at those whose turn had already come. One sad, grieving group followed another. Old people, young people and children with bundles on their backs gathered together and followed luggage-filled carts towards the ghetto. When we recognized someone, we uttered a little cry.

In the evening, we called the Katz brothers to come to our house. They were exempted because of their father's war disability status, and we wanted

1944 május 3, szerda

ORSZÁG

Megkezdték a nagyváradi zsidó kitelepítését

Nagyvárad, május 3. A polgármester falragaszon közölte, hogy a zsidókat a városban zárt területen helyezik el. Az orthodox zsinagóga környékén, nagyjából a tűzoltólaktanya, a nagypiac és az úgynevezett Kommendás-rét között laknak ezentúl a zsidók. A gettót két méter magas palánkkal veszik körül, a város felé néző ablakokat pedig bedeszkázzák.

A gettóból csak 9 és 10 óra között lehet eltávozni. Gyapay helyettes polgármester öttagú bizottságot alakított, amely végzi a körülbelül 30,000 zsidó személyes ügyeit.

Előreláthatólag négy nap alatt bonyolítják az átköltöztetést. Azon nemzsidó háztulajdonosok és bérlők, akik a gettónak kijelölt területén laknak, vagy ott van házuk, a város más helyén kapnak elhelyezést. Hasonlóképpen járnak el az ezen a részen megtelepedett nemzsidó kereskedőkkel és iparosokkal. Felhívást bocsátottak ki, amelyben felszólítják azokat, akik mű[...] értékeket őriznek, hogy három nap alatt jelentkezzenek a hatóság előtt, mert ellenkező esetben megtorló eljárást indítanak ellenük. (MTI)

"The eviction of the Oradea Jewish population has started". Article published on the pages of Magyarország (Hungary) on the day the internment in the ghetto started. Source: Jewish Museum of Budapest

In the Oradea Ghetto   53

to see if they could keep or eventually use anything from our house, in which we now felt like strangers. It was a strange sensation to walk through the house, to open doors and cupboards, to rummage through things that at one time had been so important to us. A few weeks earlier I could not have imagined anything like this. I would have been very upset if a stranger had gone through my things. Now it left me completely cold. I was looking at the whole scene, not only at the Katz brothers but at myself too, in a strange and distant way. I did not find it difficult to part with a single object. I felt that nothing belonged to me any more apart from the things already in the bags. Late at night, I listened to the English news again. In truth I was only interested in news that could directly influence our situation, mostly news about the position of the front.

On Friday, we finished our preparations. The house appeared to be in order again, but we only felt how desolate it had become. As we could not find anything else to do, we sat around, disoriented and apathetic, waiting for our turn to go.

Finally, in the afternoon, a commission of three arrived: a civilian, a clerk and a gendarme. It made me realize that at least a hundred commissions of this kind must now be at work throughout the town. Three hundred people, who had at one time been honest and respected individuals, were now visiting thousands of families to evict them from their own homes. We would never have believed that so many people would undertake such heartless work. At the time, though, we did not have a moment to think about this. The commission set to work immediately. They rifled through our luggage. They rudely asked if all the goods we had chosen were really necessary. They made an inventory of the valuables left in the house, such as carpets and candlesticks. They took away our money, our jewellery, and most painful of all, they took the wedding rings off Mother's and Magda's fingers. Poor Magda had tried to be strong, but at this she broke into inconsolable sobs. Together with the other occupants of the house, we went down to the street with our bags. With the exception of the Katz family (who were exempted) and Balogh the tavern keeper, all the tenants were Jews forced into internment in the ghetto.

The moment we closed the door behind us has remained etched in my memory. The key turned in the lock and disappeared immediately into the pocket of one our supervisors. The symbol of our home was in the hands of a stranger. Would there be any way back? Would we ever see our home again? We stepped out of the house and together with our companions in suffering put our bags onto the loaded cart. I must have been very deep in thought because I learned later that mother and Magda had suddenly remembered that it was Friday evening and they had not yet fulfilled the traditional obligations. They went back upstairs to the Katz family's apartment and lit the Sabbath candles. And the flame was lit one more time, the flame that so many times had thrown its golden light over our beautiful family life. Later, during our dreary days, I often returned to these happy times. But then I looked up one more time to the windows with the drawn blinds. Although we had decided to be strong and keep our dignity, I could not control myself. I felt drained of strength, and tears streamed down my face.

We lined up next to the cart and started off. We only looked straight ahead. I could not say if we were followed by looks full of pity or by gloating faces. Supporting one another, and trying to encourage each other with glances, we followed in the steps of those ahead, crushed and stigmatized. The sight of this sad formation wearing stars, this army recruited from stigmatized humans filled me with an indescribable sorrow.

Our circumstances had never felt so bitter. Never before had I felt so helpless, so defenceless. My strong, wise father and my loving, caring mother were both walking beside me, but I could no longer count on their protection. I was walking with them, and yet in a profound sense I was alone. From now on neither the law nor human rights could protect us. It was spring, but at the time we were not aware of it. I felt cast out, excluded, naked. I was cold.

New groups joined us at intersections. We had grown into a huge crowd by the time we arrived at the ghetto. At the entrance, I realized that as far as the ghetto was concerned we could only go in: there was no way out. When I went through the gate, I felt that I was crossing a gulf away from the world as I knew it, a world that no longer existed for me.

People we knew and total strangers surrounded us. Volunteer helpers smiled encouragement. They picked up our belongings and accompanied us to our new accommodations. At our request, we were assigned to my friend Sári Feldheim's house at 14 Váradi Zsigmond Street. Today the administration of the co-operative Lemnul is there. According to the ghetto rules, fifteen or sixteen people had to be housed in each room. Many other families had already arrived at the Feldheims' house, relatives, friends and acquaintances; forty-seven people were crowded into a small house with three rooms and a hall. Another 150 people were crowded behind this house, in homes adjacent to the courtyard. During the first few hours, I got to know a lot of these people as they swarmed through the rooms. We spent the time wandering aimlessly, putting off going to bed. We covered every centimetre with straw mattresses and blankets. We did not close our eyes that first night.

On the second day we evaluated our situation. We realized that we could not survive unless we organized our life in a way that was as unemotional and rational as possible. Aunty Feldheim rose to the occasion. At her suggestion, we took all the furniture out of the house, either to the attic under the eaves or into the courtyard out in the open. We put out furniture that had been lovingly cared for. Only places for sleeping were left inside the house. We built makeshift ledges out of the cupboard shelves and attached them to the walls. We put the most essential things on these shelves or hung them on nails that we had put into the walls. Older women lived in one of the rooms and younger women in another, mothers with children were in a third room, and the men were in the relatively small hall. There were fewer men, and they were almost all elderly, as the young men had been taken off to labour service. In other houses, a number of families lived in each room, but we thought our solution was the most sensible.

We gathered together all our food and stored it in the only pantry of the house. We established a roster and times for cooking and cleaning. We also had to regulate the use of the bathroom. As we were living in such crowded conditions, we had to follow a strict order. Outside the walls of the house a world was being born, a state within a state or a town within a town. It was difficult to compare with any other settlement. Jews had been crowded quickly into the houses of a few narrow streets without preparation. From outside, gendarmes supervised our every move.

Inside the ghetto, a five-member Jewish Council assumed control. This internal organization was in the hands of the president of the Orthodox community, Sándor Leitner, and this had a calming effect. The council oversaw the day-to-day life in the ghetto and tried to solve foreseeable problems with food, public sanitation and administration. The other members of the council were István Vajda, the rabbi of the Neolog community, Dr. Sándor Lörinc, a lawyer, Dr. René Osváth, a doctor, and Sámuel Motzen. Each member of the council had a wide range of responsibilities. Under their aegis some subcommittees came into being and these formed the essential elements of an administration. Within the limits of this mass misfortune, the council tried to maintain a semblance of civilized life.

How happy we were when in the first days young Jews serving as postmen knocked on our doors and brought us military postcards from those in labour battalions, our brothers and husbands who were suffering in the Ukraine. The postmen came from the ranks of the Jewish volunteer police. In general, the tasks of keeping public order and overseeing the housing administration had been assumed by those who had returned from labour battalions in the Ukraine, people of experience who had already endured many hardships. Leaders among these were József Gréda, a translator, József Halmi, Dr. Izsák Mihály, a lawyer, Dr. József Biró, an ex-police officer, Béla Fodor, a detective, and Jenö Pásztor, a journalist. The postal service was soon stopped, however. The city police ordered the post office to send the letters back to the front with the words "Jew interned in the ghetto – undeliverable."

The housing office functioned very well. The administrators allocated places to live and kept a clear record of who was where. They were extremely efficient – unfortunately. It is painful to write these words because these were the ghetto officials who later had to locate and notify the people who were summoned by the gendarmerie, and it happened more than once that they were their brothers, friends or close acquaintances. But what else could they have done?

From the very beginning, it was clear that many people had come into the ghetto unprepared. These people had to rely on the community canteen facilities right from the start. By the eighth day of internment, seven thousand people were eating there. As food supplies diminished, the number of those who needed the canteen kept rising. The old kitchen had to be extended and soon a new one had to be set up. But how, and with what resources? Necessity made us inventive. In an abandoned laundry building, boilers that had been used for dyeing and washing were turned into cooking vats. As food reserves decreased, the Jewish Council addressed all the people of the ghetto. Everyone was asked to hand over all food supplies beyond the minimum needed for the next two weeks. With heavy hearts we complied. At the time, we never suspected that we too would come to depend on the canteen.

Many people had arrived in the ghetto seriously ill, but in those harsh living conditions the number of sick people rose steadily, especially once the gendarmerie's torture chambers began to function. An avalanche of suicides began. We were among the first

to learn of this sad situation because the ghetto's central hospital had been set up close to our house, in the unfinished temple of the rabbi from Wisnicz. On the order of the gendarmerie, the Jewish community had to provide simple beds made of wooden planks and benches. Bedclothes, underwear and bedcovers were obtained by means of a public collection. Medical instruments, bandages and medication were obtained from the personal reserves of doctors confined in the ghetto.

The Wiznicz Synagogue, refurbished as ghetto hospital. In addition to nursing the gravely ill, it cared for people tortured and crippled by the savage beatings in the Dreher factory's torture chambers, as well as those who in their desperation chose to commit suicide. Currently it is used as a factory.

As the hospital was right next to us, we often went there to help. Overcrowding in the hospital was worse than in the rest of the ghetto. The section for internal diseases was situated on the ground floor and the head of the section was our family doctor, Dr. Vilmos Molnár, the former director of the Jewish hospital. Surgery and gynecology were on the first floor, led by the well-known surgeon Dr. Ernö Elias and the equally well-known Dr. Miksa Kupfer, who had written *Herodes* as well as numerous other historical novels. Dr. Kupfer wrote under the pseudonym Ádám Raffy, and he was the father of the writers and translators Ádám Réz and Pál Réz.

In the hospital, I found out that people with psychiatric illnesses had also been interned in the ghetto, as had people with neurological disorders and contagious diseases. The orthodox school for boys was set up for them. The chief doctor of the former hospital, Dr. Ignác Dénes, headed the section for contagious diseases. Because of lack of space, only those who were seriously ill were admitted to hospital. Instructions were given for the care of those who were ill and bedridden at home as well as those who were still ambulatory. A few exceptional doctors, who had been through the labour service experience of the Ukraine, visited the sick in their homes in addition to working at the hospital. Among these were Dr. Elemér Deutsch, Dr. Endre Popper, Dr. Sándor Bálint, and Dr. Sándor Németi.

Keeping up standards of hygiene was the most important thing in our overcrowded conditions in the ghetto. We realized this from the beginning, from the situation in our own house. The bathroom, planned for use by a single family, was now shared by nearly fifty people. In fact, we were lucky to have a bathroom. The ghetto area had been considered the poorest Jewish quarter. Here, people often still washed their clothes and bodies in a basin or a trough, and the toilets were usually situated at the end of the courtyard. Space in the ghetto was tight and extremely limited. In our house, and I would guess it was the same in all the others, it was decided exactly, to the minute, how much time each person could spend in the bathroom and especially how much water could be used because the water pressure was low. The plumbers were always busy fixing blocked pipes. Latrines were dug at the request of the Jewish Council. And so at the ends of the courtyards, huts appeared with thin wooden walls. There was a lack of wood because the wall surrounding the ghetto had been made from fences that had once separated the courtyards. Latrines were often just hidden by curtains made from bedspreads or sheets. After a few days, a stench hung over the ghetto. We were forever yielding on yet another point and found it harder to tolerate living from one day to the next. And still we continued to hope that somehow we would be able to survive the few remaining months of war. We did not realize that the ghetto, the yellow star, and the restrictions were just links in the chain leading to the final goal of total annihilation. All these things were part of a carefully calculated plan that had already been successfully carried out in the rest of Europe.

At first, communication with the town outside the ghetto walls was not completely severed. Carpenters were still working on the two-metre high fence, Christian families who had homes in the area were still moving out, and public maintenance workers still entered the ghetto. In Vámház Street, within the ghetto area itself, there was a small chemical products business, Norma, owned by István Radó, a Jewish engineer who was a war invalid. Although he was not offered another location outside the ghetto, he was forced to move his business. As he was an invalid, his twenty-year-old daughter Márta took this task upon herself. She put off the move for as long as she could, because as long as she had permission to come into the ghetto daily she could still, albeit through intermediaries and under police supervision, maintain her relationship with her grandmother, Mrs. Ede Mandel. She could not visit her personally, because she only had the right to go through the ghetto by an established route and under supervision.

There was another means of communication between the ghetto and the town: every day a number of people were requested to be used as workers in the hospital, to clear debris, to look after the cemetery, or to help in the municipal bakery. Under ghetto conditions, such opportunities might have appeared to be an advantage, but the brutality of the employers and the supervisory officials made everyone try to avoid such work.

During those days, an old acquaintance from the countryside, whose name I do not remember, sought out my father. This man offered to get my sister Erzsi and me out of the ghetto. He had a daughter who was close to us in age, and for two consecutive days when he was to be working in the ghetto he would have brought his daughter's identity card with him. When he left in the evenings he would have taken each of us with him in turn, saying that we were his daughters. When we were both outside, he planned to take us to the border point near the Félix spa where we could have crossed into Romania.

A few weeks earlier, before entering the ghetto, when we had heard rumours about girls being threatened, we might have accepted this wonderful opportunity of escape. But now, when conditions in the ghetto were deteriorating daily and every minute brought surprises, we would not leave our family. Our brother Duci was somewhere on the front line in the Ukraine. We felt that the time was coming when only we young ones would be able to be a support to our family. We could not abandon them. How could only two of us escape? If there had been a chance of freeing the entire family, we would certainly have considered it. But as for this – there was no question of it. My poor father, with tears in his eyes, tried to persuade us to leave. We discussed the matter for a few days. Much later, when only Erzsi and I were left and were suffering in the concentration camps, we often thought that if we had made a different decision then, we would have been free. But we never regretted this decision. Neither of us was sorry that we stayed alongside our parents until the last possible moment. Even if I had known that we would only be together for a few more days, I would not have left them on their own.

In the ghetto, I lived in the same house as Ági Wilkesz and her parents. To our amazement, their cousin from Budapest appeared one day with her hair dyed honey-blond and carrying false Aryan papers. She had brought false papers for Ági and tried to persuade her to leave for Budapest, where she had already found a hiding place for her. Ági reacted as we had to our offer of escape: she did not want to leave her parents. Seeing that her attempts were in vain, the well-intentioned cousin quickly left the ghetto. She went to the station and took the train to Budapest. I was with Ági in many concentration camps, until a selection put an end to her life. Only then was I truly sorry that she had not taken this opportunity. Two months after liberation, I met Ági's cousin in Lublin, and her hair, which was just starting to grow back, was raven black.

On May 9, when internment in the ghetto was complete, twenty-five hundred people were summoned for labour service. Some of them were declared reserves, while the rest were ordered to equip themselves with food and tools to leave for work the next day. Once again, the inhabitants of the ghetto had to outfit themselves from their own supplies. At first we were horrified by this news, but then we began to wonder if enlistment in labour battalions would in fact be better. People were never sent off, however. Unexpectedly, the commander of the gendarme regiment in Oradea took over the leadership of the ghetto. The role of ghetto commander was first filled by the gendarme István Garay and then by Lieutenant Colonel Jenö Péterffy.

I would not have said that life in the ghetto was monotonous until then, as every day had its own sad and sensational news. Starting that day, however, decisions that further distressed the defenceless population followed one after another with incredible speed. Immediately after the new leader's installation, the five-member Jewish Council was summoned. They were ordered to empty all their offices in the ghetto and give them to the gendarmes. They had to hand over the space used by the Jewish ritual burial society (Chevra Kadisha) and the two synagogue buildings, together with their courtyards and outbuildings, as well as the public kitchen and the hospital buildings for contagious diseases and mental illnesses. The gendarmes ordered the inhabitants of the ghetto to isolate these buildings immediately by putting up a wooden fence. Work started on this order, but after a while the gendarmes changed their plan. Instead, they evacuated the Dreher-Hagenmacher beer factory and took over their offices. This hasty back-and-forth move destroyed many of the Jewish community's archives.

Not even three hours had passed since the change of leadership when the shock waves began. New rules for the internal running of the ghetto were made public. Within one hour of the declaration of the rules, the announcements had to be posted over the entire ghetto area, on the doors of all the houses and on every floor of each multi-storey house. The yellow star, the order to wear a Jewish label, had been humiliating enough. We had been forcibly driven out of our homes and deprived of our rights. These new arrangements meant the trampling underfoot of our last vestiges of human dignity. When the fascist regime fell, the authorities sought to destroy all copies of this decree, along with other incriminating documents. Almost miraculously, Zsiga Kenyeres, one of my brother's friends, found, kept and later gave my husband a copy of this decree. These arbitrary and humiliating rules set out our bed time, waking time and meal times; they demanded total isolation from the outside world; they ordered that the ghetto should be as silent as the grave. The decree stipulated death by shooting as a punishment for escape attempts, and internment in detention camps for any non-compliance.

In front of me, framed and hanging on my library wall, are *The Ghetto Rules*. I read them from time to time, and each time I wonder why they had to

PARANCS.

A „Ghettó" felett a parancsnok-
ságot átvettem.

Parancsaimat csendőrök hajtják végre. Fegyver-
használat a csendőrségre érvényes szabályok szerint.
Minden kilengést, a szabályoktól minden eltérést
megtorolok. A táborrend betűszerinti végrehajtását
megkövetelem.

Felszólítok minden zsidót, hogy

1. azokat az értéktárgyakat (készpénzt, ékszert, arany-, ezüst nemüt, platinát, értékpapirt) amelyek még birtokában vannak, a leány gimnázium földszinti helyiségében müködő átvevo bizottsagnak ma 16—20 óra között szolgáltassa be.

2. aki kereszténynek bármilyen vagyontárgyat, bármilyen címen f. évi március 22. után átadott ma 16—20 óra között ugyanannál a bizottságnál irásban jelentse be. Részletesen fel kell sorolni, hogy milyen tárgyakat, milyen értékben, kinek (pontos név, foglalkozás, község, utca és házszám) mikor és milyen cimen adott át. A bejelentő aláirása alatt tüntesse fel foglalkozását és bejelentett lakását. A bejelentést 2 tanu előttemezze. Ugyanez a kötelezettség terheli azokat, akik ilyen esetekről tudnak.

3. akinel saját, vagy családja 14 napot meghaladó szükségletén felüli mennyiségü élelmiszer van, a felesleget ma 16—20 óra között szolgáltassa be az ugyanott müködő átvevő bizottságnak.

Holnaptól kezdve a Ghettőt csendőrökkel átkutattatom,
aki a fenti parancsaimat nem tartotta be, büntető táborba kerül.

Ezt a parancsot a ghettóban minden házban a kapu alatt, emeletes házban ezen kivül minden emeleten is ki kell függeszteni.

Nagyvárad, 1944. május hó 10.

A Csendőr Tanzászlóalj
és a Ghettó Parancsnoka.

Signed decree regarding the takeover of the Ghetto command by the gendarmes as of May 10, 1944. Source: Oradea City Archives further humiliate these people who were locked up without reason and deprived of their rights. Why did they have to specify that "inside the house – which must not be left – each occupant must stay only in the room to which he was allocated" and only be allowed to leave to perform bodily functions? Why did we have to rise at exactly 6:00 A.M., breakfast at 7:00 A.M., lunch at 12:30 P.M., dine at 6:00 P.M., and turn out our lights at 8:00 P.M.? Of what possible use was the order that nobody could go out into the street without permission, and that after 8:00 P.M. we could not even go to the courtyard of the house? What sick minds determined that after 8:00 P.M. the ghetto should be totally silent?

And indeed, after eight o'clock, the silence of a cemetery settled over the ghetto, silence and darkness. The electricity was cut off, and the windows were boarded up or whitewashed; it was forbidden to open them. Sometimes we went up to the attic and watched the town through the air vents. From the noises that stole into the house we tried to measure the rhythm of life of the town, as one does from the beating of a pulse. It seemed to me that in our absence this pulse was weaker. Perhaps I was fooling myself, wanting to believe that the town missed us.

The ghetto was divided into districts, which were subdivided into groups of houses. We had to choose house leaders from those in the building. These leaders and their assistants had to ensure that the ghetto rules were respected. I was the leader of my house, and Sári was my assistant. Usually, this responsibility was given to a man, but when my father was chosen in our house, I took on the task to spare him from the rudeness of the gendarmes.

The house leaders wore yellow armbands (again yellow!) with the initials HP (*Ház Parancsnok,* or house leader) in red beside the house number. We received identity papers but even we could not go outside without a valid reason. Twice a day, in the morning and in the evening, we had to give a report at the headquarters of the gendarmerie, where we were then given new orders that we had to enforce without question. One day, they ordered that all the women had to have their hair cut in two days' time. It was specified that it could not be longer than the earlobes. I knew that this would be greeted by protests, so I cut my own hair before I passed on the order. It hurt me to part with my blond curls. We also had to choose the members and shifts of the groups that went to do community work in the town. I think this was our most difficult job. With two hundred people living in the house, we had to be careful to divide the work evenly to avoid complaints of favouritism. We had the most trouble with those who thought their previous social status entitled them to special treatment.

People were only allowed out into the ghetto streets in groups, according to plans pre-established in writing, and accompanied by Sári or me. We had to go to the canteen every day for bread, and the sick had to be taken for treatment. We went to the public bath in the same way. The ritual bath was situated in the ghetto area, and we used it as the public bath.

My father conducted himself admirably. He had always been demanding and particular, living by certain standards, but he accommodated himself to his new situation. Our acquaintances loved and respected him, particularly our landlord's family, and supported us in our attempts to create the illusion of an ordered existence. Of course, this was limited. My father refused any privilege and seemed to be content with everything. Often I found him at the bottom of the courtyard, despondent. However, when questioned, he gave a show of confidence and tried to encourage others even if he did not feel it himself.

Our landlady was Aunty Aranka, the widow of Manó Feldheim, and she was marvellous. When we entered the ghetto, we abandoned our previous lives and our house; we knew there was no going back. Aunty Aranka, on the other hand, had stayed in her own house but no longer considered it hers. Her major preoccupation was to ensure, as much as possible, that our little community had a relatively comfortable life. It was her decision to put her furniture in the courtyard and the piano and carpets in the attic. Without complaint or reproach, she was hospitable, although in fact such hospitality had been imposed on her.

With the gendarmerie's occupation of the Dreher-Hagenmacher brewery a new phase began in the ghetto. This diabolical war machine was not satisfied with forcibly evicting people from their homes and seizing their belongings under the pretext of war needs. They then decided to take everything that Jewish families had left with friends or neighbours for safekeeping. They would allow nothing to stand in the way of achieving this goal. Within a short time the inhabitants of the ghetto began to call the administrative building of the brewery just "the Dreher" or "the mint," because it was the place where money was beaten out of people. The name reflected the atrocities committed there. This became our new terror. Every day, one to two hundred people were summoned for interrogation, as the gendarmes wanted the names of friends who held objects of sentimental or material value for safekeeping. All the members of the Jewish Council were arrested. They tortured Sándor Leitner, the president of the Jewish Orthodox community, for thirteen days. They tried unsuccessfully to force him to give a list of the wealthiest Jews. They spared neither his elderly parents nor his brother. They took and tortured the eighty-four-year-old dentist Dr. Munk, the seventy-six-year-old Dr. Samu Grosz, and the seventy-three-year-old Dr. Fisch. Women were not spared either. For days on end, they tortured Puti Steiner, who was a native of Șimleul Silvaniei and the wife of the journalist Laszló Bárdos; they also tortured the wife of the chief Neolog rabbi, Dr. István Vajda.

When people were summoned to the Dreher, the task of finding their homes fell to people trained as "detectives," who also had the job of escorting them to the ghetto gendarmerie. People presented themselves at the first summons. It did not enter anybody's mind to try to escape or to hide – there was nowhere to go. Even if there had been, who would have tried to save himself, knowing that his entire family could end up in the hands of the inquisition?

During that time, Márta Radó, who was still able to go in and out of the ghetto for the chemical products business, acquired some Romanian peasant clothing with the help of some friends. Her plan was to disguise her grandmother, Aunty Mandel, and get her out of the ghetto and across the Romanian border. But this lively sixty-one-year-old woman, who was still young in her ways, did not take the opportunity. She was afraid that if they looked for her and did not find her they would take revenge on her exempted son-in-law and his family. She was afraid they might lose their exempted status. Above all she was afraid for her niece, Anna Mandel, whom the engineer Radó had adopted to save her (the adoption was predated).

On one of the first days in the ghetto, my friend Hédi's father, the textile manufacturer József Silbermann, was taken from our house. He was brought home a few days later on a stretcher, half dead from the beatings. He was physically and spiritually destroyed. We never heard him speak a again. We learned what was happening inside the walls of the Dreher from others who had been tortured there. Gendarmes trained in the German political police interrogation course put great effort into combining medieval torture with modern techniques. First, they stripped their victims naked, then they beat them with leather belts, whips, iron rods, canes and rubber truncheons until they lost consciousness. They squeezed women's breasts in the door and, holding them by their hair, hit their heads on the wall. They chained their wrists and tightened the chain, link by link, until their bones broke. They hung their prisoners from iron bars, with their hands tied to their feet, and beat their bodies and the soles of their feet. They also tortured their victims mentally. They tortured children in front of their parents. Along with beatings they used subtler methods. They put a copper strip over the victim's head and passed an electric current through it. They put electrical wires on the most sensitive parts of the body – in the mouth, in the ears, in the nostrils, on the nipples, on the genital organs – and applied an electric current for forty to fifty minutes. They used an intestinal wash pumping enormous quantities of liquid into their victims' stomachs. People tortured in this way should have quickly given up their possessions, yet often refused to speak even when half conscious, rather than betray their benefactors. Some resisted. Others gave in. Tortures that did not produce results angered the interrogators. Successful ones encouraged them. They began to widen their radius of action. People were brought in the hundreds to the torture chambers. Music blared constantly from the Dreher to cover the screams of pain.

Fear and panic dominated those who lived in the ghetto. People sunk into themselves without hope, startled by any suspicious sound. No one knew when his turn would come. For fear of torture, many took refuge in death.

In the town, announcements stuck on walls, notices in the newspapers and newsreels at the cinema declared that there would be an amnesty of forty-eight hours for those who had hidden goods belonging to Jews. Frightened, people presented themselves in the hundreds to relieve themselves of the obligations they had taken on, while we, shut within the walls of the ghetto, trembling, waited for the summons. Some had left valuable objects with several families; when summoned, they did not know whom to declare, so as not to make things worse for those who continued to remain silent.

Hundreds of Jews were tortured daily at the Dreher. Out of their minds with pain, many gave some names. Things got more complicated, and the summons went out in waves with an ever-widening scope. On one occasion someone's hidden treasure was returned. One man, when summoned, was amazed to find his son's cradle with his son inside; the child had been left in the care of a good friend.

We were living in terror. At the beginning, people known to be rich were taken to the Dreher. Those who had been denounced followed, then those whose names had arisen accidentally during interrogation. Only those Jews who had nothing could live in relative calm. Yet even this calm soon came to an end. Bread was distributed at the public kitchen, and each house sent two people for an amount designated according to the number of occupants in the house. Every day, they lined up for endless hours before the bread was distributed. The kitchen was opposite the Dreher, and one day it occurred to an interrogator to question those in the queue too. About fifty people were lifted from the queue and taken to the torture chambers. Then new groups were chosen and then more new groups. The inhabitants of the ghetto were terrorized.

During these days of pain and fear, news began to circulate that the ghetto would be disbanded, or more precisely that the occupants of the ghetto were to be sent to a concentration camp. At the time we did not understand what this meant. In our distress we were only aware of the fact that we would be going far away from the torture chambers that were giving us nightmares. We hoped that the immediate danger we faced would be removed.

We tried to find information about what awaited us, but nobody knew anything. Once again, an elaborate plan was put into place to deceive us. The interrogators of the Dreher staged a telephone conversation with misleading information that was overheard by their victims. The victims pieced together what they had heard and joyfully passed the news along. To avoid panic, the gendarmes wanted to make us believe that we would all remain together at a place on the other side of the Danube in a centralized ghetto town. Again, we were naive. We tried to calm one another with the thought that conditions there would be different. A place of work would be assured. We wondered in what capacity we could be used, whether in factories, in workshops or in agricultural work. I had left my baccalaureate diploma with the Katz family for safekeeping, but I had my certificate of dressmaking training with me. I hoped that now I could make use of my sewing skills.

We awoke one morning, only three weeks after our internment in the ghetto, to the news that one of the ghetto streets had been closed off and evacuated. The inhabitants had only been given half an hour to get ready to leave. Each ghetto Jew could take only a knapsack and a bag for bread. That day, three hundred Jews were removed from Károly Rimler Street. Later we learnt that this group was assembled to complete the numbers of those from the province who had been evacuated and transported earlier.

The leadership of the Jewish Council asked the commander of the ghetto for an explanation. The response was the same as usual. Commander Bodolay informed the leaders that the people who had been taken would remain in the country, he could not say exactly where, and he assumed they had probably gone to do agricultural work.

The following day the deportation continued. Where? How? When? For how long? Together or separately? The terror of deportation had paralyzed all our minds. The order to organize the ghetto had been given on May 3, and after only a few weeks, on May 25, its disbanding had begun. We had gone through so much in that short period. By this time we had already begun to guess that everything we had gone through until then was only preparation for some final inevitable act.

A feverish agitation possessed the ghetto. More and more measures followed. The ghetto area was divided into a number of subunits. The evacuation was organized and scheduled by sectors, and twenty-five hundred to three thousand people left the ghetto each day. Our turn came on the day before the last.

Reverse numbering began. To avoid panic, we were forbidden to leave our houses. Only the house leaders were allowed to go outside, and only at particular times and in certain streets. Across the courtyards and gardens of the houses (the fences separating them had been used for wood from the start) we found relatives and acquaintances and kept in contact with them. We learned that Kert (Avram Iancu) and Vámház (Sucevei) streets had already been evacuated and that Kapucinus and Szacsvai (Cuza Voda) streets were next. The evacuated streets were closed, but as the gendarmes still supervised them, no one could go there.

Wishing to visit my cousin Manci Szmuk's family, whose turn was to come before ours, I wandered into an evacuated street. A terrible sight unfolded in front of me. The silence of death pervaded the street. Houses had been left in haste with their doors wide open, inviting me to look inside; they were in a state of disarray. In the dust of the street you could still see the footprints of those who had recently been deported. Here and there knapsacks, bundles, and rags tied in scarves were lying around, evidence that people were driven out hurriedly and not allowed to pick up their fallen belongings. Toys had been trampled underfoot, teddy bears once carefully guarded were now scattered in the dust of the street, and I thought of frightened, crying children. In that silent deserted street, a strange feeling came over me, as if I was walking through open graves. I was riveted to the spot. The nightmare vision only lasted a few moments. The threatening whistle of a gendarme brought me back to reality. I quickly retraced my steps to the inhabited area. I had just glimpsed what our fate would be in a few days' time.

Following the internment of the Jews in the ghetto, the population of sixty thousand in Oradea was left with only eight Christian doctors. To ensure the medical care of the Christian population, six Jewish doctors and their families had been left in the town. During the days of deportation, they were also brought unexpectedly to the ghetto. Thus Dr. Kornelia Mózes, a specialist in the sanatorium for pulmonary diseases and my friend Sári's cousin, arrived in our house. At the same time, Dr. Lajos Ertzmann, an ear, nose and throat specialist, moved into the ghetto with his wife and their beautiful twin daughters, as did the specialist for internal diseases, Dr. Artur Sebestyén, the ophthalmologist Dr. Alfréd Bock, the dermatologist Dr. László Barna, and the pediatrician Dr. Ede Aufricht. Watching Kornélia, I realized what it was like for these people, who had been in a privileged situation, to face this unexpected turn of fate. We had got used to things gradually going from bad to worse, while they were overwhelmed and virtually crushed. Only this could explain the action of Dr. Ertzmann, usually a strong man full of life, who administered a lethal injection to his wife and daughters and then to himself while they were still on the train.

Dr. Kornélia Mózes brought us news about the town. The sixteen Jewish families who had exempted status because of war disability or because of some special war merit were living in a voluntary ghetto that they had created in their own houses, isolated from the town. Although they were exempted from wearing the yellow star, they did not leave their houses for fear of insults. Those from mixed marriages tried, with the help of lawyers, to save those family members who according to the legislation had exempted status, cases that the ghetto commanders had not taken into account. The only situations where they gave way were those in which, in spite of the fact that they were Christians, the wife or the husband wanted to follow the Jewish spouse and children. Because of this the families of the lawyers Dr. Endre Fehér and Béla Friedmann were taken. Some committed suicide, overwhelmed by the terrible circumstances, as did poor Margit Kemény, the wife of Dr. Romulus Costa.

Even those with exempted status suffered abuse. The engineer Radó was denounced by his neighbour on false grounds, and members of the Katz family were summoned to an inspection in the ghetto with all their possessions and documents. Their exemption papers were torn up, they were taken out into Rhédey Park where people were being loaded into cattle cars, and they were crowded into a train that was just leaving. The chemical engineer Miklós Stern had exempt status because of war merit. At the last moment, he wanted to give some medication to his family who were already on the train. The door of the cattle car opened and Miklós Stern was pushed inside and deported. He perished with his family.

As the inhabitants of the ghetto were getting ready for the journey, not all were able to endure the tension. Some took poison. The most frequent cases of suicide were among older people, husbands and wives together. Many committed suicide because of the tortures at the Dreher, such as Gyula Stolz and Márton László.

During these last days, many wanted to get into the ghetto hospital. They thought they would enjoy more humane treatment among the sick. Others moved, with or without their luggage and their families, into the attics of those houses that would not be evacuated until the final days. They thought if they gained time they would live. Two families moved in with us as well. I condemned them at the time because I thought it cowardly to disrupt our lives for the sake of a few days' postponement. Later I realized that I was wrong. These people were courageous; they were willing to take a risk, to choose a difficult course of action. They opted for personal solutions, even if the outcome was uncertain. I heard of some who escaped through the wooden fence into town, hid for a few days in a safe place, and then crossed illegally into Romania. Others walled themselves into the cellars of evacuated houses and stayed there until the ghetto was empty and the last train of deportees had left. They still ended up in internment camps, but they survived. Dr. Miksa Kupfer and Dr. Sándor Bálint gathered a group of about thirty people on the pretext that they were suffering from typhoid fever and isolated them for a few days in the section for contagious diseases. When the deportation ended, control weakened and they managed to escape. They crossed the border and got away.

Considering the many thousands of people interned in the ghetto, the number of those who escaped was far too small. Mass opposition could have achieved more, but few thought of resistance. Although at the time we already knew about the Warsaw ghetto uprising, or maybe precisely because of that, we did not have the courage to do anything. In any case, my sister Erzsi was one of those who wanted to act, to do something. "We have nothing to lose," she used to say. "Let's unite. Let's open a breach in the wall and let's rush hundreds through it at once!" It was clear that we would be machine-gunned and many of us would die, but in such a surprise breakout many could escape.

Of course, all these plans were childish, but even now, many years later, I sometimes wonder why we did not try to organize some resistance. Some of the reasons are obvious: our strong young men had all been taken away to labour service; we were unarmed; we had only spent a short time in the ghetto; we had only just managed to get some order into our daily life. The time was not ripe for an uprising. Most of all we believed in humanity, and we let ourselves be deluded by a campaign of manipulation.

During those terrible days, we again remembered my sister Magda's Cuban passport. Magda and I went to the president of the Jewish Council, Sándor Leitner. We explained Magda's situation to him and sought his advice. Unfortunately, his reply was not clear enough, or perhaps we simply did not have the courage to take the necessary risk. We told him that Magda's passport was hidden in the attic of our house in town. He said that we must show it to the authorities. Official representatives would accompany Magda. They would find the passport and on the basis of this would intern her together with little Anikó. Magda was afraid at the very thought of separation and internment, and also of the fact that other documents were hidden in the same place as the passport, for which our father could be summoned for interrogation and perhaps tortured. We did not know what would be waiting for Magda if she parted from us, but we felt that it would be the less dangerous alternative for her. Perhaps if we had not been so afraid for our father, we would have acted. Sándor Leitner kindled a gleam of hope for Magda and her daughter. I can never forgive myself for being indecisive then. Why did I not convince Magda to take this last chance? Our generous, good, beautiful Magda, who had always let herself be ruled by the will of fate, simply could not take a decisive step this time either. She remained with us and shared our common fate. I never discussed this with her, but I am sure that she too was afraid for our father. I have wondered many times what would have happened if she had chosen internment. Certainly she and her daughter would have been saved, but I would have reproached myself my whole life if I had caused the torture of my father.

During those last disturbing days in the ghetto, many people decided to get married. People sought strength in being loved. We organized a wedding in our house. Hédi Silbermann's seventeen-year-old cousin Vita was living with her. She had taken refuge here from Vienna. Vita married Bandi, the son of the lawyer Pál Ney. Because we did not want to attract attention and get into trouble, we did not erect a *chupa* in the courtyard. As this is very important for the Jewish marriage ceremony, we substituted a prayer shawl, a *talith*, that four men stretched out like a tent. We did everything we could to create the illusion of peacetime. In the attic, from the depths of a cupboard, we found an old bride's veil. We bleached it and starched it. The bride received her congratulations dressed in immaculate white. Not even the bride's bouquet was missing, as it was mid-May and the lilacs were in bloom. The ceremony was performed according to the prescribed ritual. We were all deeply moved. Unfortunately, we could not invite guests or even our closest family members to a celebratory meal. We were, however, able to prepare a surprise for the new couple: they received a cup of hot chocolate and cake, and later the traditional golden chicken soup. After lunch they had real coffee from ground beans. Then the moment of parting arrived. The new pair left for their honeymoon. They put their bags on their backs and took pillows and blankets in their arms and left for the groom's house where the attic had been prepared for them.

Our life of constant fear was brightened by the brief spark of these moments of joy. We continued preparations for our journey to the unknown. There were no shops in the ghetto where we could buy essential articles, as business had ceased. Everything had to be done at home, with whatever we could find at hand. In a very short time, we had to sew forty-seven knapsacks and bread bags from sheets and tablecloths. We made straps from towels, and blankets from curtains and tablecloths, using buckles from belts or buttons. Each of us picked through our belongings for things to pack into a single knapsack. We had no idea what fate had in store for us or what we might need. Thinking of the cold, rain, and frost that was coming, we chose raincoats and warm pullovers with long sleeves. But we would also need underwear, detergent, cooking pots and of course food and blankets. We each packed separately because we had no way of knowing where any of us would end up. Forty-two people raced through the house getting ready for the journey. We sewed, we chose and we packed. We tried out our knapsacks, thinking about what we would miss and what we would need most. Since there were hardly any chairs, each of us was doing all this crouched down on the floor.

Aunty Feldheim, who used to seek advice from the rabbi of Páva before making important decisions, turned to him now. The rabbi gave her a laconic answer: "You don't need to prepare bags; you don't need to pack anything; you don't need anything." Two days later, the rabbi was deported with his family, and we observed, smiling, that on this occasion his prophecy was not correct. In fact he was right, but we did not know it yet.

Time was passing with astounding speed, and the day of departure drew nearer. The butchers at the Dreher came up with a new plan. Just before a new section was due to be evacuated, they took about fifty people from each group of houses for interrogation. Trembling at the thought that they could be separated from their families, these people confessed everything.

We were to go on Thursday, June 1. We spent Wednesday in a state of great agitation, waiting to see what would come from the Dreher. To our amazement, nothing came. By Wednesday evening no one cared about keeping the rules anymore. We sat outside in the courtyard, ignoring our curfew. As a body we refused to obey, because now that we were being deported, we believed that nothing else could happen to us.

News items from the local press of the times: "Never again will the Jewish spirit reign within the City of Saint Ladislau"; "The publication, distribution and borrowing of the work of Jewish authors is forbidden." Detail of the speech given by Dr. László Gyapay – known as the "executioner of Várad"– on July 15, 1944, on the occasion of his appointment as Mayor of Nagyvárad. Source: Oradea City Archives

Soha többé nem uralkodhatik a zsidó szellem Szent László városában

Éberen fogok minden erőmmel őrködni azon, hogy az elmult idők zsidó destruáló szelleme soha többé be ne juthasson ennek a városnak a falai közé.

Ha akadnak a város polgárai közül olyanok, akik még most sem értik meg az idők parancsoló szavát, akkor nélkülük, ellenük fogom megszervezni mindazokat, akik tudnak és akarnak dolgozni a közösségért, az egyetemes nemzeti érdekekért, Hazánk fennmaradásáért, szebb és boldogabb jövőjéért.

A vezetésem alatt álló tisztviselői kart kívánom elsősorban ebbe az új egészséges, keresztény, magyar, népi és szociális szellembe beállítani, mert csak így övelük együtt tudom feladataimat teljes egészében teljesíteni.

Az én szociálpolitikám alapja nem az alamizsna, hanem a tisztességes kenyér, a család jólétének emelése, a munkás jövőjét biztosító munka nyújtása min-maradása s ez az új nemzeti szocialista szellemben újjáébredő Magyarország megerősítése nem lesz lehetséges.

Erre az összefogásra, a lelkek megbékélésére hívok fel mindenkit s ennek a keresztény nemzeti társadalmi egységnek megteremtése érdekében kívánom beleültetni a váradi lelkekbe a jobboldali, magyar nemzeti fajvédő irányzatot.

Tekintetes Törvényhatósági Bizottság!

Ma, amikor egy roppant gigantikus méretű háború kellős közepén áll az ország, reális és részletekbe menő programmot nem adhatok.

Nagy alkotásokról a háborús anyaggazdálkodási és munkaviszonyok korlátolt lehetőségei keretében nem lehet szó.

Elgondolásom, tervem, programmom sok van, amelyeknek megvalósitására az épitő, alkotó munkáról majd

---

Zsidó szerzők müveit kiadni, terjeszteni és kölcsönözni tilos

A kiadóvállalatok és könyvtárak példányait megsemmisítik és hulladékpapírké értékesítik

A hivatalos lap vasárnapi száma kormányrendeletet közöl a magyar szellemi életnek a zsidó szerzők írói müveitől való megóvása tárgyában.

A rendelet értelmében zsidó szerzők írói müvét többszörösíteni, közzétenni és forgalombahozni nem szabad. Tudományos tárgyú írói mű többszörösítésére, közzétételre és forgalombahelyezése közérdekből a vallás- és közoktatásügyi miniszter a miniszterelnökkel egyetértésben kivételesen engedélyt adhat.

A rendelet mellékletében felsorolt zsidó szerzők müvének a kiadónál, nyomdavállalatnál, kereskedőnél és általában a forgalombahozatallal vagy terjesztéssel foglalkozó — akár természetes, akár jogi személy által fenntartott — vállalatnál levő és forgalombahozatalra szánt példányait terjeszteni, kölcsönadni, vagy bármi más módon használatba bocsátani nem szabad.

Az említett vállalatok, úgyszólván a könyvkölcsönzéssel foglalkozó vállalatok, valamint a nyilvános könyvtárak, továbbá az egyesületi, iskolai, intézeti és egyéb olyan könyvtárak vezetői, amelyekből könyveket bárkinek vagy a személyek bizonyos körének (egyesület vagy társulat tagjainak, iskola tanulóinak stb.) olvasásra vagy egyéb használatra átadnak, kötelesek a fentebb meghatározott müveknek forgalombahozatalra, kikölcsönzésre vagy könyvtári használatra szánt példányait e rendelet hatálybalépésétől számított 15 nap alatt kimutatásba foglalni és a kimutatás több példányban az említett határidőben a sajtóügyekért magyar királyi kormánybiztoshoz (Budapest, I., Uri utca 18.) bemutatni.

A sajtóügyek kormánybiztosa a jelentések három példányát a Mag Papirosipari Nyersanyagbeszerző F nek küldi meg. A Kft. a beküldött jelentések alapján felhívja a b lentőket, hogy a példányokat ho mikor szolgáltassák be.

Az állami, törvényhatósági, köze egyházi, alapítványi és közinté müveinek a bejelentett könyveinek példányait elkülön kell őrizni s azokat csupán indo esetben tudományos kutatás célji adják ki.

A rendelkezéseket alkalmazni azoknak a zsidó szerzőknek írói veire is, akiket a rendelet hatál lépése után a Budapesti Közlöny közzétett ujabb jegyzék felsorol A hivatalos lap közli az jegyzéket is azokról a zsidó szerről, akiknek müveit ki kell von közforgalomból.

A Kft. a beszolgáltatott példá kért a hulladékpapir hatóságilag állapitott árát téríti meg és a be gáltatott példányok megsemmisíti ről összezúzás útján késedelem né gondoskodik.

---

ztositani akarja

THE JOURNEY TO AUSCHWITZ

*M*ost of us had spent the night without any sleep. After agonizing hours in the grip of the terrible unknown, the dawn was finally upon us. The knapsacks, closed and ready, were on the floor. We were waiting for the signal to go when we heard a loud, coarse police voice in the courtyard below, urging us to hurry up. "Line up! We are leaving!" Without a word of protest we took our bags and left. Once again we were leaving a place that we had begun to think of as "home." It occurred to me that we had wasted our time trying to create some humane living conditions. We had fallen into the trap again. We had thought that we would remain in the ghetto longer. I did some calculations: our sad life in the ghetto had not lasted a month, yet it seemed like years. And in truth we had aged years.

We stepped out of the house, and we did not even think to close the door. Who cared what we left behind us? Following rude orders spiced with obscenities, we formed a column in rows of five in the courtyard and then joined the caravan that had stopped in front of the house. A group of about seventy people had formed up. In front, cheerful, loquacious, mounted police, wearing tall hats with plumes, rallied the groups. They were determined to keep the number at seventy even if that meant separating some families. Then greed and desire for profit overtook the police again. They yelled at us threateningly:

"People! Watches, pens, and money must be handed over! No one should take more than one pair of shoes with them!"

To show that they meant business, they rummaged impatiently through our bags. After this humiliating interlude was finished, we set off.

I remember it well: it was June 1, a Thursday. We were very warm, as we had put on two or three layers of clothing to leave more room in the bags for food. We had tried to make sure that we had winter clothing, such as sweaters and coats, as well as summer clothing. Using towels, we had made aprons with oversized pockets that we had tied around our waists. At the time, who cared about what we looked like? We had put soap, a toothbrush and toothpaste, shoe polish and other useful little things in the pockets. We still had illusions. We still hoped that "there," in that uncertain place to which we were heading, we could meet our basic needs.

Troubled, we staggered on, our steps hampered by the heavy burdens on our shoulders and backs. With a heavy heart, I took a furtive glance at my parents. I had never seen them so crushed yet so heroic in their despair. My poor father was carrying such a heavy bag that I could scarcely move with it, but he carried it as if he could continue for many kilometres if necessary. My dear mother walked as one who did not know what was happening around her. It did not matter where the road was leading, as long as she had her family beside her. The muscles in Magda's neck were tight, and only her great love and concern for her child stopped her from throwing down her heavy bag. Her little girl, Anikó, had had her fifth birthday a few days earlier. Although she was wearing too many clothes for June, including a winter coat and a raincoat, she endured it patiently and with incredible tenacity, as if she understood that this was not a time for indulgence. And we all went on in silence, like machines. We had no thoughts in our heads but a single weary wish: to reach the train as quickly as possible and put down our heavy bags.

Slowly, we reached the walls of our prison, which opened towards Vámház Street. From here on we continued outside the ghetto walls. I think that the inhabitants of the town had been forbidden to walk freely through this part of town because I only saw people watching us from the windows. We went on dumbly along this deserted route. For the majority of us, this was the final journey. The street later justly acquired the name of the Avenue of the Martyrs (Mártirok). For a few minutes we tasted freedom again. And to make the illusion complete, we passed under the superb, shady trees of Rhédey Park.

The Silbermann family was in the row in front of us. Right at the start, the blanket had fallen off the bag carried by my friend Hédi's father. A gendarme immediately appeared on the scene beside him. He picked it up and hurled it far away, so that there was no way of retrieving it. Here there was no difference between a clerk, a factory owner, a doctor, a shopkeeper, or a beggar; here there were only "dirty Jews." The gendarmes made this very clear during the journey. The Silbermann family was distressed about losing their blanket. Then one of the straps on Mr. Silbermann's knapsack broke. Hédi tried to help her father. It was heart wrenching to watch her carry her father's heavy bag as well as her own heavy bag. Soon she could only drag the bags along the ground until she gave up the struggle only a few steps before reaching our goal. In this way many people abandoned their bags along the way. The fallen bags looked like anonymous graves at the side of the road.

We moved forward like a slowly heaving flood into the unknown, stumbling along in the steps of those in front of us. Those who could not keep up with the convoy – the elderly, the sick, and disabled – were abused by the guards. There was no indication of any humanity in those who drove us; if it existed, it was hidden with great skill.

I breathed freely when I reached the leafy trees of the park. I took a deep breath of the fresh air. This sensation only lasted a few moments; I could not escape the claws of merciless reality. The railway tracks were already under our feet, and we had to be careful how we trod as our view was impeded by those in front of us. Under the fresh, green trees stood a long train made up of cattle cars, with narrow platforms leading up to the doors. Orders were rattled out and hundreds of people – teenagers, children, old people, the healthy, the sick, and the disabled – all clambered up the narrow planks and disappeared into the darkness.

When we found ourselves up there and squeezed into the cattle car, we understood why we had been counted. Seventy people were crowded in cattle cars intended for twenty horses or forty people. In some cars there were even more. We were completely at a loss and did not know what to do. Terror completely overcame us the moment the door was closed behind us, as the iron rods were ground home and the padlock shut. Now we knew for certain that we were prisoners.

Only a weak light crept through a tiny, wired window. We guessed that a long journey was ahead of us, and for that reason, we lowered ourselves to the floor, with knees raised, supported by the bodies around us. We had taken our places in family groups. Those who could not find a place to sit down remained standing. Later, we traded places. In one corner a barrel of water had been prepared for the journey, and in another corner a similar receptacle had been placed in which to relieve ourselves. While we were still struggling in that miserable, tight space, we heard the wheels grind and the train set out towards the unknown future.

Where was this train going? Where were we being taken? Without my wishing it, an image formed in my mind, an image that I had never seen but had often imagined. We had heard that Czech, Slovak, and Polish Jews, in locked cattle cars full of distressed people, mad with thirst, had passed through stations and disappeared into "thin air." We had never believed that this could be our fate too. Now our train was moving on, exactly as in my imagination. It was a frightful image, an ill omen. I did not talk to anyone about it. What would have been the point of frightening people who were already so terrified?

The air in the cattle car was suffocating and stifling. I cannot explain how such a thing is possible, but with the exception of the wailing sound of an occasional burst of sobbing, I cannot remember anything about the journey. Certainly there must have been very sick people among us, perhaps people who were dying, dissatisfied, indignant, or fussy, but I remember only those who were sitting or standing next to me. And here in the cattle car, as in the ghetto, we gathered one another into a close circle of family and friends. Most of us sat, deep in our thoughts. Our mouths were so dry that we could not even chew the cakes our caring mothers had baked in the last few days. Perhaps because of our anxiety we were not hungry. However, we were suffering from extraordinary thirst that was compounded by our dehydrated bodies soaked in sweat and the lack of air. The last few glasses of water from the bottom of the barrel had been distributed by the person in charge of the cattle car, virtually mouthful by mouthful, but in the end the barrel was completely drained and there was no more to be had. When the train stopped, as it rarely did, those near the windows stuck out some saucepans. From all the windows one could hear heartbreaking, imploring cries: "Water! Water! Have mercy on us, give us water!"

Hands reached to take the vessels and occasionally kind faces followed us, but much more often we saw malicious, grinning faces. Some snatched the saucepans and ran away with them, never to reappear. Others tried to lift vessels full of water to the thirsty, but the gendarmes chased them far away. With my parched and dry mouth I gazed yearningly at the great jet of water that was pouring out, and I thought that the cruelty of the guards could not be simply inborn wickedness but had to be the result of systematic training. Was it by chance that they took us from our homes, banished us from our native land, robbed us of our belongings, and now looked on with indifference as we were dying of thirst? From many cattle cars came the sound of banging. People were pleading to take off the dead, some of whom had committed suicide. Not one cattle car was opened. There was no mercy.

A very meagre amount of light and air came in through a window the size of a hand. Besides the thoughts that tormented us and the unbearable thirst, we were suffering terribly from the heat of our sweating bodies, the lack of air, and the overcrowding. We had to find room for seventy people as well as the knapsacks and layers of clothing we had taken off.

The children suffered even more than we did, but they understood the extraordinary nature of the situation. We took turns telling stories to our little Anikó to distract her from the thirst that was torturing her. She listened with resignation. Only on the third day, when the thirst had become truly unbearable, did she murmur in a voice wracked from exhaustion, in a dying voice: "This time tell me a very long story." She whispered to my sister Erzsi, who could master the longest stories and knew best how to calm her.

The wheels of the train rattled indifferently and monotonously under us. The train advanced without pity. We tried to orient ourselves by reading the names of the train stations we passed through to see in which direction we were heading. We could no longer imagine that we would be settled on the other side of the Danube. When this became obvious, faces became more apprehensive and tongues more silent. It is true that we hurry to share our joys with others, but pain requires solitude.

Our despair reached its peak when during the third night, rattling words of command woke us from our lethargy. We followed every word with bated breath. For the whole journey we had been waiting for a sign from which we could deduce the fate awaiting us. Our suspicions were confirmed within a few minutes: we were to be given into the hands of the Germans. Our worst fears were realized. We were going to an internment camp; there would be no ghetto town, only defencelessness.

When we had heard about the deportation of Slovak, Czech, and Polish Jews, we had said that nothing like that could ever happen to us. The Hungarian Jews were so closely linked to the Hungarian nation, so well assimilated, that the Hungarian people would not allow such a thing. Now they had not only accepted German aggression, but having robbed us of everything by their own hand and used their own trains, supervised by their own gendarmes, they were delivering us to the Germans to do anything they wanted with us.

We spent the night in the train station. Towards sunrise, the locks clicked and the doors opened, but not to let us get down and stretch our stiff limbs or to draw some clean air into our lungs. After they had ordered us to be quiet, the guards announced with resounding voices that we were in Košice and as we already knew, we were to be handed over to the Germans.

In those final moments they robbed us one last time. In spite of the many threats, a few among us had still kept some small trifles, either because they could not part with some beloved keepsake or because they thought that they would be able to exchange these objects for a piece of bread in even harder times. Now the guards wanted these valuables too.

"People!" sounded a threatening voice. "Wedding rings, earrings, pens, and money must be handed over. You will be searched and if anything is found punishment will follow. Let it stay in the country, because the Germans will take it for sure," they added, not without a certain amount of cynicism. The rings, the last sign of the link between husband and wife, fell into the gendarme's now extended hat. At this sight, tears welled up again in poor Magda's eyes, although her ring had already been taken. Probably only now did she understand that she would never see her husband again.

In those critical moments, we thought of those we loved, whom fate had spared from the end that awaited us. In those moments, the idea came to nearly all of us to say farewell, to send a last greeting, a message to those whom until recently we had worried about and who from now on would know nothing more about us. In our apron pockets, in addition to things necessary for hygiene, we carried postcards, and impelled by a sudden idea, we started to write. Father wrote to my brother Duci and my sister Ibi. Erzsi wrote to her husband-to-be Józsi, and I, to Karcsi Mózes, to whom (and it was then that I realized this) I felt the closest. I wrote those lines cautiously, not mentioning the place from which it was sent. From

Magyarország jövő békessége és felvirágzása — a szovjetoroszországi harcmezőkön dől el!

TÁBORI POSTAI LEVELEZŐLAP.

Cím:

Dr. Kovács Károly

k. m. r.

A feladó

neve: ....

foglalkozása: ....

címe: ....

Ára : 1 fillér.

A tábori posta száma: **B. 509.**

A címzett csapattestének, alakulatának megnevezése szigorúan tilos!

En route to the unknown, my goodbye postcard to Karcsi from Kosice. The date (upper right) mistakenly indicates May 4 rather than June 4. Our postcards, thrown from the cattle car, were forwarded by a good-willed railway worker.

the postcard one should not be able to discern in what surroundings it was written, as this could jeopardize its delivery. I could not write the entire truth because the addressee was also in a difficult situation and he too was in need of strength of mind to be able to cope. Karcsi brought this card home, along with all the other postcards from me and those he received from his parents. That is why I am able to quote those lines word for word:

> Dear Karcsi! I am still in a position to write to you today and I want to use the opportunity to say farewell to you. I hope that we will meet again and that pleasant days will be ours once again. Because until now we have not had many. We will try to send you news about us. I know that now the situation is reversing and it will be you who will worry about us. We will hold together and we will take care of one another. Take care of yourself. May God be with all of you and with us. See you later. Teri, June 4, 1944.

Did we really believe that we would see each other again, in a happy reunion, or did I only write this to reassure him? I do not know, but if I recall my later hopeful behaviour and incredible optimism, I guess I truly believed it.

The postcards were written and the train was slowly preparing to leave. I elbowed my way towards the window and waited for an opportunity to give it to someone. I had already begun to lose all hope when a railway worker appeared who seemed to understand what I wanted. He covered the postcards with his red signalling flag, and in a few moments he had disappeared, taking them with him.

How often I thought about those postcards sent from the shadow of death. It preoccupied me. I wanted so much to know what had happened to them. Only after the war did I find the answer to my worries: all the postcards had reached their destinations.

Writing and sending the postcards had a calming effect and shook us a little from our lethargy. The monotonous rattling of the train, our grief, and the unknown places coming into sight from time to time soon threw us back to our previous state of numbness. We stared into nothingness in front of us. Much later, my father's whispering voice broke the silence. It seemed as if he was talking slowly to himself; perhaps he was thinking out loud.

"They will put the young people to work, but they will not feed us old people and the children for nothing."

At the sound of these prophetic words, I was struck by recognition. I knew that he was right. I knew that I should say that he was wrong. I should contradict him, convince him of the opposite. Yet I felt that it was not the place to dispute or to console, because every word would sound false. We all remained quiet, not uttering a word until we arrived. The thirsty and hungry did not complain. No one objected. In those moments of great danger, it became perfectly clear to us what was important. We all knew that all these things were insignificant compared to what awaited us.

4
AUSCHWITZ

When the iron bar was pulled aside and the door of our cattle car opened, we were greeted by brilliant sunshine. We did not have time to look around, though, or to evaluate where we were, because with shouts and beatings they drove us out of the cattle car as quickly as possible. From all directions we heard:

"Alle heraus!"

"*Los! Los!* Alle heraus! Schneller heraus!" (Get out, get out, quickly, get out!)

"Alles dort lassen!" (Leave everything there!)

What happened then lasted only a few minutes. We did not have time to think. We simply knew that we must do what they ordered.

"*Los! Los! Schneller!*"

This hassling had a profound psychological effect as it stripped us of the last shred of our ability to judge what was happening.

Almost all of us left the cattle car at once. On the platform we were surrounded by frighteningly experienced black-uniformed SS guards. Within minutes, they lined us up in rows of five. The women were separated from the men. For a fraction of a second I followed my father with my eyes as he disappeared into the distance. After the three-day journey, his face was covered in stubble, but he still held himself with dignity and self-assurance. He was supporting my friend Hédi's father, and this was his fatal mistake. My mind only recorded that my cousin Harry Klärmann, who was just a few years younger, was beside him.

I found myself in a row with my mother, Erzsi, Magda, and little Anikó. The column moved on without stopping. Ahead of us, we saw that the elderly and mothers with small children were being separated from the young and strong, who then continued with a group that led off in another direction. Men in prisoners' clothes who appeared to be helping the SS guards mingled in our rows and whispered in Yiddish in our ears.

"Leave the children with the old people! ... Make sure twins present themselves."

The appearance of the prisoners was strange and their advice confusing, but it was not the time to ask for explanations. The column continued to move forward. Erzsi offered to go with Anikó. Magda was just on the point of agreeing when our row arrived in front of an all-powerful SS officer. Naively Magda addressed herself trustingly, without being asked, to the elegant, smiling officer with the pleasant appearance:

"Mein Kind (my child)," she said, and the young officer who inspired such trust smiled and with a nod of his head, "Gehe mit ihr (go with her)!"

We returned the smile, full of gratitude, and we headed in the directions he indicated to us. Erzsi and I went to the right; mother, Magda and Anikó went to the left. Without a word of farewell, without putting up the least resistance, we were separated forever. I would never have thought such a thing possible, that with smiles on their lips and with faces that inspired trust and feigned good intentions, these men could send hundreds of thousands of unsuspecting people to their deaths.

A few steps further on, my friend Sári told me with joy that because of the intervention of her cousin Dr. Kornelia Mózes, a place had been found for her younger sister Agi, who was very weak, in the Red Cross car. The same benevolent officer who had approved their request, we discovered later, was none other than the notorious Dr. Josef Mengele, SS Hauptsturmführer, the doctor who had performed the selections. They too had fallen into the trap of their own naiveté.

All this happened with incredible speed, practically in passing. As with other groups, our column was made up on the basis of differing criteria and headed off in an unknown direction. We did not have time

On the day of our
arrival at Auschwitz,
my sister Magda and
her little daughter
Anikó both died a
martyr's death.

to think what was bad and what was good or what we should do. We were not able to assess what was happening around us. All we knew was that we had arrived in a detention camp whose size surpassed imagination. From where we stood into the far distance, all we could see were many giant concrete pillars against the horizon, surrounded by barbed wire, rising towards the sky. Hundreds of barracks, surrounded by watchtowers, formed orderly columns. Whichever way we looked, we saw frightening SS soldiers wearing black uniforms and carrying death's head automatic pistols in their hands, their fingers on the triggers ready to shoot.

Just as the stigmatization with the yellow star and the internment in the ghetto had the sole object of facilitating our deportation, so here everything was well planned and moved like clockwork. They had to move people quickly before they could shake their bewilderment and break into panic, even more so because each transport brought twenty-five hundred to three thousand people. Hungary was ceaselessly churning out trains, with three or four trains arriving each day for a total of twelve to fourteen thousand people.

So we young women went along the route that had been indicated to us. Young men in great numbers were going in another direction. The sick, the disabled, the children, and anyone over fifty years old were taken in yet another direction. Each group by itself formed an immense mass of people.

The SS men, who had surrounded us, moved around like demigods. They dismissed us and looked down on us. We did not dare address our burning questions to them. Prisoners in striped clothes were helping to keep order. We did not yet understand what their role was. We simply understood that they had a privileged position, in spite of the fact that they were prisoners. So we assailed them with questions. Some knew Hungarian, but most spoke Yiddish or German.

"Where are they taking the elderly, the sick and the children?" we asked, alarmed. "When will we see them again?"

They did not really reply, and when they did their replies were evasive. Some of them told us indulgently what we were expecting to hear:

"You can meet every evening.... You will see them again tomorrow. They will be looked after. They will be fed. They won't have to work."

Others bluntly and cynically pointed to the sky and only said,

"They are being taken to Camp H." Later they explained that the H was for *Himmel*, which means heaven.

In the distance, tongues of flame were darting out of huge chimneys. The air was heavy with the nauseating stench of burnt flesh. Although the allusion was unmistakable, this was too horrible for us to accept. A sound mind could not bear this sudden confrontation with reality. We all unconsciously shrank from this cruel and brutal truth. We did not allow what we were hearing and seeing to enter our consciousness. We consoled ourselves with answers that were clearly lies. We kept repeating the comforting words we had heard and passed them on from one to another so that the good news would gain the greatest weight.

We talked like this while we were marching forward. We were advancing steadfastly, seemingly hypnotized, along the designated path between the high barbed-wire fences. Beyond the fence, we could see hundreds of barracks. In front of one of the nearer barracks, characters clothed in long, shapeless dresses were running about. One of them, with a cane in hand, was chasing them towards the barracks. I had never seen anything like it. The shaved heads, looking like small balls, swinging to and fro, reminded me of Goya's painting *Scene From a Madhouse* and his engravings titled *Caprichos*. I was convinced they had brought the sick of the psychiatric ward from some town, and now these unfortunate people were just running around.

One of the women stole up to the fence and called my name.

"Teri, if you have any food on you, throw it to me over the fence. They will take it away from you anyway. We are starving here…"

Unfortunately, all our things had been left behind. Apart from the clothes we were wearing, we did not have anything with us, so I had no way of granting her request. I searched her face, but it did not remind me of anyone. Her voice, however, sounded familiar. With horror, I suddenly realized that the woman in front of me was one of my former classmates, Ági Guttman, whom I had seen three days earlier in the ghetto in Oradea. She had been young, healthy, and confident. What had happened to her in the space of a few days?

"Dear Lord, what is happening here?" I asked myself. "Where have I come to? Do the civilized people of Europe have any idea what is happening here?"

As we learned later, they knew. Suddenly I was overcome by the feeling that we were in the middle of an enormous ocean, on an isolated island where the SS could do anything they wanted with us and between us and the world was an insurmountable distance about which we could do nothing. I did not realize how close to the truth this sentiment was. Indeed, not only could they, but they actually did do anything they wanted. The only difference was that we were not far from Europe. We were actually in its middle, in the southern part of Poland, near an insignificant little town called Auschwitz, in the concentration camp of Auschwitz-Birkenau.

Our column was stopped in front of one of the barracks. They led us into a big room and ordered us to undress. At first we were shocked. Around us, many SS soldiers and prisoners in by now familiar striped clothing moved about. As on our arrival, they did not give us time to think. Commands of "*Los!*

Los! Schneller!" resounded and we were already taking our clothes off. We had a lot of clothing on, and we folded it carefully, one thing on top of the other. Erzsi folded her new camel-hair coat with special care, with the lining outside. The SS guards and the people in striped clothing moved about, unaffected and indifferent to us. They looked right past us as though we were mannequins.

They steered us towards the other room where "barbers" sheared us like sheep with a shaving machine that removed all the hair off our heads and bodies in minutes. Stark naked and bald-headed, we stared at each other and did not even recognize our own sisters or closest friends. At this point Hédi, just as one time at school when we could not stop her spasmodic crying, broke out into maddening hysterical laughter. We did not know how to calm her. The guards, however, were there for a reason, and with blows and brutal words they quickly reduced us to silence and hustled us out to the other room in the direction of the showers. We could only take our shoes with us, holding them up above our heads. We started to suspect that we would not see our clothes again and I wanted to salvage something from my belongings. At the last moment I took my toothbrush in my mouth. There were a number of toothbrushes in Erzsi's apron. She also took one, hiding it in her shoe with a deft movement. During the long and bitter period of our slavery, when we did not even have water to quench our thirst, let alone the luxury of brushing our teeth, I sometimes used to look at the toothbrush, the last symbol of our existence as human beings.

After Auschwitz we passed through many camps and we learned that the showers were not necessarily a place to get cleaned and that in them, stark naked, people were often killed. And we learned we would never again see the things that had been left in the previous room, that some of us had risked our lives to hold onto. And indeed, from my life at home, I have no memento other than the toothbrush that I still treasure to this day.

In the shower we had hardly soaped ourselves when the warm water suddenly turned to boiling water and was then immediately turned off. How pleasant it would have been to wash the dust and sweat of the four-day journey from our bodies. But that was not the aim of the shower. Our place was taken by another group that just arrived, and we were hustled farther on. In the next room mounds of underwear and clothing were piled on the floor. We went past the piles of clothing quickly, as directed, and picked what was closest at hand. With disgust we dressed in the worn, ragged clothing. One got a tight, short dress while another had a long dress without a belt. When we looked at one another, we recognized with astonishment that bald and ragged, we now looked exactly like those we had seen behind the barbed wire fences, characters whom we had thought were mad. In less than an hour our human appearance had been taken away. Our disheartening appearance was emphasized by a special mark. It was not enough just to wrap us up in these dreadful rags. On the back of our clothing, a broad vertical stripe was painted with red oil dye. We left the room, crushed and outraged. In the midst of blows and yells, we were driven on further until we arrived in an enormous field. Lined up in columns, in rows of ten, we stood and waited. Time passed, but we were not left to stand on our own. However tired we were, we were not allowed to crouch down. From time to time, they ordered us to squat or sit down on the ground, but we had to do it in military style in set rows of ten and all at the same time. Later we were told to present ourselves at tables in front of us, where all prisoners were registered in alphabetical order. We wondered what to do. In the end we decided not to present ourselves for the time being, thinking that perhaps it would be better to remain anonymous.

For the whole day we stood, sat and squatted under the burning sun. We were hungry and thirsty. We had almost got to the point where nothing hurt anymore; we had no interest in anything and we did not care about anything anymore. Suddenly, our attention was drawn to a group similar to our own. They were standing opposite us, about a hundred steps away. Our exhausted and subdued minds sprang to life and began to function again. We looked for familiar faces, and we seemed to recognize acquaintances in the group opposite. Exclamations of joy could be heard.

"Oh, do you see that little old woman! I'm sure it's Aunty Etelka!"

"And the broad-shouldered woman beside her, in the black dress, is mother! And there on her own is Ágica."

In at least six or seven pairs of women, I thought I recognized my dear mother and Magda. The fact that I was wrong seven times did not discourage me, tried my luck again and again and again, was more and more convinced that I had recognized them. Cries, or more accurately imploring screams, were heard from the lips of tormented women. We wanted to know if our loved ones were among them. We wanted to transform our memories of them into palpable reality. We wanted to know that they were alive. We wanted to see them. And so we saw them! Then suddenly we witnessed a horrifying scene: a German female SS guard started to hit an older woman who could not accept being separated from a woman who was either her sister or daughter. Because the woman continued to stretch out her hand to her companion, the SS guard impulsively took the belt from her skirt, wound it round the throat of the woman and began to drag her on the ground, like a dead dog. As if unleashed from one throat in a single cry, we all screamed "Mother!" Indeed the unfortunate woman could have been the mother of any one of us. At that moment, I felt that I had lost my mother then and there. Tears filled my eyes. I saw before me my small beloved, proud mother who no longer had anything to lose and was ready to give up her life for the only daughter who still remained with her. The German SS guard dragged the rattling, suffocating woman about twenty metres and then shot her like a dog.

We stood, shocked and numb, our eyes fixed on the lifeless body. We wanted to believe that what happened had only been an illusion. Each person protected themselves as best they could from accepting reality. Some lost their minds. Lilly, my cousin Harry's wife, started to hallucinate. She was no longer aware of what was happening around her. Her thoughts were far away somewhere in Székelyföld, where she was waiting for her husband in a sunlit field. Frightened, we tried to calm her, imploring her to be quiet. We were terrified that they might discover she had lost her mind.

Because of this upsetting scene, which had actually only lasted a few minutes, our orderly rows were now broken. But the women brought in to maintain order waved their whips and told us with sharp, high-pitched voices that if we did not calm down they would shoot us on the spot. We knew that here this was not an idle threat.

It began to get dark. Exhausted from all the standing around, we had to move, again in those rows of five to which we were now becoming accustomed. We arrived somewhere in darkness. We had no idea where. We passed through some open doors and went down a few steps. In the impenetrable blackness we could find no clue as to where we were. We tried to work out by touch what this new space was. The room was wide. We had not reached the walls. We could only touch the bodies of those around us or on the floor. The floor was cold and damp; we did not want to sit down for fear that we would catch cold, so we remained standing as long as we could. We stood for hours until we collapsed on the floor. In the end I did the same as the others and squatted; when this position became intolerable I tried to sit cross-legged. It was a long and sleepless night. Then I had time to think and to reflect on all that had happened that day. I remembered every word that had been spoken, even intonations and gestures, and in the end I could see it all clearly. I saw the hands raised, pointing to the sky like a vision. I looked at the young women next to me with whom I was crowded on the floor. For the most part we were about twenty years old; those younger than twenty or over thirty, possibly forty, were the exceptions. It was there, in the deep oppressive darkness, that I suddenly realized that my loved ones were no more. I stayed crouched on the floor and cried silently. Hunger, thirst, and exhaustion no longer tortured me, only unimaginable pain. I was sure that I was not the only one struggling with these frightful thoughts. Many others must have reached the same conclusion.

When dawn came I was awake. At last I could look around and found that we had spent the night in an enormous bath chamber or *Washraum*. Around us everything was damp. No wonder we had shivered on cement that was as cold as ice. Desperately wanted water was dripping from the pipes. As we threw ourselves on the pipes to quench our thirst, we heard shouts from several directions: "Don't drink it. The water is poisoned!" Many did not pay any attention to this warning, but unfortunately I and those immediately around me were scared by this rumour, and we did not drink.

As day broke, the shouts of *"Los! Los! Schneller! Alle heraus!"* started again.

We were driven to the *Appelplatz* (assembly or roll-call place). The sunlight made me forget the horrors of the night. I was no longer as sure of what I had thought. I was already inclined to think that my earlier conclusions had just been imaginings of the night. I and those around me made great efforts to accept and pass on any news that would have a calming effect. Most of it came from our imaginations. We wanted to believe that our relatives were still alive and so we wove a web of lies through which we assured each other that we would soon see our families again.

We lined up again in rows of ten, and guards with whips taught us something new: "Stillstand! Stillstand!" (Stand to attention! Attention!). Endless hours of standing or squatting followed. After three or four hours of torture under the scathing sun, we began to miss the dark, stinking place where we had spent the night, although at the time it had seemed to be the most terrible place in the world.

It became clear that all the orders of the SS guards were to drain our last drop of vitality. Those overcome by this torture had hysterical reactions. Right beside me, Ági Wilkesz begged to be killed on the spot, crying that she could not stand any longer and that they should put a bullet in her head. She threw herself onto the ground. We desperately tried to cover for her. Luckily at that moment they gave the order for everybody to sit, and she was spared.

Later, they appeared again with the registration tables. We had time to think about what to do. In the end, common sense prevailed and we decided to register. We naively thought that perhaps one day those from home would try to trace us with the help of the Red Cross and then the lists would be useful.

It was a clear, hot day. It became more and more difficult to cope with the heat and to stand still. There was no shade and not a drop of water. We had nothing to protect us from the sun. Several days had passed since we left the ghetto, but with everything that had happened we forgot our hunger and thirst. Now, however, standing idle in the sun brought to the surface the losses we had suffered. Many fainted. Lilly continued to be delirious. I cannot estimate how many hours we spent like this. We had lost our sense of time. After a seemingly endless period of time, a big soup kettle was brought. The news spread like lightning: "They are distributing food!" We had to keep the strict rows of ten while we waited impatiently to get our first prison meal. Perhaps if we had known what would follow we would not have anticipated the food so excitedly. Much later I saw how low the threshold of horror could be taken, how human beings can be defeated, how victims of fate can be reduced to animals.

They gave out small bowls of a soup that looked like something meant for animals, a sort of porridge. It was served from a broken and rusty tin that at home would not even be used to feed chickens. I was as amazed at the sight of these hideous bowls as I had been at our clothes. We could not imagine where such trash had been found. Each bowl, without a spoon, was given to ten people. The bowl was passed from hand to hand. Anyone who managed to get their hands on it would certainly get a bigger mouthful if the others let them, but the bowl of soup had to be divided into ten portions. Therefore the rule was that each person could drink five mouthfuls. Those around attentively watched the one who was gulping, so that she did not take too big a mouthful from the bowl or add an extra gulp.

I watched the eager mouths, the eyes bulging out of their sockets, the trembling hands, the shaved heads, the ragged and starving, a horde of people not themselves, gulping this disgusting soup, and I recalled the image of how we had once been. What had we been changed into? And the word rang in my ears, the word that I heard for the first time there in Auschwitz: *Häftling*. Yes. In less than forty-eight hours we had become perfect *Häftlings*, concentration camp prisoners, stripped of our identities and the capacity to put up any resistance.

As I watched this horrible liquid being swallowed my stomach turned and I was about to be sick. I decided that when my turn came, I would not touch the bowl that had been licked all around. And yet, when the awful bowl arrived, I was overcome by an incredible desire to survive. I tried to weigh up the situation. I had to eat not only to assuage my hunger but to be able to resist and to survive. I gulped from the bowl. The cold broth with the dubious appearance felt gritty between my teeth. I could not decide from what it was prepared. One thing was certain: it had not been washed. I felt sand in my mouth. With difficulty, I made myself force down four more mouthfuls, and I was glad that I did not vomit.

We still had not been given water. Five or six days had already passed since we had had anything to quench our thirst. We were desperate. We felt relieved when another magic word was issued: "Feierabend" (evening rest).

So we had survived yet another day.

They drove us into one of the barracks. Here they were called blocks. We learned later that it was an unfinished barrack. There were no places to sleep in it as it was probably intended for temporary use. About five hundred of us were already crowded inside when another group of women was shoved in with us, so that we must have numbered about a thousand. The pushing and shoving started, and the struggle for a tiny standing space began. Once again our group tried to stay together. It included Sári Feldheim and her two sisters, the other three Feldheim girls, Irénke Goldmann, Hédi Silbermann, Ági Wilkesz, Erzsi, Lilly and me. To avoid a quarrel with the others, we took turns squatting.

Once we had found a spot we could at last think of our bodily functions for the first time since we had left the train. Ten people were allowed out at once. We had to wait in line for a lavatory designated for an enormous number of people. We were greeted by an indescribable sight. An endless row of women with dresses rolled up, with bare bottoms sitting side by side. A new way of humiliating and shaming us.

It was already dark when a new group was crushed into the already overcrowded room. The situation had become intolerable. Already more women were standing than squatting. On top of that, as time passed, we became more tired and irritable. Our thirst grew worse and worse. Outside, the air was pregnant with clouds, then thunder and lightning, and eventually rain. The tension inside eased a little, but not for long. Rain came in through the poor roofing of the building. Water streamed down the walls and the support posts. Everyone tried to get near the wet walls. When we moved away from our places, the minimal order that had been established was undone. We had to get to the water that was pouring through the roof! And when we got to it, we wet our hands and licked the walls. A threatening voice from outside warned us that if we did not stop moving about and making noise, we would all be shot. Soon the door opened and a powerful lantern swept over us. The silhouettes of many SS men stood out in the doorway. One had sheets of paper in his hand and started to read the names on them. We listened in an eerie silence, holding our breath as if hearing our death sentence. After many unknown names, I suddenly heard "Sári Feldheim, Erzsi Feldheim, Márta Feldheim," and the others with the surname Feldheim, as well as others with the initial F. We held their hands, ready to stop them if they made any movement. But nobody moved. Hundreds of people stood stock still, their hearts in their mouths. Then the guards, enraged, began to drive people out of the large room without referring to the lists of names.

At first we were glad of the fresh air, but soon we were drenched with rain. The luckiest among us had shoes, but those who had taken their shoes off because their feet were swollen did not find any in that unexpected jumble. We staggered through the dark night. Neither Erzsi nor Hédi had found more than one of their shoes in the darkness, and they were both for the same foot. Erzsi gave her shoe to Hédi and she walked barefoot with cold feet until someone who was more enterprising had pity on her and thrust into her hands a pair of tattered sandals.

After what seemed to us another endless march, we reached a railroad track. Day was already dawning when we found ourselves again facing a long line of freight cars. It had only been forty-eight hours since we had arrived and now we were travelling again. However, we were quite different from what we had been when we arrived. Now we were *Häftlings*, humiliated, dispossessed, and drained of our will to live.

On that June morning, we did not realize how lucky we were that we had only spent a few days in Auschwitz. At the time we had no means of knowing from what we had escaped or why. We did not know that Auschwitz-Birkenau was the largest extermination camp, or *Vernichtungslager*, of the German Nazi empire. We did not know that it was a death factory where, with industrial technology, an enormous number of people were gassed and then burnt in crematoria and in enormous open burning pits. We did not know that in Auschwitz-Birkenau alone 1.5 million people perished. We did not know that months earlier, when we were still able to walk about the streets untroubled, Auschwitz was preparing to receive the Hungarian Jews. They had reinforced the incinerators and raised the number of the *Sondercommando* (the prisoners who operated the gas chambers and incinerator ovens) from 224 to 860. They had moved the arrival point for the trains closer to the crematoria, or as they called it, "the death platform."

We did not know that 437,000 Jews were deported from Hungary between May 15 and July 8, 1944, among whom 160,000 were from Northern Transylvania alone. We did not know that of those who arrived there, only 10 per cent were selected for work, the others being exterminated immediately. About 400,000 were murdered on arrival. We did not know that after the first selection, some of those chosen were kept at Auschwitz, while the rest were dispersed through the other 386 concentration camps functioning in the Nazi empire. Fewer than 5 per cent of these deportees ever returned. And we did not know that those who were kept at Auschwitz probably suffered the most, partly because of the terrible living conditions but also because they had to face the smoking chimneys of the crematoria that worked night and day. They always had the sword of Damocles hanging over their heads, always with the possibility of being picked for a new selection.

We had deceived ourselves when we believed that no one knew of the existence of Auschwitz. A great many soldiers and SS officers passed through Auschwitz. Among those, many ended up at the front or were sent to other regions. We believed that the Nazi empire had "resorts" where the SS who knew too much were also liquidated. Nevertheless, news about Auschwitz spread, as Randolph L. Braham documents in his excellent two-volume work, *The Politics of Genocide: The Holocaust in Hungary.* Many prisoners attempted the impossible goal of escape.

Auschwitz. High
tension electrically
charged barbed wire,
with camp blocks in the
background.

Auschwitz. The
camp inmates were
under continuous
surveillance from
watch-towers.

Five of those risked their lives to make known to the entire world what was happening in the concentration camps and to stop the continual deportations. The first escapee tried to warn the Jews of the Theresienstadt ghetto about the extermination of the Czechs in Auschwitz. A written record was prepared from the testimony of the others, which was sent to Hungary in time to draw attention to this criminal action being prepared against the Hungarian Jews.

We did not know that with a little good fortune, we could have been saved. Based on the oral testimony given by Rudolf Vrba and Alfred Wetzler, who masterminded the second escape from Auschwitz on April 7, 1944, a written statement was prepared at Zilina, Slovakia. This written statement was sent to Jewish organizations abroad, to the Papal Nuncio in Bratislava, and to Dr. Kasztner in Hungary, through whom the message would have been given to regent Miklós Horthy and Cardinal Jusztinian Serédi of Hungary.

A few weeks later, at Liptószentmiklós, the reports of two other Auschwitz escapees were registered, in which attention was drawn to the fact that Auschwitz was already making preparations to receive the Hungarian Jews. Unfortunately, these very important documents only arrived in the hands of Governor Horthy at the end of June, by which time some of the Jews from the country and from Budapest had already been deported and liquidated. It is likely that because of these two reports, the request of the

Pope, the appeals of President Roosevelt, and the warning of King Gustav of Sweden, deportations from Hungary were stopped and part of the Jewish population of Budapest was saved.

5

In the Latvian Camps

*T*hey counted fifty young women to each freight car. After we boarded, our group was split into two and lined up in rows of five to the left and right of the door. We were ordered to stand at attention until the train started, and then to sit cross-legged. We changed position a few times during the journey, either sitting down or standing up on order, all fifty of us at once. I do not know whether to attribute this torture to German precision or to Nazi sadism. The door of the car was open throughout the entire journey, which might have calmed us if it had not been so cold outside. As it was, the cold penetrated to our very bones.

One young SS soldier watched over us. He was dressed entirely in black and sat as still as a statue between the two groups, facing the door. He did not speak during the entire journey, and he forced us to be silent as well. He did not even deign to turn down our first request. He sat unapproachable, with an automatic pistol in his hand.

Before we set off, the soldiers had distributed food. Everyone received a piece of bread and a single slice of something like salami. I looked suspiciously at the meat, which was an unusual colour. A doubt seized me that I could not articulate. I did not touch it.

Two pails were in opposite corners of the car. One was full of drinking water, and the other was for us to relieve ourselves. We were not able to drink when we felt thirsty, but only when ordered to by the guard, when we passed a chipped enamel mug from hand to hand. It was worse when we needed to relieve ourselves. The guard would not allow two women to make a screen to hide the barrel. Because of this, we only used it when we were really desperate. I have never been sure whether his cruelty was a response to orders or his own initiative.

The train traveled very fast. We tried to decipher the names of the stations, but they were German or Polish-sounding names we had never heard before and we could not get our bearings from them. We could only judge our surroundings by the vegetation that rushed past the open door. The shade of the forests and the cooling of the air indicated that we were traveling north, but even knowing this, we could not deduce much more. We did not know what the conditions were like in German concentration camps, and we had no way of knowing what might await us.

A crushing fear gripped me throughout the journey. I recalled the fate of the Slovakian girls who were taken to the front for the soldiers. Even though we were ugly in our shapeless rags and shaved heads, I could not get rid of this thought. But I would not have shared my worry with anyone even if I were allowed to speak. We were helpless, and it would only have scared the other girls.

Erzsi's period had begun. Even at home, Erzsi suffered terribly every month. She could only endure her cramps under strong sedatives. Now, without any hope of basic comfort or hygiene, her agony was intensified. We were lucky that in place of her undergarments she had received a cotton shirt, while I got a cotton undershirt. We used these as sanitary napkins. Erzsi's pain got worse and worse, especially when she had to stand to attention. We were glad when darkness fell and she could stretch out on the floor of the freight car. However, it was our bad luck to find ourselves right over the wheels of the car, with so much jolting that she could not rest. I drew her over me so that I could absorb most of the shock. We both passed a painful night.

We were cold in our rags. Some of us had received summer dresses with short sleeves, and one girl just had a lace evening dress. Even a belt would have helped, if just to tighten the rags around our bodies. Without our cotton undershirts, Erzsi and I were even colder than our comrades.

After two days, the train stopped in a pine forest. Rain was pouring down. We got out of the train and lined up in rows. SS soldiers surrounded us here too. We did not try to speak to them anymore, but one of the soldiers heard us talk and addressed us in Hungarian.

"Where are you from?" he asked. We took courage on hearing our native tongue and started asking questions.

"How do you know Hungarian?" we asked him. "Where are we?"

He was a Swabian youth from near Satu Mare (Szatmár). He had been to Oradea several times. He named the shops on our main street, and our eyes filled with tears. But he would not tell us where we were.

Then we had to go to the baths. This time, they let us wash ourselves properly, and we badly needed it by now. Apart from the "shower" at Auschwitz, we had not bathed in over a week. We took great pleasure in the warmth of the water as well as the feeling of cleanliness.

Here too we came out of a different door than the one we had entered through. This time we were glad to be rid of our dirty rags. We received grey dresses with short sleeves. Some dresses were too short and tight, others too long or loose, but by this time we were not bothered with such trifles. We were just glad they were clean. Looking around, we realized that later we might be able to swap dresses. We felt stronger now that we were looking a little more human. Our joy was even greater when we received thin jackets like pyjama tops. The blue and grey striped clothes made us look like prisoners, but they alleviated our shivering.

On our way out, we were assigned numbers. We lost our previous identities. Piroska Kovács and Klári Nagy no longer existed, only *Häftling* 567 243 or 567 875. I never understood the purpose of these numbers, considering that no one took the trouble to read them when they ever spoke to us. If a soldier called out an order, he simply yelled "Du verfluchte Hund!" (You cursed dog). Our numbers were not even noted when we were transferred to another concentration camp. We were numbered simply at random. Two hundred, five hundred, a thousand people, as many as they needed at a particular time. We suspected that the numbers of the dead were redistributed, so they were not even useful in counting the total number of prisoners. It was simply another means of degrading us.

Along with our numbers, we wore coloured triangles. We Jews wore the yellow that has been used to shame us since the Middle Ages. Political prisoners wore red, prostitutes wore blue, common criminals wore green, and homosexuals wore black. The last three categories supplied the supervisors, and they did their jobs without mercy.

The new clothing and labelling absorbed our attention for a short time. We had not yet been able to get our bearings when we were moved again. Soldiers loaded us into big trucks, and once again we were rolling toward the unknown. The wind whistled through our thin dresses on the open trucks. The cold penetrated our very bones, we were freezing, and we were terrified of what the future might have in store for us in this unfamiliar environment.

Eventually we arrived in a strange place. A lot of dilapidated and crowded buildings surrounded a small square in which an immense crowd of people in threadbare clothes swarmed around. At first, we were surprised to see men and children among the women. They all looked thin and exhausted but their heads were not shaved. I did not see a single bald woman.

From these fellow prisoners we learned that we were in Riga, the capital of Latvia. We had been in Kaiserwald, in another district of Riga, which was an enormous concentration camp like the one at Auschwitz.

We were now in the Riga-Spilve district. This camp was situated in the centre of the former milling industry, which at first had been used as a ghetto. We met people here who had lived in it since it was a ghetto, which was why there were still families that had not been split up. Convoys of deportees from Germany, Austria, and Poland had joined the ghetto's inhabitants when it became a camp. There were infants among them. Because we were the first

Hungarian transport to arrive at Riga, the others looked at our shaved heads in amazement.

We were to sleep in little rooms crammed with three-tier bunk beds. We tried again to stay together; we were joined by a few strangers, who had been assigned to our room. We settled ourselves in as best we could and then looked around. We were shocked to see hundreds of rats running through the courtyards and rooms in full daylight. We would soon learn that at night they climbed into our beds and devoured the carefully guarded precious bits of bread saved for the next day.

The Latvian, German, and Austrian Jews already living there received us with interest. They saw us as a link to the world outside the camp and beyond the borders. They asked us about the position of the front, the attitudes of the European nations, the difficulties of the journey, and the circumstances we had been living in just before our deportation. Almost everyone spoke German and Yiddish. I understood some Yiddish, but I had trouble expressing myself in it.

Although we were exhausted, hungry, thirsty, emotionally shaken, and grotesque in our rags and shaved heads, there was a great difference between us new arrivals and the *Häftlings* we met in the camp. These people had lived for years eating just enough food to survive, and they were aged before their time and thin as skeletons. They looked like shadows. We still had some flesh on us. We still looked well, strong, full of life, and above all young. The others registered this difference with amazement, especially as we all seemed to be the same age. After this, we tried to look at ourselves with their eyes. We were overwhelmed again at the thought that we, only in our twenties, were the only survivors. Yet there was little time for reflection. Soldiers ordered the evening roll call and then sent us to our rooms. We put our troubled heads down to rest, struggling with fatigue. We lay half asleep and half awake, in a state of preparedness to protect ourselves at any moment from the attack of the rats.

The morning began with the roll call. In that way our numbers were checked every morning and every evening. Over two thousand of us were in the camp. After roll call, we were sent to work. Early in the morning, we were cold in our thin dresses. We walked five kilometres to an airport. For as long as we stayed at Riga-Spilve, this was our workplace. There I saw an airplane and an airport up close for the first time. I learned right away what ground turbulence was. The landing and takeoff of the first plane sent most of us falling to the ground. Nobody had warned us to find safe cover if possible or else to lie flat on the ground.

Our job was to camouflage the airplanes. They split us up into teams and entrusted different phases of the work to us. One of the teams built a hill with gentle slopes. Another group cut sod in the forest, while still another covered the newly erected hills with grass. Before long the hoes and the shovels had blistered our hands. Our backs hurt from the continuous bending and lifting, and our legs trembled from the unusually long workday.

Our small group was responsible for cutting the sod. We were taken to the forest by truck. We cut the grass-covered earth into rectangles, lifted these with the hoes and shovels, and then placed them in a pile. Then we passed them from hand to hand into the truck. After that we climbed up ourselves and rode with the sod to the airport. Forming a chain, we again passed the sod down from hand to hand.

We had a hard time with this work, which was not at all suitable for women. The sod, cut with a thick layer of earth, was very heavy. Nevertheless, we considered ourselves lucky because we could rest during the drives, and while we were on the truck we were not exposed to the abuse of the supervisors.

After a number of days working, the driver of our truck, a Viennese man of forty-five, suddenly began to look at my friend Sári with astonishment. He said that she reminded him of his own daughter who was twenty years old. It was then, in fact, that he began to pay attention to us. He became more communicative. He also said that if he knew his daughter was in such a situation, he would commit suicide. From that day, our driver urged us to finish making our fixed quota of sod as quickly as possible and then he let us lie down on the grass for a few minutes to rest. That feeling was heavenly. We rejoiced at the chance to rest as if it were a gift from heaven; after the terrible rudeness we had borne, we were now electrified by this good will. And then one day, the driver brought us a few pieces of unhemmed material. The girls who seized these happily tied them on their heads, covering their humiliating baldness. On another occasion we were delighted to receive a few pieces of bread and a little marmalade. Because we were so many and we were all terribly hungry, we each got only a very small portion, but his humane tone of voice and the compassion that he showed made a deep impression on us.

One day a jeep pulled up near our work teams. After perusing our sad appearance for a while, the driver exclaimed indignantly:

"Is this your work?"

"No, it's yours, the Berliners," came the retort.

At that moment I felt great hatred towards the Germans because I saw in them everything that was evil. Only in the evening, remembering this dialogue, did I realize that I was mistaken. I was judging an entire nation because of the behaviour of one man, or a few people. I had almost forgotten what the Austrian fascists had done in 1938, at the time of the Anschluss. I remembered things my father had told us. I remembered the Austrian refugees who had arrived in Oradea. Vita was one of these, the only survivor of her whole family. After she had found a new home in Oradea, she was deported with us. The Austrian fascists were no better than the German

Nazis. There were exceptions to the rule both here and there. There was no difference between those sporting the swastika and those with the arrow-cross, the Hungarian fascists. The difference was between a Man with a capital M and a scoundrel.

Our privileged situation in the woods only lasted for a few days, and then we went back to our permanent work at the airport. A cold north wind blew over the wide-open field. Starving and dressed in light clothing, we were terribly cold that June.

Chance, or perhaps necessity, gave one of our fellow inmates a brilliant idea. In one of the airport barrack stores, she found a few empty cement bags made of paper. From this "material" she tore pieces in the shape of a vest and she wore it under her dress so that no one would notice. Those of us who worked near her followed her example. We shook the cement out of the bags and reversed them so the clean outer side was towards our skin. The cement dust irritated us even then, but we did not let it bother us. At the time, the cold was the greater danger and the paper proved to be a great protection against the wind.

Once when we were working in the barrack storage area, Erzsi was told to go to another team. She was already on her way when I remembered that I had her spoon. I ran after her to give her the spoon so that she would have something to eat lunch with. I was already by the door when the German supervisor came up behind me. He had probably misinterpreted my intentions because he took hold of my shoulder and dealt me a terrible blow. It took me unawares. I stood stock-still as if I had turned in to stone and just remained there with my arms out and with the spoon in my hand. I think that he realized he had made a mistake then. Of course, he did not ask my forgiveness. He continued to walk back and forth as if nothing had happened. Later, in an obvious gesture, he put his lunch wrapped in newspaper on the windowsill next to me and left. I stood one step away from the food I was craving, not knowing what to do. The rational part of me was telling me to refuse it, not to touch it. On the other hand I could feel the concentrated gaze of my starving companions on me, full of reproach. I did not have time to think, as I had to join those who were working outside. So I put the precious treasure inside my breast and I went out. A moment later, I already regretted what I had done, but there was no going back. That humiliating gift of charity burned my skin all day. For a long time afterwards, even until the present day, I have not been able to wipe it from my memory. In the evening I gave the food to the girls. We were about ten amongst whom it had to be shared. Each of us only received a very little portion. I could not swallow any of it.

We were in the country of white nights. Because of this it did not get dark as we had been used to. We did not have a watch, so we did not know when the working day had ended. Every day seemed interminably long to us. We were glad when *Feierabend* was declared and we saw the sign to start off. We were longing for the crowded rats' nest, without air, where in the steam of our own bodies, we too could at last warm up.

The road to the camp went past vegetable gardens. On the ground here and there stalks of green onion or stray beetroot lay about, but we were not allowed to bend down to pick them up and there was no question of leaving our row. The guards watched over us and if the lines were broken, they fired a few warning shots. I proved to be extremely unskilful. I could never acquire, or as they used to say, *organize* something. *Organizing* was nothing like theft. A *Häftling* would not short-change another *Häftling*. Nothing would be taken from a *Häftling* or from the common bounty. *Organizing* was much nearer to the notion of acquiring. The long years of suffering had given rise to camp jargon. Certain notions were described with the same word in different camps a hundred or even a thousand kilometres away from each other.

I was incapable of *organizing* anything. Erzsi, on the other hand, proved to be an expert. Sometimes she managed to collect a few onion stalks. We used them to improve the so-called *Dörrgemüse* soup, a broth prepared with dry vegetables that always had the same dreadful taste. Erzsi even gave from it to others. Lilly, Harry Klärmann's wife, *organized* with the greatest skill. On the way she managed to grab some nettle. As she spoke good German, she befriended some of the old inhabitants of the camp and cooked nettle soup at their place. This consoled her to some degree, giving her the sense that she was supplementing food that was poor in vitamin content. In fact our food was not poor in vitamins, it was totally lacking in them. In the mornings we were given a glass of dark-coloured liquid, with no taste, which was called coffee; at lunch we had a mess tin containing about a litre of soup; in the evenings we had a piece of bread and sometimes one spoonful of marmalade or one or two ounces of margarine. Some people ate their whole bread portions all at once. The bread was black, hard, and felt like sawdust. Erzsi and I cut it into thin slices, splitting it into three portions. Each morning, lunchtime, and evening we ate a little piece so we would not have empty stomachs.

The strain, the hard physical labour and the poor food broke Erzsi before her time. One morning she collapsed and could not get up. At a loss concerning what to do, I appealed to one of the older inhabitants of the camp. He calmed me down, telling me that I could announce that she had fallen ill. There was an infirmary where perhaps she could get help. He also pointed out that in other places you had to keep quiet about illnesses, because sooner or later sick people were exterminated.

Although the infirmary was in the courtyard, I parted from Erzsi with a heavy heart. A Jewish doctor from Germany had begun to look after her, a *Lagerarzt* (camp doctor). In the absence of any adequate laboratory and X-ray apparatus, he could only give an approximate diagnosis. He suspected some kind of stomach disease. In the absence of medication and a prescribed diet, he could not do very much, only ensure a few days' rest. Under those conditions, this was an enormous gift. The fact that Erzsi did not have to go out to work, that she could stay under a roof in a sheltered place, that she could rest and did not have to stand up at the lengthy roll call meant a lot. And the infirmary food was marginally better. I remember that one day she received a small piece of cheese. Erzsi could not eat it without me and gave me half. I, however, wanted to save it for the next day, and because there was no other place, I hid it in the bed. In the morning, I was very surprised to discover that only a small piece of bread was left. The rest, with the cheese, had been taken by a rat. I was glad that at least it had not chewed my ear.

One cold, windy day when we were returning to the camp, it occurred to me that we would warm up faster if we marched to the beat of a song. Memories of school came back to me, with a picture of girls returning from an outing singing, and almost unconsciously I began to sing. "Through mountains and through valleys the train rolls…" I had hardly begun to hum the well-known children's song when the tune spread and was heard on the lips of over a hundred young women. With hoes and pickaxes on our shoulders we marched in time. The whole episode lasted only a few minutes and the song died on our lips as it had risen. We did not plan to sing, nor to stop. But the same thought had certainly been in all our minds: did we have the right to be happy and to sing when we knew nothing about our loved ones? What would the inhabitants of the town think about us, seeing us so happy and seemingly untroubled in the concentration camp, as if we were on a Boy Scouts' outing? For a moment, we wanted to forget our gloomy, tormenting present. And indeed, it had all lasted for a single moment. Pain, despair and discouragement soon overtook us. Once again we were plunged back into our previous state of indifference.

Erzsi was still in the infirmary when the weather suddenly changed. The wind stopped, the sky became clear, and the sun was burning hot. If before we were afraid of the cold, now we were suffering because of the burning sun. We carefully folded up our paper shirts and put them in our beds for the hard days ahead. We left behind our thin jackets that we would only have needed during the mornings and evenings, because we had nowhere to put them out in the field. The suffering caused by the strenuous physical work was exceeded by the burning heat. There was not a trace of shade. Along with the other girls with fair, pale, sensitive skin, I suffered terribly. Within a few days all the places that were exposed to the sun – arms, legs, neck – were covered with giant blisters. In a few days these split open and became infected because dirt got into them and they became full of pus. I was in unimaginable pain. We did not receive any kind of medication or gauze. I was glad when, a few days later, someone bound the wounds with toilet paper procured from an unknown source. But I did not have time to worry about my pain. Bad news had reached the camp. Word went from mouth to mouth that a selection of sick *Muselmanns* was being prepared, and that they were to be sent to an unknown destination. Those not seriously ill, including Erzsi, were hastily discharged from the infirmary. A Latvian man, a former opera singer, explained to me what the word *Muselmann* meant. This was another example of camp jargon. It described the *Häftlings* who were in a declining physical state, very thin and incapable of work. My new acquaintance examined himself with fear. He told me that in the last few weeks he had lost a considerable amount of weight. He was skin and bone. I could see that he was truly frightened.

At the time, we still felt safe. Although we had lost a lot of weight, we still had some flesh on us compared with the older inhabitants of the camp. Only later, when we had become *Muselmanns* like them, was the dramatic reality fully apparent. Only then did I understand this terror.

The Latvian opera singer told me about the tragedy of the Latvian Jews. Following the occupation of Latvia by the Germans, the order was given for the yellow star to be worn as it was everywhere else under German control. After the Jews had been identified they were locked up in their homes; under the eyes of their neighbours, they were robbed and entire families were murdered. People were taken from the street, imprisoned, and then group by group, taken to the woods and shot so that they fell into ditches that they themselves had dug. For the survivors, the ghetto was organized according to the already known prescription and the situation became worse. Exterminations took on mass proportions. Ceaseless streams of people poured from the ghetto to the woods of Rambul. Groups of two to three thousand surrounded by a chain of guards were driven to the place of execution.

On the way, in front of and on both sides of the columns of Jews, SS soldiers went on foot, on horseback or on motorbikes. Most of the prisoners believed, as had happened in the other places, that they were going to work or to another camp. Out in the woods, the prisoners were told to undress to their bare skin. Then they were driven in groups towards the ditch and ordered to lie down with their face to the ground at the bottom of the ditches. After they had been shot in the back, the SS soldiers made the following unfortunate group lie down on top of the dead. This went on until the pit was full. Then they dug a new ditch and the mass extermination continued. My Latvian acquaintance had survived such a place. Yet he felt there was no escape from his fate. Not only the *Muselmanns* were terrified. Also in fear were those few husbands, wives and children who had managed to stay together until then.

The anxiety only intensified when one day a new group of two thousand women arrived in Riga-Spilve. They were carefully isolated in one part of the courtyard, cordoned off by a rope, and we were forbidden to go near them. As far as we could tell from a distance, many of our acquaintances from Oradea were in their group. We recognized some who had lived in the Ullmann palace during the time of the ghetto and had left the town on the last day of deportation. From a distance, we recognized the wife of Dr. Jenö Adonyi, the dentist, and his daughter Zsófi, who had been a schoolmate of mine. I would have loved to speak to them, but any attempt proved to be futile. We made signs to each other. I would not have believed then that there would be a time when I would bring the last news about them.

In the meantime, we were gathered together and seated in rows of five. The first group was loaded without delay into the truck that had arrived for this purpose. We had barely spent a month in this filthy place and had scarcely got used to this new way of life, when once again we were on our way, not knowing where. We were filled with terror. In spite of the fact that it was very bad here, we feared the unknown, and we used every means at our disposal to remain. We even got Lilly to plead a case for us and she had asked the *Lagerälteste* to keep us. Fortunately her pleadings were not heeded.

Later, we learned the terrible fate of those who had remained there. When Russian troops were advancing in force, a large-scale selection was launched around the Riga area. They selected and exterminated the sick and weak. Those who were still capable of work were sent by different means, on land and water, by vehicles and on foot, to those areas of Poland and Germany still under Nazi domination. In the final days of the offensive, those who remained, including the prisoners who had taken our places, were drowned in the sea. From the trilogy *The Storm*, by the writer Vilisz Lácisz, I learned how the execution took place: people from the camp were loaded into trucks and taken to the port, where they were driven onto barges. A boat towed them into the open sea. The guards moved onto the ship. The barges were untied. As the people on the barges stood uncomprehending, a formation of airplanes appeared. The raid lasted five minutes. By the time the planes disappeared, the barges were already sunk. All this happened after, when it was clear that the Russians were coming and the Germans were no longer able to evacuate Riga. Not knowing what the future held, we envied those who remained behind. We tried to discern what the future held for us.

As we discovered later, the trucks took us back again to the main camp of Kaiserwald, where we were sent, after the pattern we now knew, to the baths. Following the rules of entry, we stripped to the skin. Those who had managed to acquire a small piece of cloth for a headscarf could only kiss it goodbye. We stepped over the threshold with our shoes raised above our heads. I managed to keep the toothbrush on this occasion as well, without knowing quite why. This time, however, there was no hot or cold water from the tap. At the exit we grabbed at random from the pile of clothes on the floor, dressed, and were carried along by the current of people.

"*Los! Los! Schneller!*" sounded incessantly.

In all the haste and confusion, I lost sight of Erzsi. She became agitated and frightened trying to find me, constantly looking to the right and to the left. I only caught sight of her at the moment when an SS woman brought her back to her senses with a heavy blow. In a fraction of a second I made my way to her, arriving in time to stop Erzsi's hand, raised to respond to the blows.

They took us out to the big square again where it was just like a slave market, as an agitated crowd was split up and classified with amazing speed. Erzsi was put in a smaller group while Lilly was earmarked for another. At that point I tried to explain that Lilly was a Klärmann, our sister, and that we wanted to stay together. Who was interested in such trifles? On the contrary, I had not even finished mumbling my request, when I too was given an enormous blow on the back that propelled me away from Lilly, ensuring that my request had no chance of success. Fortunately for me, this is how I managed to stay with Erzsi. I looked around. There were only six of us left from our old group from home of more than twenty: Hédi Silbermann and her cousin Ági, Éva Ritter, Irénke

Goldmann (Sári's cousin), Erzsi and I. The loss of our ghetto comrades hurt us very much. It helped us to share our pain and our memories with each other. However, we had no time to lament. A *Wehrmacht* officer made a short speech to us. This was something new: somebody was addressing us. Throughout our travels, the SS gave us directions, orders and commands, but they never talked to the Jews.

The officer told us that where we were heading, hard physical labour was waiting for us, fit for men. He invited us to think about whether we would be able to do it. I took the appeal seriously. I stepped out of my row, showed him the sores on my arms and legs and also told him that Erzsi had stomach problems. The officer took a long look at us and just said, "It does not matter."

There were a hundred young women in that group. We climbed into a truck and started out for the new camp. Night had already fallen when we arrived and the kitchen was closed. Our commandant arranged for supper from the army reserves. We were given a wonderful pilaf of white rice and meat. We had not seen other cooked food since we had left home, apart from the dishwater-like soup they called *Dörrgemüse*. The tempting smell of home-cooked food awoke old memories for us, and moved us to tears.

We had learned that we were still in Riga, at a relatively small camp. Most of the old Jewish inhabitants of the camp, about a hundred in total, were Polish, but among them were some women from Germany or Austria.

After the powerful impressions of the previous evening, we had the chance, on the second day, to get to know the place in which we found ourselves. The camp consisted of two big barracks, built formerly for prisoners of war. The original inhabitants lived in one of them, and we, the women from Transylvania, in the other.

They gave us big rooms with bright windows. In one room, there were seven bunk beds and as many closets. We looked at the closets in a disoriented way. We only had the dresses we were wearing; even our scarves had been taken. What could we have put inside them? A new surprise: the *Lagerälteste* (prisoner assigned with managerial responsibilities) gave us soap, toothbrushes, and even small-toothed combs and toilet paper. It is impossible to describe how we felt at the sight of all these treasures. Until then we had not even had enough water to quench our thirst. Who could have dreamed of using a toothbrush? We had only washed extremely rarely in cold water, and we had not seen soap since we had been taken. We thought that from now on we would probably be able to wash ourselves. In the absence of a handkerchief, we used to wipe our nose with leaves if we happened to have trees nearby, and if not, on the backs of our hands. Now we had this seemingly enormous quantity of paper. As our hair had scarcely begun to grow again, we had not needed combs. Now, however, we raked the skin on our heads with great pleasure. Our delight grew even greater when they gave out mattresses filled with fresh, clean straw. We prepared comfortable sleeping places.

We spent the first day scrubbing the floors, doing the cleaning and giving ourselves a wash. The atmosphere was good, with nobody pushing us or hurrying us. We did not hear "*Los! Los! Schneller!*" once, which we hated so much and to which our ears had begun to grow accustomed. The mere absence of it had a beneficial effect on us. For the first time since we were carried off, I had a restful night, free of worry. We were so happy not to be under the authority of the SS any longer. We were now under the *Wehrmacht*, and we would not have to work under the open skies anymore. Here we worked in a military clothing depot, with a roof over our heads. Unfortunately, the *Wehrmacht* did not supply us with food. This continued to come from the central camp, and it was as bad as it had been up until then. We were given a small amount of poor quality bread and the tasteless *Dörrgemüse* made from dry vegetables. However, with the exception of the food, everything else – the accommodation, the working conditions and above all their treatment of us – was humane.

The next day started with a surprise too. The hated, exhausting, body- and soul-destroying roll call was discontinued. The *Lagerälteste* shouted "Moskauer Strasse antretten!" They showed us the trucks, which were waiting for us beyond the fence. We climbed into them without being numbered. They stopped in Moskova Street, near a small Russian church with many turrets and an onion shaped cupola.

Erzsi and I, together with two Polish girls, were assigned to a storage area on the ground floor of the warehouse. We had to sort sheets for military tents. We undid bundles of five and inspected them. The rejects had to be separated from those without defects and put in new piles, and then the bales had to be tied and put aside. From time to time a new load arrived. We had to bring the packets inside and put the tarpaulin we judged to be in good condition into a space cleared for that purpose. One military tent sheet is very heavy on its own. To lift five at a time meant an almost superhuman effort for a woman. Even arranging them was tiring, but the most difficult task was getting them in and out of the truck. We were unlucky to get this work, perhaps the hardest of all. The other women were sorting shirts, boots and scarves. Hédi and Ági were packing gloves.

Work was from 7 o'clock in the morning until 4 o'clock in the afternoon, with a fifteen-minute break for breakfast and thirty minutes for lunch. We had lunch in a canteen where we sat down at tables. What an exhilarating feeling it was for us to eat from plates, to drink from glasses and to eat like human beings, whereas before we had been spooning our soup crouched down on the floor, from mess tins held in our laps. In the morning we each received a glass of warm coffee. The coffee did not taste like coffee and it was not sweet, but it was warm and we drank it at the table while we were talking. The coffee reminded me of an anecdote I had heard when I was still at home, from men who had returned from labour camps, and that we had thought very amusing at the time. The coffee presented an advantage, a disadvantage, and a riddle. The advantage was that it contained no coffee substitute. The disadvantage was that it did not contain any real coffee. And the riddle was why is it black? We could not work it out, but at the time it did not bother us. The important thing was that we felt human again.

The two Polish girls were very reserved toward us in the beginning. This reserve went as far as a kind of hostility. We also saw it in the Slovakian Jews, but especially in the Polish. In time I discovered the cause.

At the beginning, we worked almost without a word. After a few days both Erzsi and I suddenly became ill. We became white as ghosts, we had the chills, and we were running to the toilet all the time to vomit acid. The vomiting was probably caused by the heavy physical work and the poor diet. Danka, the younger girl, took pity on us and laid us down from time to time on a pile of tents. She watched the door and helped us to our feet again if the supervisor was coming. Her concern for our fate, the feeling of solidarity and common destiny we shared, gradually made her more compassionate toward us. Danka became less reserved and more talkative. She began to show an interest in our former life and became more communicative. I learned that she had been sent to Auschwitz from the Warsaw ghetto and then had been moved again. This was fortunate for her. She was worried about her fiancé, whom she had last seen in the ghetto and about whom she had heard nothing since. She had an iron ring on her finger, the symbol of their engagement, which she used to twist in a pre-occupied manner. After she had begun to trust me, I thought the time was right to ask why she had not trusted us before.

"I don't envy you because you were still able to en-joy yourselves or that you could go to the swimming pool or on holiday at a time when we were already being tortured in the ghettos and camps. But I feel deeply revolted that although you knew, or at least suspected what was happening to Jews in neighbouring countries, you did not prepare any kind of resistance. You did not seek refuge, you did not hide, but let yourself be led like lambs to the slaughter."

She talked to me about the Jewish partisans who had fought for survival with weapons in their hands. Their resistance had cost them their lives, but they often caused great losses behind the front lines.

To those of us who just a few weeks ago had still been living in normal conditions, these things seemed unlikely. After we had arrived back home at the end of the war, my brother and Karcsi told us a lot about the Jewish partisans whom they met at Volynskyy in the Ukraine. They had crossed the Strij River with their help and managed to get back to their unit. The partisans also freed them from imprisonment by the Ukrainian nationalists who were on the side of the Germans. Danka also talked to me about the Warsaw Ghetto uprising, about the weeks of heroic but hopeless fighting and the struggle of the young Jewish heroes, events that those in the camps only learned about later.

I thought Danka was absolutely right. And even now, I still blush to think that I was on holiday at Lake Balaton at the time of the Warsaw Ghetto uprising. I was mortified that I had not then listened to my father.

Until then, we had not seen events in their context. After that, whenever I found myself face to face with the hostile attitude of the Poles, I understood their behaviour better, as well as the greed with which they fought for a bowl of food. After all, this was their fifth year of captivity, and they had suffered great privations.

After the tension between us had ceased, Danka drew my attention to the fact that it was still possible for us to put up some resistance in the situation in which we found ourselves. She obtained a razor blade and made a hardly visible slit in the tent sheets that did not have any defects. She encouraged us to follow her example. It was a dangerous occupation. With great anxiety but also great satisfaction, we too took this initiative.

Seeing how often we felt sick, Danka persuaded us to tell a doctor. A kind elderly woman doctor, an Austrian Jew, lived in the camp and worked with us. She helped her comrades willingly and although unable to offer medication or a special diet, she gave good advice.

"Does your stomach hurt when you eat the bread?" she asked us when we went to her with our complaint.

"It hurts terribly," I replied. "It feels like it sticks to my stomach and burns me."

"What happens if you don't eat your portion? Is the pain bearable?"

"There's not a great difference. It hurts anyhow."

"If it hurts in both cases, then at least eat the little you receive, because otherwise you will die of starvation. What they give us here is the minimum necessary for survival."

She advised us to try to change our place of work. Our pain was intensified by the heavy lifting and the hard physical work.

However, there was no chance of that. We did not tell anyone about our problems. Hédi, on learning of the doctor's advice and being full of good intentions and the desire to help, insisted that we swap with her. She said she wanted to take our place because the drivers who brought the consignments gave us a present of a little food from time to time. Naturally, we recognized her sacrifice and we did not want to accept it. Hédi closed the discussion and went straight to the supervisor to arrange our move with him.

The following day we were packing gloves.

We had to put three hundred pairs of gloves into each bag and then mark it with our personal signature by way of guarantee. We continued Danka's sabotage activities here too. We opened the seams of the good gloves a little at the fingertips, knowing that they would unravel further when they were worn. As for the defective ones, we opened their seams even more so that they would be more difficult to repair. I had pangs of conscience when I thought of the unsuspecting soldier who would wake up in his tent, wet through to the skin, or with his fingers frozen stiff during the heavy frost. I immediately reproached myself for my sentimentality. I was ashamed that I could not hate more strongly. Had I not suffered enough yet, I asked myself? I reminded myself again of all they had done to my loved ones, to us, and to hundreds of thousands of unsuspecting people, and I continued to spoil the gloves, more and more enraged. Erzsi often put twenty to thirty gloves fewer than the number marked on the bags. The work continued at a feverish rhythm. No one took the effort to verify our work. As for complaints from the front, it was questionable that we would even be alive when they were made.

Sometimes Erzsi managed to get into the next room. From old torn shirts she would tear off pieces of cloth for scarves and smaller pieces that we used as handkerchiefs. We were searched in the evenings when we left the workplace. Fortunately they never found anything on Erzsi, even though she had to *organize* something quite often, not only for us but also for our less skilful roommates. If the opportunity arose, she searched the pockets of clothing, where once in a while she found trifles that were of inestimable value to us. That was how we got a needle and thread.

From four o'clock in the afternoon until the next morning we could use our free time as we wanted. The Germans stayed away from our barracks. We washed ourselves, we sewed and we rested. We usually preferred to stay in our room, but sometimes we sat on the grassy strip that bordered one side of the barracks. Knowing how to sew, I fixed Erzsi's dress and mine so that they almost fitted us. I even had time to sew a white collar on each dress. At the end of the week they changed our dresses and underwear. But after we fitted our dresses they had become ours and we preferred to keep them and wash them ourselves.

We wished that we had paper and a pencil with which to write down our thoughts, or a book to read, perhaps aloud. We had begun to realize that our intellects were becoming dull. Until then, all our efforts had been concentrated on survival and appeasement of our hunger. It seemed that there was only one way of keeping our minds active and that was by playing *bar-kochba* or charades. Others joined our little group from Oradea to play. The wheels of our minds moved with difficulty, but we got into it and enjoyed the new activity. Once we had worked out whether the game was about a person, an object, or an idea, our attention invariably turned to the relationship between the word's meaning and our past and present living conditions. There was no way to break away from this approach. We often thought about our loved ones. How were they? Where could they be? Were they still alive?

The girls from northern Hungary and Slovakia, overcome by despair, resorted to spiritualism. Late at night, when the sky started to darken into the mysterious light of the white night, they organized a séance to call on the spirits. They obtained a stool from the kitchen, squatted around it as close as they could, and made the chair dance. They put questions to their closest relatives, whom they feared dead, and the loved ones replied with one, two, or three knocks. I had never had any inclination towards mysticism and did not believe in that kind of thing. When I once went to a fortune-teller in Oradea, I only went to observe her expressions and behaviour and to try to figure out the logic of the responses she gave to different questions. I did not learn anything from her.

In spite of this experience, however, I could not remain an indifferent observer during the séance. The scenes that took place shook me profoundly. It was strange to see the companions whom I knew so well in trances, crying, whispering, and pleading to their brothers, mothers, and children, whom they believed lost, to say a word or to give a sign. When they recovered their senses they screamed out in pain. Following these séances, some believed beyond a doubt that their loved ones had died and promised to keep a time of mourning according to Jewish tradition, to tear their clothes and to sit *shiva* in the hours after work for a week. Those with the most common sense condemned the conjuring of spirits. We reached the conclusion that perhaps it was a sin to sit *shiva* for people who might still be alive. In this way, they managed to end these gatherings that needlessly stirred up people's feelings. Controls were put in place for a while to ensure that the séances did not occur in secret.

Riga is set on both banks of the Dvina, fifteen kilometres from the Gulf of Riga. The windows of the buildings in which we were working overlooked the river. The tempestuous waves of the wide river reminded me of the Budapest section of the Danube. As I watched the flowing water for a long time, my thoughts followed the foamy waves as they disappeared into the distance. The uninterrupted flow of the water provided an irresistible temptation to freedom. In my imagination, I threw off my prisoner's clothes and the stigmatizing number and saw myself leaving the warehouse. My imagination did not reach further than that, to where I might land and on whose help I could count. Before the German invasion, Riga had been the centre for Germans from the Baltic countries. Who would take care of me with my shorn head when I could not even speak Latvian? I went on gazing at the water, fascinated. My common sense told me that there was no hope for escape.

One day, the German supervisor got drunk and went for a swim. A few girls followed him, but they soon returned, frightened. The supervisor had been swept away by the current and drowned! We were in a great panic, afraid that we would somehow be held responsible. However, this did not happen, perhaps because of the bad news that was arriving from the front. The rapidly advancing Russian army was threatening Riga, and there were many indications that the Germans could no longer defend the town. A feverish though systematic evacuation of the town had begun. This included our warehouse. No more transports arrived. We were now packing everything hastily, without any kind of sorting. Before we finished packing the boots, our well-meaning superiors encouraged each of us to choose a pair. I would have liked to keep my soft brown shoes, which I had brought with me from home, but we were not allowed to have two pairs of shoes. In Erzsi's case the choice was clear. She was still wearing the tattered sandals that somebody had thrust into her hands when we were leaving Auschwitz. In the end we both chose boots. We knew full well that in the July heat it would not be easy to walk in heavy boots, but we had to think ahead to winter. We could not miss such an extraordinary opportunity. As well as the boots we also received a gift of thick grey cotton stockings. Later, in the −40°C weather, we often thought with gratitude of the leaders of the *Feldbekleidung* (military clothing depot). We did not realize at the time that good footwear would later mean survival.

We tied the packages in big bales, took them down to the front of the building and then loaded them onto the waiting truck. By now we were all doing the same hard work. The trucks headed for the port. One of our teams was there unloading the bales and storing them. Those of us who were working at the warehouse in town sometimes accompanied the goods. The attendant sat on the bundles in the truck's trailer. If a bundle fell, the attendant had to get the driver's attention by hammering on the side of the driver's cabin with a long wooden stick. Once, when I was the attendant, the driver went into a side street and invited me into the cabin. To my great surprise, he told me that he was going to show me the town. He set off immediately. After repeated journeys, I had formed an image of the town; I had always looked around with interest but without really knowing what I was seeing.

"Riga ist ein uralten Stadt" (Riga is an ancient town), the driver began like a professional guide, and he showed me all the notable places in Riga on the way to the port. He told me that Latvia, also called Livonia or Latvija, was the biggest of the three Baltic States and had entered the Hanseatic League in the thirteenth century. This was the reason for the medieval German character of the old town. He slowed down in front of the fifteenth century gothic castle that later became the governor's palace. He showed me the parliament and the theatre. Later, smiling, he showed me to a statue in the centre of a square. It was the silhouette of a woman with three stars in her hand, symbolizing freedom. He said that because of its similarity to the label on bottles of cognac, the statue had been named "The Cocktail Lady" in their circles.

By inviting me to sit next to him this young man took a risk. This was an exceptional moment. As we were approaching the port, I knew I would have to go back to the trailer in a few minutes. Unable to postpone the moment any longer, I asked with a trembling voice,

"Is there any hope that we will be liberated?"

He did not reply but nodded his head reassuringly.

During those days it must have passed through the minds of many Germans that the unpredictable nature of the coming days might prove fatal for them.

The soldier who accompanied us in the truck that took us to work in the morning broke the rules by throwing his gun carelessly on the bench next to him. A young girl who was sitting near him, probably influenced by the good news floating around and giving in to the generally optimistic atmosphere, suddenly picked up the gun and mischievously pointed it towards the soldier. The boy went pale and it was clear that his blood froze. We too were terrified. The whole scene only lasted a fraction of a second, and the girl put the gun back in its place. When the soldier felt the gun in his hands again he only said, "Well, that's life. Today I guard you, and perhaps tomorrow you will be guarding us." That said, the case was closed. There were no repercussions from what had happened.

With the reduction in work at the warehouse they started to reduce our numbers. One evening, fifty women were selected, and Ági Wilkesz was among them. Hédi said straight away that she wanted to go with Ági. Someone was found immediately who was anxious to swap with her. After Hédi lost all her relatives she had become like a sister to Ági. I could understand this feeling because in a concentration camp, being able to count on someone with complete certainty often meant survival.

As always, nobody said where the new group was going. In fact, they only said, "You will be taken to another camp." No one said a word about what that would mean for their future. Like everything else at the *Feldbekleidung*, the selection was more humane than in the other camps. Sisters were allowed to stay together, as well as mothers and their children.

It saddened me deeply that only four were left from the group from Oradea. I asked Erzsi and the other girls to join Ági's group. They did not agree. I debated it with Erzsi all night, but she could not be persuaded. She declared that she was a confirmed fatalist and she was not going to try to interfere with the workings of fate. In the end, unable to resist my insistent pleas, she asked for time to think.

We left for work while those who had been selected remained behind. I worked on Erzsi all day until in the end she agreed. We would go with Ági. But when we got back they were no longer there.

The separation was extremely painful. I was annoyed with Erzsi, but I was more annoyed with myself. Why had I not been more insistent? Later, at Kaiserwald, we learned that two weeks later Ági and Hédi had gone through another selection, this time their last. Stripped naked, they were ordered to turn with their faces towards the wall and all those with the tiniest sore, no matter how small, had been taken aside. This was the last news about them. They were seen alive for the last time by someone who had escaped this selection.

The fate of poor Ági and Hédi had a decisive influence on how we dealt with our future. From then on we no longer exercised our own initiative. We let ourselves be carried along by events. Of course this does not mean that we made the right choice. There were cases where only those who had the courage to break away from the crowd were the ones who survived. But then who knew what was the right thing to do? Not even whose who were carrying out orders. Sometimes orders would be changed as we were on our way somewhere. I have never lived through greater uncertainty than at that time. Any kind of lucid, logical judgement of the situation was of no use at all. In spite of all this, we had to believe in something.

We enjoyed our privileged situation at *Feldbekleidung* for three or four weeks. Yet we knew the day was rapidly approaching when we would not be needed any longer. We were afraid of the changing situation, and yet we expected our liberation to come sooner because of it. And the Russian attacks were increasing.

Working outside at the port we were witnesses to an agonizing scene. A large unit of SS, dressed in black and armed to the teeth, formed two long, tight rows like walls on either side of the harbour road leading up to a ship's gangway. Russian prisoners of war, crushed and hopeless, passed between them and boarded the ship. We knew that five thousand prisoners of war were living a few hundred metres from our barracks, but we had no contact with them. We had hoped that the approach of the front would mean their liberation too. Yet here was the proof that Hitler's war machine did not want to give up this cheap labour force. We were immensely sorry that they had been taken away. At the time we did not know that this was their good fortune. I think they were taken to Germany to work or exchanged later. Others who remained behind were killed in large numbers.

After seeing the utter despair of those Russian prisoners we began to wonder if the Germans would have time to transport us. Would they have time to annihilate us? We could not dare to hope that they would simply hand us over to the Russians.

A few days later we had the chance to see for ourselves something that we had read about once in the newspapers at home: the German army in retreat. Everything, including even the signposts and the posters on the walls, was transported to the port. They even took the nails out of the walls. Absolutely nothing was left that would have indicated what the building was used for. Following the final orders, we took out the window frames, loaded them into the trucks and took them to the port. Was there a window shortage in Germany or did they just want to make life as difficult as possible for the advancing Russians?

Once the stripping of the buildings was complete, any justification for our presence disappeared. We felt that it was only a matter of hours before we would have to leave when the air-raid siren went off. The German corporal, who almost never stepped over our camp's threshold, now came and led us in orderly rows to the underground bunker. For the first time in my life I saw a bunker that had been made for German soldiers. They made us sit down around a long wooden table in the flickering lamplight. They warned us not to speak as we exceeded the permissible number and talking would consume too much air. Astonished, I realized that the German soldiers were afraid. This was such a new and powerful impression that I forgot to be scared myself.

The Russian raid did not last very long. After the siren ceased, we went back into the building. They made us remove the closets and then our bunks. All of a sudden the idea came to me to write a message on the inside of the closet doors. A message to whom? We had no idea. Somebody found a pencil stub, and we started to write on the doors, in large letters, the names of those who had been in our room and the time that we had been at Riga, from the middle of June until the end of July, and before that in Auschwitz. We asked those who read the message to send this information to our families, and we gave a few possible addresses. It seems to me now that this was as hopeless as if we had been lost at sea, putting messages in bottles. I never saw any other closets in a concentration camp, before or after, and I never met another *Häftling* who ever had a closet. So we could not put too much hope in our message reaching its goal. Yet when we scratched those lines, we did it with great conviction.

We showed our naiveté before we started our journey when we asked our supervisors to ask for us if they ever needed workers again. They did not tell us where we were being taken.

In fact, during the whole period at *Feldbekleidung* we were never given any orientation. They offered us everything they could within the limits of prisoner regulations, did not bother us needlessly, and addressed us in a humane tone. They only said what was required for working relationships, not a word more. One day, for example, they asked for volunteers for extra work. The request was unusual and only a few presented themselves. Erzsi at the time was still full of initiative and presented herself. As it turned out it was to remove the eyes from sprouting potatoes in the cellar of a nearby military warehouse. Those who presented themselves were generously rewarded with half a bucket of pickled herrings, a great delicacy for us. We would have been more reassured if we had known beforehand what kind of work they had in mind.

We were very interested in the attitude the *Wehrmacht* soldiers had towards us. Was their decency due to their humanity, their view of life, education or merely cold calculation? Obviously, in better conditions one gets better results. Their reticence was also puzzling. Perhaps we did not count, perhaps they were indifferent, or perhaps they were afraid of their superiors. They never said a word about the situation at the front that had such an important bearing on our fate. We deduced what little we could from external clues.

We left our clean and healthy barracks with a heavy heart, as if we knew that our camp life from then on would not be anything like this. Once again the truck carried us on. We soon arrived at Kaiserwald, the central camp in Riga. We had been there twice, but only now could we really get to know it. This time we immediately found ourselves in the thick of the pulsing camp life. They did not take us to the baths, which we were very glad about at the time as it meant that we were able to keep the things we had obtained in our privileged situation. Nor was there a selection, which meant that we could stay together, not only we four from Oradea, but our whole group. They crowded us into a huge barrack meant for five hundred people in which there were already about a thousand before we arrived. Each bed had three tiers, with two people sleeping to a bunk. In fact, as I learned later, there were actually twice this many people. Each work shift lasted twelve hours, and the two shifts rotated themselves on the bunks. This dreadful slum shocked us after our nice, small rooms. Our neat appearance attracted immediate attention. Compared with the existing inhabitants we looked like we had arrived from a Swiss boarding school or a resort. As a matter of fact we did behave as if we had just dropped in from Lausanne. When we learned that all the camp inhabitants had lice, we looked fastidiously around us and avoided approaching anyone. We were hanging around in groups near the doors because we would not sit on the beds. While they looked with envy at our neat dresses and kerchiefs, they smiled at our naiveté. They knew very well that we were hoping in vain that someone would come and take us back to the *Feldbekleidung*. They also knew that in a short time we would look like them.

We were assigned to the night shift and put to work at the workshop where batteries were recycled. On the very first day, we had met Babus Kemény, her younger sister Zsuzsi, and many other acquaintances from Oradea. We walked to work in strict rows of five. We passed many of the camp streets, the *Lagerstrassen*. It was then that I realized just how immense this concentration camp was.

The anode works was made up of a great number of barracks crowded together. We worked at tables, sitting on benches without back supports. We dismantled worn-out batteries. After we had laid out the metal case we had to separate the carbon sticks and put them to one side. This was the fourth year of the war, and the Germans needed to reuse their resources. They could do it because they had an enormous number of slave labourers at their disposal.

The work was not hard, but it was tiring to bend over without support for twelve hours at a time. The nights were especially difficult. The most disturbing thing, however, was that in a few minutes we were as black as if we had been working at a coal mine.

We slept for a few hours during the day, and in our free time we got to know the camp. Enormous blocks were lined up one next to another to form streets: the *Lagerstrassen*. Street next to street formed a labyrinth too vast for the eye to take in. We did not dare wander too far because we were afraid that we would not find our way back. We soon learned that the toilets and *Waschraum* (bathhouse), built to accommodate large numbers of people, were the principal meeting places in the camp, and here we met many people from Oradea once more. I met my old friend Sári Feldheim and her sister. We wanted to know where we had each been since we had been separated from each other, and we had no end of things to talk about.

Our food at Kaiserwald contained a new ingredient: peas. The soup was prepared from dried peas, and we eagerly attacked this new dish. As a result, in a few days we had terrible diarrhoea, though we did not make the connection at first. We also developed a very itchy skin rash. We were afraid it was typhus. We heard there were many cases of the disease in the camp, and we already knew that we should not give in to sickness. We did not dare to go to the infirmary. It was no secret that the sick underwent continuous selection.

I learnt from Sári that Kornélia Mózes, a doctor from Oradea, was in our camp. There were so many doctors at Kaiserwald that there was no point in registering as one. Kornélia worked with all the others. In the end I went to her with my problems. I had not even finished when she made her diagnosis: the peas.

"Okay, okay! But then how do you explain the itching, the rash?" I asked her anxiously.

"Have you looked at the seams of your underwear?" she asked me impassively, with her usual humour. I looked at her puzzled, not understanding the connection with my rash.

She appeared bemused by my ignorance. "Oh, you don't yet understand? Your skin itches because of the lice bites. Lice make their first nests in the warmest place in the body, the seams of underwear."

Kornélia's reply reassured me on one hand but horrified me at the same time. We had escaped the certain death awaiting those struck by typhus but ... but lice? And we had been so careful.

After being convinced that my life was no longer in danger, I looked at Kornélia more carefully. She had become a shrivelled old woman since we had last seen her. Her long dress, without a belt, hung on her body in a dishevelled manner. Her head was covered with white bristles. Her hair was just beginning to grow back, and though it had been black only a short while ago, it was now as white as snow. In Oradea, Kornélia had been one of the Jewish doctors exempted from internment in the ghetto. Deportation with all its accompanying horrors had taken her unprepared. Probably because of this, she had worn out faster than the others.

Once back in our hut, I racked my brain about how to get the better of the lice. I had no private place of my own to which I could retreat. In the end, I crouched in the corner of the bunk bed and in the seams of my underwear I found the unbearable lice.

What could I do? Along with the others I began to crush the disgusting creatures between my nails. It made me sick, but I went on. I cracked them one after another without pity, almost with relish. I wanted to eliminate this mass invasion of lice once and for all. I thought that the most logical thing to do would be to get rid of the seam in which they were nesting. So I took out the waistband and tied it round my body on the outside, but this did not help. I had destroyed the lice but not their eggs. All my attempts failed. The lice multiplied exponentially. They nested in the underarm of the dress sleeve, because this too was close to my skin, and then they teemed over my whole body. They bit without pity. My skin was so itchy that I felt I would go out of my mind. With my hypersensitive skin, I was badly affected. As well as the physical suffering, the invasion of lice caused a great mental trial, because lice were emissaries of another danger. I remembered what Karcsi had told me when describing the living conditions in forced labour detachments: lice are typhus carriers. We had very little opportunity to wash in that mass misery, and there was no chance of boiling our clothing. Our only weapons were our ten nails. With these, we could reduce the number of lice without ever being able to eradicate them.

A campaign to track down typhus sufferers began, causing great panic. They were collecting stool samples from everybody, and we all wondered whether to give our own stools or to ask for a sample from those whom we considered to be in good health. We asked Kornélia again for her advice. Her answer immediately ended the debate:

"A healthy person can also be a bacteria carrier. There is no point in taking the risk."

We stuck to Erzsi's theory: don't try to influence fate. Whatever will be, will be.

In the end the Germans gave up testing stool samples. They found a simpler way to reduce our numbers. Today when I think about what happened I cannot believe that they were really interested in special testing. I suspect it was just one more way to frighten us and to weaken our resistance.

Those *Häftlings* who had lived for many weeks or months in Kaiserwald complained of monotony and boredom. Our life did not seem at all monotonous to us. For us it was all new; every day brought new events, usually bewildering and agonizing ones.

In those miserable days, one meeting was a pleasant surprise. One of my former classmates, Böske Rosenberg, and her younger sister Éva sought me out. They considered themselves lucky because they were working outside the camp in a vegetable garden in the town. They had heard of our arrival and they wanted to surprise us with a few carrots. Such a delicacy, which reminded us of the food at home, was a rare thing. Their kindness was even more unexpected. In the world of coarsened, hardened morals in which we lived it was an unbelievable event. After recovering from the initial shock, Erzsi remembered our toothbrush, which had survived the searches and to which two had been added in *Feldbekleidung*. To return their kindness, we gave them each a toothbrush.

The most memorable of all the events in our lives at that time was on July 23, the day when we heard news that an attempt had been made on Hitler's life. I do not know who brought the news or how it reached the camp, but it spread like lightning. Unfortunately the attempt failed. We discussed the news in whispers: the attempt had been put in motion by army generals, there were many dead, Hitler only sustained minor injuries. We also heard that by way of reprisal many generals had been executed immediately. We only learned the details months later. Colonel Klaus von Stauffenberg had placed the bomb in Hitler's general headquarters at Rastenburg. Of the twenty-five people present, Hitler's stenographer died instantly and many generals were fatally wounded. After the failed conspiracy, many thousands were arrested, of whom over five thousand were executed.

We tried to imagine what would have happened to us and to the German nation if the attempt had succeeded. Perhaps the war would have ended; perhaps we would have been freed. Completely uninformed from a political point of view, we were not able to make any analysis of the event. While we regretted that the attempt had not succeeded, we were glad that it had been made and glad that organized resistance was still possible in spite of the awful terror instituted by the SS and the SD. All this made public the existence of a deep internal conflict within the German command, a fact that was itself sufficient to fill us with joy.

Another tragic event in camp life followed: they sought out and discovered all the children under age fourteen. Sixteen children who were under the age limit in the Riga ghetto had miraculously escaped their death sentences. Over the years they had been hidden in different places in the camp and even in the workshops. They had been moved constantly and secretly fed. These children who never saw the light of day had lived under permanent dread, for they knew that once they were discovered it would be the end. News of their existence somehow reached the SS, and when selections became methodical and regular they ordered the surrender of the children. Several dozen armed SS soldiers with barking dogs began combing the camp grounds in all directions. When they began heading for the electrical station, I felt that the fate of the children hidden there was sealed. And indeed, a group emerged shortly, led by a sickly boy of about fifteen with head held high and blinking eyes. His face showed that he knew very well what awaited him and that there would be no point in trying to change the verdict. He proceeded courageously, firmly leading two younger boys of about five or six by the hand. The boys were constantly looking behind at the soldiers. They were crying, wailing, kneeling down, and pleading. It was a heartbreaking scene. For a few minutes I watched those children, frightened and condemned to death, followed by the dogs sniffing and barking with their tongues hanging out, and the detached, merciless SS men. The voices and the expressions on the faces of those unfortunate children are imprinted on my memory forever.

By the evening they had found all sixteen children. The mothers also appeared. They could have saved themselves but chose to give themselves up to accompany the children on their last journey. And the Germans granted them this favour. I saw them when they got into the truck. Without exception, the mothers were dressed in old, shapeless, bright green dresses. They looked awful, but they did not mind. With great love, they embraced the children whom they had hidden and anguished over for years.

While we suspected it, at the time we did not know their destination. The next day, we found the following message that had been written with trembling hands on the inner wall of a truck, as we had prearranged. "We arrived in the forest. The passengers of the first truck were already ordered to get off and undress. They moved away from us. In a little while we heard the rattle of gunshots. It won't be long before we too will be at rest."

The following day, they took another group, wearing the same bright green dresses. Since then, I tremble whenever I see a woman dressed in bright green.

Each time I unwillingly remember those days and the death they brought.

More and more new *Häftlings* arrived daily from smaller camps that had been closed. We were told that following preliminary selections only a small number of them remained. In the main camp, selection had become a daily event, and we lived in a permanent state of terror. We returned from work more than once to find that a selection had been made while we were away. They took Flora, Éva Vadas' younger sister, while she was sleeping. The poor girl had come back from work tired and exhausted and had gone to bed without washing, still covered in soot. This caused her downfall. She was classified as sick, weak, and useless. Other times we had to file past a commission in rows of five and a judgement about our life or death was made on the basis of a fleeting glance. Sometimes they only took one unfortunate out of the row and at other times a whole row was taken aside with a simple gesture. Those chosen were strictly isolated in a special barrack that had been emptied for this purpose and had its doors and windows boarded up. They were kept in the darkness without food or water for one or sometimes two days. When we returned from work the barrack was empty. Then it started all over again.

It would be impossible to describe what mothers and sisters were going through. To know that your loved one was a few steps away from you and condemned to death was unendurable. When their tears dried, the women fell into a state of apathy and stared into space. How terrible it is to feel death nearby, to know that at any moment you can be snatched away and to fear for those close to you. We experienced this feeling so often that in the end we barely endured it without going mad. Those who deserved the most pity were those awaiting execution behind the boarded windows and doors. I was not afraid for myself. I felt sufficiently strong, but I was very worried about Erzsi. At every selection I trembled for her. Each time I heard the nails being hammered into the doors and windows, I felt as if those nails were being hammered into the lid of my own coffin. I imagined Erzsi alone, abandoned and crouching in the darkness. My heart was breaking. As much as I believed that I would survive, that I would come out alive from those terrible trials, as much as I wanted to live, I had decided that if fate decided otherwise, I would not abandon Erzsi but would accompany her in death. I did not speak to her about this, but after I had reached this decision it was easier for me to cope with the uncertainty. My decision did not mean that I had given up the struggle to survive: Erzsi and I struggled constantly to make ourselves appear as healthy as possible. After work, we said we wanted to go to the toilet before returning home and we washed ourselves there. If we were not able to do this, we wiped the soot off our face and hands. We were always washing our kerchiefs so we would appear fresh and cared for.

Emotions reached a fever pitch when we heard that Mengele himself was coming from Auschwitz to lead a commission of selection. We wanted to look good at any price. I made shoulder pads from discarded paper for Erzsi and myself. In the same way, I padded Erzsi's thin, flabby breasts under her dress. I felt overwhelmed by good fortune when I found a small piece of red paper in the dust by the road. We used this to colour each other's lips and cheeks. Thus armed we walked with a sure step past the commission, and we succeeded. We had gained some time.

By then Riga was being bombarded daily, mostly at night. The light was switched off in the workshop because we did not have anything to cover the windows. Motionless, we watched the amazing fireworks through the window. After a few days, we realized we had nothing to fear. No bombs were dropped on the camp, not even by mistake. We thought it would have been better to be killed by a bomb than to be executed by an aberrant fascist inquisition. One of the night bombings I experienced inside the camp remains imprinted on my memory. On that night Riga was bombed with incredible force. Hundreds of Stalin lights lit up the town. Planes were flying over us and heavy bombs were exploding in the vicinity. Women woke up terrified by the thundering racket and the bright light. Many rushed almost unconsciously to the door and windows. There was no point in going out because the *Lagerstrassen* were no safer. However, most of us thought that if a bomb hit our barrack, we would all burn inside. Our hut only had one door with a narrow exit, so we would not have been able to get out quickly. Before panic could break out, our *Blockälteste* (it was said that she had formerly been registered as a prostitute in Germany and that was how she got to be in charge of us) shouted in a sharp voice:

"*Ruhe! Ruhe!* If you are not quiet, I will shoot! Go back to your beds immediately! If anyone moves after that, I will shoot her like a dog."

The fact that she did not even have a gun did not cross anyone's mind at the time.

Her authoritative tone had its desired effect, and the barrack quieted down. Fortunately for me, my bunk was near the window and I could watch the extraordinary rain of fire through the entire night. It was a dangerous game, a confrontation of life and death. Shot-down Messerschmidts burst into flames and plunged into oblivion. Bombs exploded, and fire engulfed the whole area. We saw the incandescent sky and heard stupefying thunder. It seemed as if our barrack would be burning as well at any moment. As far as I remember, I was not paralyzed by fear; on the contrary, I was glad. I felt the end of the war was near. I cheered the Russians and wished for the defeat of the Germans, which promised our liberation. I was not afraid that I would die. Such an end seemed more acceptable to me than death as the result of a selection. We thought that this might be the final battle, that perhaps tomorrow we would be free.

6

THE BOAT JOURNEY

*T*he day after the bombing, they did not take us to work but began evacuating the camp. It happened just as it had with the Russian prisoners of war. The SS assault detachments lined up along the route, and between their rows our sorrowful convoy set off without hope towards the port. I do not know how many thousands of people we were, but we were many, very many.

We boarded a military transport ship. There were five levels inside the ship, and we were on the lowest. In a closed, oppressive room, they squeezed twelve people onto each three-tier single-width bunk bed: four *Häftlings* to each bunk. By now, we were used to discomfort, but the hardships this caused were intensified by many other factors. There was no air. Air only reached our room from a narrow stairway leading to the deck. Those of us on the lowest level suffered the most. I do not remember exactly if it was the end of July or the beginning of August. While we were under such strain, I lost my sense of time, and even now, trying to remember, I cannot orient myself in terms of time. One thing was certain: it was very, very hot. The heat was even harder to tolerate because of the lack of air and our bodies' perspiration. We undressed to our underpants and many were even naked, but sweat was streaming off us nonetheless. The rocking of the boat, people's distress and the overcrowded bunks falling apart made our situation even more intolerable. Thus more of us were crouching on each bed, and many more lay on the floor where there was no longer any room to walk. They gave us nothing to eat or drink. In any case there would have been no way to distribute any food. While I did not suffer from hunger, I felt my thirst all the more. The toilet was on the deck. To reach it, I had to stand in line for hours on the stairs. Once I had already reached the third floor when the line was driven back with a rubber stick and I had to start all over again. Not all the women managed to contain themselves; some emptied their bladders helplessly wherever they happened to be at the time, which only worsened our misery.

During the three days of the journey, I only got up to the deck once, on the third day and then only for a few minutes. I envied Erzsi who had fainted and was taken up before her turn, able to lie there in the fresh air. The hunger and thirst also had a positive effect:

my diarrhoea stopped, and for others also. We paid dearly for this recovery.

The three days on the ship went past as in a fever dream. We endured overcrowding, lack of air, stifling heat, a stench that penetrated every corner, the perspiration and the closeness of moist bodies. Inevitably we touched one another, but what was even more terrible was facing the undisguised truth. At the same time I was both the object of suffering and an objective observer of the staggering, tragic sight. I saw bodies of just skin and bone, limp sagging breasts, and slack wrinkled stomachs. The women from Poland and Germany who had suffered for several years were substantially worse off. We looked at faces worn out with hunger, thirst and despair, and I was sorry that I did not have paper and pencil to immortalize what we lived through. I wondered if there was a writer or an artist among us who could depict this terrible frenzy. Forty years later, I met such a woman in Budapest. Her name was Piroska Hidvégi, and she was an artist. She did not pass through Riga or travel by boat, but she had been taken from her home and locked up in cattle cars with bars on the windows. She had been in Auschwitz and in Bergen-Belsen where hundreds of thousands of people died of starvation. She experienced different things, but like the horrors we experienced, they weighed on her for the rest of her life. On her huge canvases, she used sombre colours, broad brush strokes and dramatic power to bring to life the lighting of the candles on Friday evening in the cattle car, the death of her older sister and the disorientation caused by psychological trauma. During those three endless days and nights on the boat, I had time to recall my experiences of painting, the theatre and literature. I pictured Goya's shockingly realistic bronze engravings and Gorky's *Night Shelter*, Dante's *Inferno*, and *Les miserables* of Victor Hugo. Frightful pictures! When I had seen them, they had all upset me terribly. And yet they did not even touch the horror of those days spent at the bottom of the boat. The closeness and touch of the tormented, sweaty bodies, wet with perspiration, and the women's immeasurable despair drove me to utter hopelessness. But what was our sin? That we were born Jews? That we were God's "chosen" people?

Since I was young, I had had a doubting nature. There, however much good it would have done to believe, to hope, to trust in someone, and however much I tried, I was unable to think about God except to accuse Him or to deny Him. Where was God when millions of people were taken and many old people, sick people, innocent children and strong young people full of life perished? What kind of God would tolerate such horrors? What natural or supernatural power could cause such a cataclysm? I did not find a single reassuring answer. One thing I knew for sure: I had to endure, to survive this inferno and emerge to live as a witness.

I felt that I would never have the power to express in words what I had lived through, and I decided that if I ever returned home I would find Joe Pasternak, a film director originally from Şimleul Silvanei, and persuade him to recreate the mad world of the concentration camps through the power of film, both as a memorial to the dead and so that this tragedy might never be repeated.

I was plunged into despair when I realized that I could no longer hear the noise of the engine. We had probably reached the end of our journey and the ship had stopped. Normally this would have cheered me, but I was afraid because Erzsi was not beside me. I was afraid that I would lose her in the confusion of disembarking. I spent a few hours in this state of alarm. I do not know how Erzsi managed to figure it out; perhaps, having reached the deck, she realized faster than I did that we were nearing land, but she did return in time. When I felt her hand in mine I was at peace. At that moment we were not interested in the future. We only wished to stretch our limbs and breathe some fresh air. It took a few hours to reach the shore. It was then that we realized how very many we were, even without all of us being there. Later, when we met up in another camp, and after liberation, at home, I learned that some of the *Häftlings* from Riga and Kaiserwald had been transported in another ship and a bigger group had made the whole journey on foot; those whom they had no more time to transport had been drowned in the sea.

Our boat stopped in an uninhabited gulf that gave us no idea of where we were. Each time we had arrived at a new destination we did not know in what part of Europe we were because the German empire encompassed a very great area. They left us for hours on the shore without supervision. We lay down and stretched out, enjoying the fresh air and the cold sea breeze.

Night was already falling when the tension rose again. Barges had been brought to transport us farther on. Once again we found ourselves in the bottom of a ship, but this time cool, fresh air reached us from above. We also had more freedom of movement. I tried to go up to the deck. To our great surprise the workers and sailors on the ship were the only ones with us. Our SS guards had stayed behind.

The captain of the barge, who was otherwise uncommunicative, told us that we had been in the Gulf of Danzig and that we were now sailing down the Elblag Canal towards Stutthof. These names did not tell us a great deal at the time. Until then, we had never heard of Elblag or of the Stutthof concentration camp, so the only thing that registered with us was that we were somewhere in the north of Poland.

We were probably not the first prisoners who had traveled in this barge. The ship workers knew what we were dreaming about. Many buckets of water were hoisted up from the canal, and they indicated that we could wash. It gave us incredible pleasure to wet ourselves with the cold water and to wash off the sweat of three days spent in that sauna. They were not able to give us drinking water, but this wash gave us the feeling that we had quenched our thirst. The cold, fresh air, the wash and the words of good will made us feel reborn.

It was dawn when the barges stopped and we got out onto the shore. We thought we had reached our goal, but a long journey was still ahead of us, to be covered by foot. SS guards appeared again and led us through a small town. The houses reminded me of those gingerbread houses in children's stories. The lace curtains at the windows were white as snow, the flowerpots of geraniums on the window sills breathed peace and calm. We found it difficult to believe that in those days people still slept in soft, white, clean beds. We did not meet a single person in the streets. The town seemed to be uninhabited. They had certainly organized our passing through so that no one saw our wretched convoy. They probably wanted to hide this shameful sight from the residents.

We walked for hours. Yet this felt good. After sitting and sleeping in rigid positions for several days, we craved the rhythmic movement of walking.

After many hours of marching, we arrived at an abandoned building of whitewashed brick. Our guides left us alone until evening. After the first uncertain steps to investigate, we began to find our way. In front of the building was a water pipe with lots of taps. We stormed them. Again and again we filled our receptacles with water. We could not get enough.

We wanted to quench four days of thirst all at once. I remembered once more a warning from Karcsi. At the beginning of the war, when he was home on leave from his work detachment, he described to us how many of the soldiers from the detachment had perished because they had drunk too much water from a questionable source. His words sounded in my ears and I wondered about the possible consequences, and yet I was unable to resist the freely running cold water. I drank an extraordinary amount, and we were seized with a kind of giddiness. There were no unfortunate consequences.

After we had calmed down, we went into the empty building. A new surprise awaited us. From the floor to the very top, the walls were full of tightly written inscriptions. There were millions of names, dates, and places of origin, messages for those who might arrive at later date, such as Piri Weisz from Cluj, July 5, 1944; Sarolta Grósz from Debrecen, July 10, 1944. We lingered for hours in front of the walls with a tightness in our chests, searching for a sign that our beloved parents, or perhaps Magda, had been there. Our search was in vain. Yet shouts of joy also sounded in that room. It suddenly seemed very important that we too should leave a message behind us. Stumps of pencils that had been carefully kept suddenly appeared and were passed from hand to hand. However, insecurity had taken root in us; no one could be truly happy because we realized that between the date of the inscriptions and the present, many things could have happened.

Those walls covered with the writing of confused and trembling hands left a deep impression on me. A quarter of a century later, I was in Prague with my family. We wandered through the old Jewish district and visited the Pinkas synagogue. On the white-washed walls were written in red and gold 77,289 names, the names of Jews from Czechoslovakia who had fallen victims to Nazism. The big, empty temple was filled with the cries of pain of tens of thousands of murdered people. And the names on the walls reminded me of the walls of Stutthof. And then, again later with my family, we started off on my former deportation route to recall the past, following Auschwitz-Birkenau to reach Stutthof. I found no trace of this building in front of the concentration camp. Inside, in the museum set up in the location of the old camp, I learned that only Polish prisoners had been held there; there was not a single mention that Jewish prisoners had ever been held in this camp. This is how easy it is to falsify history.

The guards left us on our own for a whole day. Night was already falling when they appeared again. They lined us in rows of five and prompting us with the usual "*Los! Los!*" they led us into the camp of Stutthof.

7

STUTTHOF

"Stutthof" was written in huge letters on the gates of the camp. Above it was the ironic inscription *Arbeit Macht Frei*: "Work makes you free." The barbed wire fences charged with high voltage electric currents, the watchtowers set up close together, the frightening shouts of the SS, and the prisoners' barracks crowded together in tight rows all made it obvious that we had arrived at our destination.

"Erzsi, Teri.... If you have got any food or clothes, throw them over the fence and we will catch them!"

Ragged, parched, weary creatures, all women, gazed at us over the fence. Who was speaking to us? Who could possibly know us? They all looked the same. It was hard to identify anyone whom we might once have known. Yet the voice reminded me of someone. As we passed on our way, I recognized Tizi, the wife of János Spitzer, a produce merchant, with whom we had once lived in the same house, down the same hall. I threw her my kerchief.

Our arrival at every new camp brought new and unpredictable events. At Stutthof, they did not take us to the baths. They did not give us clothing. They did not take anything away from us. In the barracks to which we were assigned, our supervisors were a woman of dubious past by the name of Ilse and her friend Max. According to the rules, roll call had to take place three times a day, but in reality it was whenever it took their fancy, sometimes several times a day. Ilse and Max, one with a club and the other with a whip, struck us full force as we passed through the door. We were so scared of the thrashing that we preferred to jump out the window, and we were not the only ones. When the signal was given, we would take flight. Nevertheless, after a few days, our backs and arms were covered with injuries and our legs and arms were bruised from jumping out the window.

We were not put to work. We spent many hours a day at the dreadful roll calls. In between them we were free, but we were eternally vigilant because we could be called at any time. In the little time we had, we hurried to the fences, trying to find relatives or acquaintances in the neighbouring barracks. After much probing, we discovered Lilly Klärmann, our cousin's wife, and some acquaintances from Oradea including Edith Kenéz, the Feldheim family, my friend Sári and her sisters, the other three Feldheim

Watch-tower in the Stutthof concentration camp.

girls and Dr. Kornélia Mózes. They had come from Riga by train. We were overjoyed at seeing each other again. We could not stop questioning each other. Of course we were determined to do anything to stay together. Because there were more of them, we were the ones who had to act. We decided that we would escape into the neighbouring barrack by creeping under the fence. This proved to be quite complicated. We had to find an equal number of people willing to take the risk of transferring to our hut. After a while, Sári reminded us of what poor Hédi Silbermann and Ági Wilkesz had experienced, whose fate had been much more unmerciful than ours. In the end, we returned to our original position, having decided not to interfere with what fate determined. We remained where we were. After our return home, we found out that the Oradean girls from the next barrack had arrived at a work camp similar to the one where we were. Their camp was liberated at the same time as ours, but they managed to get home much quicker. Edith Kenéz and Tizi Spitzer also survived the disaster. A few weeks later poor Lilly Klärmann was a victim of selection and she went to her death. We met another neighbour of ours from the ghetto, who was by now completely destroyed and in a terrible state of self-neglect. She was unrecognizable. Her skin was dirty and she was full of lice up to her eyebrows. It was clear she had given up the fight. On the other hand, Suzi, the younger daughter of the owner of a grocery store on our street, had been more adept. She had become a *Lagerschreiberin*, a clerk. She was dressed nicely and looked sufficiently fed. She worked in an office where she had to register the number of prisoners arriving at Stutthof in a huge book. We also presented ourselves to her. We no longer hesitated. We too hoped that one day somebody from the Red Cross would take an interest in us.

Thus two more weeks passed in which we went around and learned all about the camp until unexpectedly we were lined up once again and found ourselves on another journey to the unknown. When we left the camp, they made us stop in a field, undress to our underpants and leave behind our prison garb. Everything else we had to leave in a pile on the ground. In another pile was a vast amount of ragged second-hand clothing, from which each of us had to pick up a blouse, a dress and a coat as we moved along. Each rag was worn, dirty, and full of lice. After a few minutes, we looked as we had been a few hours after our arrival in Auschwitz: a pitiful ragged army. Yet I considered myself lucky. I had pulled from the pile a blue cotton dress with short sleeves and a mikado coat, a thick, three-quarter-length coat worn by boys in the winter. Erzsi had picked up a black cotton dressing gown and a navy blue light spring coat. In the scorching heat of August the black gown absorbed the heat of the sun and proved to be much too warm, and I could hardly drag myself along in my heavy three-quarter length coat. Our attention had been so absorbed by our physical transformation that we did not notice until we were already lined up in rows of five that the SS stormtroopers had surrounded us again and were driving us forward. They were as unapproachable as before. We asked where we were going, but they did not reply. They looked through us, their glares piercing, cold and stiff. After a long journey on foot, we arrived at the railway station. On the track, a long train of cattle cars was waiting for us.

THE CAMPS IN NORTHERN POLAND: DÖRBECK AND GUTTAU

*A*fter a train journey of a few hours, we continued on foot. It was pitch dark before we reached our destination. As had happened so many times before, we were without any idea of where we were. We found ourselves in front of an opening through which we had to step. Ten of us were counted to go in, but it was very crowded even for ten. We were hitting our hands and our heads against something soft and elastic, and everything was cold and damp. We groped around but could not figure out where we were.

As soon as day dawned, I put my head outside and looked around anxiously. A strange sight unfolded before me: an enormous forest of tents. Set up with military precision, at an equal distance from one another, in ten rows of ten, were military tents, or

Zelts, of the kind we used to pack at *Feldbekleidung* in Riga. All became clear: we had spent the night in a tent. It was like a big Boy Scouts' rally. For a moment, I nursed the idea that our summer holidays had just started and we were on a trip. However, when I turned my gaze to my companions and saw that ten were crowded into a tent meant for four and that they were ragged, unwashed and at the end of their reserves, I realized that my hopes had strayed into fantasy. The sad truth soon became apparent. We were somewhere in northern Poland, on the edge of the village of Dörbeck, of which none of us had ever heard. We had been brought there to dig ditches and trenches. Soldiers handed out spades, shovels and pickaxes. Each morning we went farther and farther with our tools on our shoulders to work wherever the last ditches had been dug. Each morning we walked four, five, or six kilometres, to be retraced on the way back in the evening. We got up at dawn every day, and after a long and tiring roll call, we set off to work. We came back when it got dark. Even for men, it would not have been easy to dig and shovel the earth without a break. Poles from work detachments were our supervisors, but SS guards also bustled among us. They watched to ensure that we did not take a break from our work or start talking to our Polish bosses.

On the first day they brought us lunch. It arrived in kettles on wheelbarrows, and it was the same soup that was at once so despised and yet so eagerly awaited. With our tin cups in our hands, we lined up two by two awaiting our turns. The most enterprising among us wolfed down the food quickly and then stole into the queue again, so that many were left without food. The distribution of food would have been done better if we had been left to supervise it ourselves and to manage the lineups on our own because the guards did not exercise any control. On the second day it became apparent how little they cared when they did not bring any food because transporting it was an inconvenience for them. Starting that day, the soup was distributed in the evening. On that first day without lunch we nearly fainted from hunger, and in the days that followed we suffered terribly. It affected even Erzsi and me, and we were among those who coped with hunger reasonably well. The marches on foot and the heavy physical work in the fresh air required frequent meals and substantial food, yet we became accustomed to the hunger as we had to so many other things.

In the morning, before setting off, we received a small mug of warm water, really a brown liquid without sugar and taste that was called coffee. As bad as it was, if we went to get it early enough, it was warm and it helped on those cold mornings. That was all until the evening. When we got back, they gave us soup. In place of the usual *Dorrgemüsse*, we received a soup made from fodder beets cut into cubes, sometimes with cabbage and a few carrots. Extremely rarely, a shred of meat might be found floating in the soup. The *Blockälteste* distributed the soup among a hundred people, who lived in ten separate tents. Each woman received a ladleful. Those who were amongst the first to receive a spoonful from the surface of the pot found themselves with thinner soup. Towards the end of the distribution, at the bottom of the pot, the soup was thicker. Naturally, most people tried to hang back towards the end of the row, however impatient they were to get to the food. As a result, the distribution of food often turned into a big quarrel. I cannot remember whose idea it was, but in our group of a hundred, we resolved the problem by distributing the food alternately from the beginning and from the end of the queue. In this way, the differences were settled. Today I can no longer remember how Renée Rachmudt, the *Lagerälteste*, a math teacher from Dej (Dézs) in Transylvania, became head of our group. I am certain that it would have been difficult to find someone who would have represented our interests better. She was young, both considerate and honest, and her kindness earned respect. Her deputy was Lilli Hirsch, a girl of great vitality who was sometimes impulsive. Renée could moderate her impulsiveness when she sensed a need for it. The two of them managed to remain fair and honest even in the most difficult circumstances. This was partly because we had a good group. I am not saying that among a hundred women there was not some dishonesty; some would even steal a piece of bread that had been kept carefully by a suffering companion. When thieves were discovered they were excluded from our ranks, even if only for a short time.

As for the distribution of food, we were given a daily portion of 250 grams of bread and the *Zulage*, which was a 20 gram slice of salami or a 30 gram piece of margarine, or, once a week, a spoon of castor sugar or even marmalade; it was different each time. All this combined contained far fewer calories than necessary for a restful lifestyle, let alone to sustain a woman engaged in heavy physical work.

The bread and the portion of *Zulage* were distributed by tents, and it was the responsibility of the tent supervisor (in our case Erzsi) to apportion it. Erzsi managed to divide the bread and the margarine into ten portions with great precision. Nine pairs of eyes watched her closely as she undertook this operation, and each person waited, trembling with impatience, to receive her portion. Éva Klein, who had been a student with me at the Jewish Gymnasium, swallowed her portion all at once. "What will be, will be. I just want to feel as if I have eaten something," she said. Erzsi and I carefully cut each piece of bread into six thin slices. We ate two in the evening with the soup because we were starving, two in the morning so that we did not set out on an empty stomach, and two at noon in place of lunch. It took us a week to get used to this schedule, but in the end I stopped feeling faint.

Sometimes the coffee tasted and smelled strange and for a while we did not know what to think of it. Each day a different person went to get the coffee from the camp kitchen. When my turn came I could not find a bucket. I looked around in confusion and saw an SS soldier washing himself with soap in a bucket of water. He yelled at me to take the pail from him. As soon as I had the bucket in my hand, the cook threw coffee into it. The next person was already following. Now I knew where the strange taste in the coffee came from, and my stomach turned over. I took the coffee, of course, but I also told the others what had happened. After that, many gave up their portions, while others were glad to receive more. Neither Erzsi nor I could swallow a drop more coffee. We did not taste it, we did not smell it, we just gave it up once and for all. In spite of the cold in the morning, which made us miss the warm drink very much, what human dignity we had left gave us the strength to refuse it.

After each day of heavy work, we badly needed to rest, especially at night. Unfortunately, this was impossible in the camp's conditions. Ten of us were sleeping in a tent designed for four, and each of us had received only one thin blanket. We split into two groups of five. We spread two blankets on the ground, rolled one up into a kind of pillow, and covered ourselves with the two that were left. Five of us slept on the width of two blankets. Of course, we all had to sleep on the same side. If one person turned over, the other four also had to.

The trenches had to be dug with engineering precision: 70 cm wide and 170 cm deep. If someone had told me a few weeks earlier that we – students, dressmakers, teachers, clerks, young mothers, or just girls from good families, unused to hard labour – could make such perfect trenches, I would not have believed it. Now the fertile earth was crisscrossed by a network of trenches that we had dug. Had we not been preparing this line of defence against our own interests and against our own possible rescue, we might have been proud of our work. The most difficult part was at the surface, when the guards could still see us. It became a little easier when we were concealed in trenches a hundred centimetres deep; one of us would stand guard to warn us when an SS officer was approaching. Swapping places with each other, we managed to catch our breath a little.

Not all the Polish supervisors had the same attitude toward the *Häftlings*. Some of them made no attempt to hide their anti-Semitic feelings and were no better than the SS. Yet some among them were more enlightened, having traveled abroad, especially in France, and who, when no one was looking, very cautiously said a word to us in secret. Once, one morning, one of the Poles "accidentally" left us the remains of his breakfast wrapped in a newspaper. It was only a slice of bread and butter, which was not a lot for eight or ten people, but his gesture of goodwill was what mattered. Equally important was the newspaper in which it was wrapped. We could hardly wait to get back to our tent where we could pore over it in secret. The Polish man had not left it by accident: it contained sensational news. The newspaper announced that on August 23, in Bucharest, King Michael had crossed over to the Russians. From that day, our interest was drawn even more to news from the front, as each advance increased our hopes of liberation. We were a thousand people in the camp. When anyone in the group got hold of any information, they immediately passed it on in secret.

As a result of the very poor diet, those of us who had the energy and the courage tried somehow to supplement our food. Some hung around for hours trying to get an extra portion of food after it was distributed. Others tried to organize a few potatoes from the fields. Such opportunities arose very rarely. The SS were very watchful that we did not get anything that would exceed our daily allowance. We used to go along a country road to our workplace. The dusty, stony, difficult road had wild apple trees towering over it, and we often trampled fallen apples underfoot as we passed. It was strictly forbidden to bend down to pick them up; if anyone tried, an SS guard would strike her with a rubber truncheon. Such a scene happened one day with a young girl. Three local villagers were coming along the road in the opposite direction from our group. In a reflex action, one of the men picked up a rolling apple and gave it to the girl. A young SS guard immediately hit this man savagely on the face. We learned that he was later beaten to a pulp in the village hall. Under threat of harsh punishment, the people of the village were forbidden to say a word to us or to help us in any way.

Yet some women among us did not give up hope and were ready to attempt the impossible. Such was the case of a young girl from northern Hungary, Lilike, who lived with her mother in the camp. One day at dusk, Lilike sneaked out of the camp and went into the first house up the road. She believed that she had escaped all danger when to her surprise, she was captured with her meagre acquisitions. The SS commander wanted her punishment to be an example for all the others. He announced that she was to be executed, but first she had to dig her own grave. He picked a place visible from all corners of the camp and made Lilike dig the hole there. We thought her poor mother was going to go out of her mind. She cried, she wailed, and she threw herself on the ground to implore mercy. It was in vain. Lilike's tears poured down her face, but she dug without protest. We all stood helplessly in front of our tent.

Night fell and Lilike was still digging her grave. After a long time she finished, and they told her to undress and lie in the hole she had dug. They announced that she would be executed in the morning. No one closed her eyes that night. The next day, after roll call, the soldiers took us out to work. When we got back we learned that Lilike had been pardoned. Her short bristling hair had turned white. We never knew if they had decided to pardon her at the last minute or if they had only really intended to frighten us, but whichever it was, the incident affected us deeply.

The scorching days of summer passed, but not easily. Many of us had sunstroke. Many girls burned so badly that their skin turned red and their arms and backs were covered in sores. This was made worse by the blows we received from others. A lot of us suffered from infected wounds. Then grey, rainy, windy days began to follow one another with dreary monotony. We rose at daybreak. There were endless dreadful morning roll calls, long days of hard labour without food or drink, and restless nights. The deadly work, the hunger, the awful exhausting weather, and the rough treatment broke us mentally and physically.

Constant fear, concern for our loved ones, and the desperate struggle we waged against lice wore us down. Each of us reacted in our own way. Some women lost their minds and were no longer aware of what was happening around them. These women lived in imaginary worlds, usually thinking about their old lives. Others endured everything with complete resignation. Still others became indifferent and insensitive to the pain of their companions. Some became self-centred and proved capable of taking the last piece of bread that their comrades had carefully preserved. And then there were those few who not only remained human but became better people and proved capable of great sacrifice. These people became a support for those who had given way. They had nothing to give but they helped as they could. We realized that in the camp one could not survive alone. Mothers and daughters, sisters or cousins made happy pairs. Where family was not present, a friend or even a stranger became a so-called camp sister. When one of us felt that she had lost all strength, the camp sister did everything she could to put her back on her feet. Solidarity was not only desirable but vitally important. That is how fellowship developed among camp inhabitants. Among those from Oradea the following people formed pairs: Éva Rosenberg and Böske (Mrs. Halmi and Mrs. Blau); the Kemény girls, Babus and Zsuszi; Erika Markovics and Margit Goldstein; Kati Kajári and Éva Vadas; Magda Roth and Olga Berger. I witnessed many incidents of amazing humanitarianism.

I also met women who remarked with satisfaction that they had purposely remained alone so that they did not have to worry about anyone else. Later, when I was at home, I learned that some people had deliberately separated themselves from those they were close to because they thought that they could better fight for survival unhindered by friends.

Days and weeks passed, and we went on ceaselessly working in the fields and on the land. The trenches crisscrossed the agricultural land in all directions. By now, the morning and evening journeys to and from the trenches covered eight kilometres every day. We completed the work in complete physical exhaustion, and we left Dörbeck the next day.

No packing was necessary. At Dörbeck, nobody really had anything. Besides a dish and thin blanket, the clothes we wore were all we could call our own. The soldiers lined us up in rows of five, and we set off for the station. Unlike our arrival, our departure took place in full daylight. The locals had grown used to our presence, and it had been made clear to them that contact with the prisoners was undesirable.

To our surprise, a train of passenger cars awaited us at the station. We boarded and sat on wooden benches. The journey caused an incredible and unexpected sensation, for sitting on benches made us feel human. I recalled journeys to my grandparents in Sighetul Marmaţiei. Each one among us had an image to hold on to, an event to remember. We did not want to know where we were going. We were all thinking about the past, and we had cut ourselves off completely from the present. We were so happy to admire the beauty of the scenery through the window. We stepped onto the railway buffers and no one stopped us. A gentle breeze caressed our faces. We felt like young girls. For the first time in months we really felt as though we were twenty years old.

The journey only lasted a few hours. It ended sooner than we wished. We had arrived in Guttau. At the time, we did not know that this would be the last stop on our journey through the camps.

The surroundings could have been confused with the camp at Dörbeck. Here too our tents had been set up in a field. Here too we walked kilometres to get to our place of work. Here too we worked for the *Organisation Todt*, the German state construction agency. Here too we dug trenches. The food was just as scant. The opportunities for washing ourselves were even fewer. Ten tents, that is, a hundred *Häftlings*, shared only one washbasin, which was used in strict order by a different group each day. When the day came for our turn, washing went on into the night. After we had washed ourselves, each person also washed her dress and underwear in the same water. At Dörbeck, we had brought water from a nearby lake. Here, we had to go to a river that was much farther away. We brought the water in tins, and we used to hang five or six of them on our fingers at a time. We brought five or six litres of water in one hand, of which half was spilled on the way. It was not easy to wash once in ten days and keep our clothes clean, or even to create an illusion that we were clean.

We did not dig trenches much longer: we moved on to digging tank traps. The anti-tank trench was five metres wide on the surface of the earth and became gradually narrower towards the bottom. It had to be three metres deep. This work was much harder as the earth had to be thrown from a greater depth and the sides had to be finished diagonally. Following the directions of the head of works we left a protruding rim here and there on the trench walls.

Those who were working at a greater depth threw the earth to the rim, and others threw it further up to the top. At the end, we gradually hollowed out the earth underneath a girl who was standing on the rim, until the wall was smooth. When we had finished, even we were amazed at the results of our work. A thousand young women stood in trenches digging and shovelling without stopping from dawn until dusk. We dug and shovelled in the heat of the sun, in the cold, the rain, and the wind. Secretly, we were indignant when we were forced to work in dreadful weather. We did not know that we would be sent out into the fields even when the harsh winter of the northern regions arrived and the ground was covered with snow.

The days passed with an exasperating slowness. Our hands hurt from the handles of the hoes and the shovels. We did not even have rags to wrap them in. We suffered from the whims of the weather and the exhausting work, from the dirt and the hunger. There was no respite. To our dismay, we discovered that the endless hardship was brutalizing us. All we were interested in was the approach of evening, when we could break off from work, if only for a short while, to receive a dish of food and to go to bed at last. Some of those who suffered the most from hunger thought constantly about the tasty dishes of home and remembered them with delight. While throwing the earth, they used to make up food menus, changing the recipes and describing the tastes of different delicacies. The rest of us tried in vain to explain to them that this only increased our suffering.

In our narrower circle, we became all the more aware that we had to do something to keep our brains working. We decided to resolve mathematical problems in our heads. In the past some of us had been good mathematicians. Of course, we did not try to solve problems that were too difficult. We constructed equations with two unknowns, and we tried our powers with geometry problems too. We drew geometric shapes and angles on the ground with the end of a stick. We inverted problems on our own and were glad when we remembered the formulae we used to use. We tried to carry out multiplication and division in our heads. Another way of putting our brains to work, and perhaps an even more successful one, was to reminisce about books we had read in our previous lives. We had befriended two girls from Debrecen, Éva Vadas and Kati Kajári, and during working hours we tried to arrange to be near one another. We started recalling *The Tragedy of Man* by Imre Madács. It took weeks on end for us to recount the tragedy in all its details, scene by scene, from the appearance of the first couple until the final act with the Eskimos. We told the story as we dug with our shovels. If a guard drew near, we stopped. When the next opportunity arose, we continued. When one of us got stuck, another helped. We corrected one another. We struggled together with Adam, covering all the meandering of human history. We wanted to believe that life was not devoid of meaning and that our struggle was not devoid of hope. However ruined we were, we would not take Lucifer's part, which meant doubt. We did not want to accept that the most awful end was inevitable. We would not let ourselves tread in the steps of Lucifer. We were always repeating Madács' words, "Man, fight and believe!" Even today I still believe that Madács gave us trust and strength. We followed with the novels *Flood in India*, *The Field*, and *On the Wings of the Wind*.

Three girls from the sub-Carpathian region became the leaders of our camp. Arany Friedmann had become *Lagerälteste*, and she had named one of her younger sisters her assistant, while the other had become responsible for Block 1. We were in Block 10 here too, and fortunately our leader was the same as in Dörbeck. The camp doctor, of course, was also one of the leaders. Even in the camps with a number of doctors, only one could work as a doctor. As it happened, our camp had only one doctor, and she never did anything for anyone. She did not insist that the weak rest from work. A woman in our block had been suffering from a kidney problem since before she had left home. It was difficult for her to cope with the work, and since her shoes were worn out, she used to work practically barefoot. Even when the weather got cold and rainy, she did not manage to find another pair of shoes. Seeing her suffering, we implored the doctor to let her stay in her tent with disabled status or to put her to work in the kitchen. The doctor did not do anything for her. Sadly, the woman died before our eyes.

I know that it was not easy for the doctors to cope either, but I was disturbed that she had not even tried to help. What revolted me most was that even during the most difficult times she looked well cared for and wore a different pair of shoes each day. She had shoes for autumn, leather boots, and shoes in white canvas with wooden heels. I did not envy her warm dress or her clean, well cared for clothes, but when I looked at her feet and saw her shoes whitened with zinc talc, I felt the blood rush to my head. I will never forgive her for seeing our suffering without trying to alleviate it.

Because of the cold, our situation grew worse each day. The north wind blew stronger, and it began to rain a lot. We reached the end of our strength. More than ever, people were getting sick. There was no respite. The SS and their assistants the *Kapos* drove us on without pity, to roll call and then to work. More and more women were not even able to leave their tents. Their comrades had to drag them to work. Even if they collapsed on the way, everyone had to be present at the reading of the lists. The roll call could last an hour or two. We lined up by Blocks in groups of about a hundred. The *Blockälteste* numbered us first, and then if the numbers agreed, they reported them to the *Lagerälteste*. Only after this did the *Lagerführer* appear with his entourage. Those who collapsed in the meantime were held up by their comrades. And the numbering started again. They demanded that we stand upright in a military, orderly fashion. This was part of their systematic torture. We were glad when at last we set off for work. They allowed a limited number of the most seriously ill to help in the kitchen. The others left with difficulty. On the way, the weakest collapsed, but not for long. The SS brought them to their senses with a whip, forcing them to get up. Tormented, they continued on their way, dragging themselves to the field.

Our first death was an eighteen-year-old woman from Košice. Her death shook us. Could it have been diphtheria? Who would know in such surroundings? We cried for her, and many of us accompanied her on her last journey. We buried her. We marked the grave with branches of a tree. I can remember how hard we tried to remember the place where she was buried. We used the surrounding shrubs as a reference point to help the parents find the earthly remains of their only daughter at some later date, because after the war she would certainly be taken home. How naïve we were. We had not yet understood that her parents were perhaps no longer alive, or that in Germany, Poland, and other occupied countries the number of unmarked graves had risen to hundreds of thousands. Those who did not even have a grave could be counted in the millions.

The first death was soon followed by many others. After a few weeks, we could no longer keep count of our losses. It was unbelievable how easy it was to die. Those who left for work forced themselves to their limits, but in the end were no longer capable of keeping up, and perished in turn. Those who worked alongside the sick took their shovels and pickaxes when they could and tried to support them too. At work they tried to protect them. When the SS noticed those who lagged behind, they spared none. Often neither blows nor gunshots had any effect. The sick simply could not get up. However much our hearts went out to them, we had to go on. What happened to those who had been left behind, those helpless ones, we could only guess.

Our work became especially difficult when it rained torrentially. Besides suffering from clothes saturated with water and from wind that blew through our wet rags, we constantly marched through mud and mire. We used to slip with every step, and we were covered in mud. The soil was much heavier when wet, and lifting the earth and cleaning our tools became more difficult. Sometimes the trenches were filled with half a metre of water. When that happened, we tried to find work on the surface, for example, to level out the earth we had already thrown, but in the end we were forced into the trenches. In such circumstances, each day was unbearably long. Whatever happened, they would not take us back to the camp until night fell. There we had nowhere to dry our clothes. In the evening, we swallowed our soup quickly, got undressed and went to bed. We spread our wet rags over the blanket. In the narrow tent they dried from the warmth of our bodies.

Erzsi and I had good boots. This was our luck. We also had long cotton tights. These things meant life, and we looked after them very carefully. We oiled our boots with small pieces of margarine that we had been given to eat. Shoes were even more important than food. Many walked in useless worn-out shoes or in sandals. Those whose shoes were no good at all could be considered lucky. It was not always the case, but sometimes if there were any available in the stores they were given a pair of cloth boots with wooden soles. These were usually men's sizes, three or four sizes bigger than what the women needed. It was difficult to walk in them, but they were better than shoes with holes.

The clothes that had been assigned to us in Stutthof were so tattered they were unrecognizable. Confused by the sufferings we had borne, we no longer noticed what we looked like. The day came when our eyes were suddenly opened and we discovered with amazement what a plight we were in. It happened once that we finished digging an enormous tank trap before the next work had been identified. Of course they did not give us a day off, and we were kept there until darkness fell. To occupy us, they made us carry stones, enormous quarry stones. It was a dry sunny day. Only about ten guards were watching us, and they were gathered in two groups at the ends of the area. For the first occasion in a long time, we were able to move about relatively freely. As we passed beyond the view of the guards, we relaxed our pace. Until then we had only seen the backs of those walking in front of us, but now, for the first time, we could study each other's faces as well. Never in my life had I seen such a miserable collection of tattered human beings. Our appearance was frightening. Eva Halmi, for example, in the absence of stockings, had torn strips from a mustard yellow silk dress with green flowers and had used these to wrap her legs. I had not noticed that until then. We were glad of this unexpected rest, for even lifting rocks seemed like a break after so much digging and shovelling. It made us feel good to walk on that sunny road and it cheered us to exchange a joke. We imagined how we would look marching in these rags along the main street in Oradea on a Saturday afternoon during the time for promenading in front of the Japport cafe. We imagined meeting acquaintances who were still living civilian lives. With the eyes of strangers, we weighed each other's appearance. It was then that I really understood the state to which we had sunk, and I realized that we had already endured much more than we would ever have believed possible. Yet at that time we did not know what great trials were to follow.

Winter came early that year: the first snow fell at the end of October. We were still sleeping in army tents designed for four people. At dawn, when we got up, the fields around us were white, and the blankets covering us were covered in frost. All this would have been wonderful if the beautiful winter had not been yet another cause of suffering for us.

One day, when we came back from work, we were welcomed by the pleasant sound of hammering. They were erecting cylindrical tents with pointed roofs. We were happy that they were being prepared for us. As we were living in the tenth group of a hundred tents, many days passed before we could take over the block that had been assigned to us as our new home. In these Finnish tents called *Zelts*, the middle area was left clear. The outside of the circle was split into twelve circular sections. Of these, ten sections were used for sleeping, one was the entrance, and the piece of the circle opposite the entrance was kept for leaders. The *Lagerälteste* and *Kapo* organized the allocation of bread here and saw to the other administrative duties. Five *Häftlings* slept on the floor in each section. Altogether there were fifty. A metre above the places for sleeping, a wooden story had been added in which another fifty women slept. So one hundred people were crowded into a single tent. Our SS guards had allowed us to fetch as much hay as we could carry from a distant haystack. Unfortunately, a lot of hay fell to the ground over the long journey, and we had to be satisfied with a very thin layer. Erzsi and I settled on the ground with a few other girls, which proved to be a very bad idea. Our hay disintegrated, turning to dust underneath us, and soon we were sleeping on a bare board. Besides that, the boards above us were full of cracks. Bits of hay rained down on our heads, and sometimes a liquid of dubious source flowed down with it. There was nothing we could do about it; the status quo could not be changed. We folded one of our blankets in two and put it underneath us. For a cover, we used the other blanket as well as all our clothing.

The wind blew fiercely through the thin walls of the tent. At first we were terribly cold, even colder than we had been in the small tent, where the heat of bodies had warmed us a little. But as more and more snow fell, the situation improved. Learning from the inhabitants of another tent, we surrounded the wall from the outside with a thick layer of snow. It proved to be a very good insulator. When the frosts came and the temperature fell to –25°C, cast-iron stoves with long pipes were installed in the middle of every tent. For heating we used brushwood that had been gathered from the surrounding area. It was dark all day long in the tent. The only light came from the door when it was opened, or if it was closed, a small window above. We were only in the block in the evenings, though, and then the flames from the stove gave enough light to keep us from bumping into one another. We had a lot to do in the evenings, so we had to do something about the light problem, and indeed we did. We made lamps from a few hollowed out potatoes. We gave up the small portion of margarine we received to use as lamp oil, and for wicks we used woollen threads taken from our dresses and our blankets.

The flames that rose in the stove and the weak light of the lamps made a peaceful, pleasant atmosphere. After our evening meal, we used to squeeze around the lamps with pieces of underwear in our hands, while we diligently cracked the unbearable lice with our thumbnails. Water was always being heated on the cast-iron stove in the only washbasin or in our kettles. Once every two weeks, observing a strict order, we washed with warm water from top to toe. We also washed our clothes, which we dried by morning on the long stovepipe. All this was performed as if it were a ceremony on which our life depended. The truth is that these moments helped greatly to raise our morale and helped us survive.

The other advantage of a hundred of us sharing a hut was that we got to know each other better. We found girls with beautiful voices who were good at reciting or story-telling. I do not mean that we organized literary evenings, but when we were not too tired, after each one had nestled in her rags, Renée called on the gifted girls and women, and the songs and verses they recited created a warmer atmosphere. In the midst of our grief, we resorted to beautiful thoughts and noble sentiments. It was there that I heard for the first time the sad song of the Polish Jews about their native land, *Mein Städtele Beltz*. The song made an impression on all of us because each one of us had left behind a "Beltz" for which our hearts now grieved. A girl from Maramureş went from block to block to sing the heart-breaking song *Es brennt*.

In our imaginations the flames broke out and our homes fell prey to fire. Memories of the past were so very, very painful.

In my moments of quiet, if I wanted to think of something nice and pleasant, I recreated in my thoughts the atmosphere of holiday evenings at home. I saw again the tablecloth white as snow under a napkin embroidered with Hebrew letters, the smell of the plaited *challah* bread with the crisp crust. I saw the flames of the holiday candles rising from silver candlesticks. In the stove, sparks of fire cracked and spread, and we, the family, were gathered around the table. On such occasions my father, a man who was not given to much speaking and was rather introspective, forgot all his cares and relaxed in the pleasure of being with his family. He used to tell us stories from his memories, incidents from the First World War and adventures he had during his travels. He had traveled a lot in countries that at the time had seemed very far away to us. He had been in Vienna, Paris, London, Berlin, Leipzig, and he had at least one interesting story to tell from each place. During the dark nights, muffled up in my rags, I saw the candles in my mind's eye. Their light fell on the faces around the table, and it seemed that I could hear my father's voice and see my mother following my father attentively. The light of the festival candles left a deep impression on my inner world. After I returned home, each anniversary and every family celebration unfolded to the light of candles. Even today, a celebration is not really a celebration without candles.

The sixth of November arrived: my birthday. The monotonous flow of time had made me forget it. But not Erzsi. She gave me an even bigger surprise than I had given her on her birthday six weeks earlier. With some coffee grounds obtained from the kitchen, I had mixed margarine and sugar with three spoonfuls of jam saved from my portion to model small balls the size of nuts. Erzsi had surpassed me: she surprised me with a present of a *dobos* cake. To this end she had sacrificed half a portion of her bread. On slices of bread cut as thin as onionskins, she had spread jam and margarine sweetened with sugar. Then she had put one on top of the other and decorated it. It brought me great pleasure. It was not only the fact that she had not forgotten me in such bitter days, but that in trying to produce cakes such as we had at home she had managed to create a family atmosphere.

I had a wonderful dream the night before my birthday. I was at home, and everyone overwhelmed me with gifts. Nothing darkened my joy. The next day I awoke rested and in good spirits. It is interesting that generally at night I dreamed that I was at home. I do not remember ever dreaming about life in the camps. So my nights were peaceful, restful, and regenerating. Perhaps that also explains why I was able to put up a good struggle in those difficult days. I held on to the belief that I would survive. I was convinced that if I was not killed on purpose, I would escape with my life.

My hardest struggle was with my sister Erzsi, who had lost all hope. She was overcome with despair. She used to cry, sometimes all day, for our poor parents, and she was worried about Józsi, who was later to become her husband. She did not believe that she would survive or that she would ever see Józsi again. She saw no sense in making a superhuman effort to survive, because life showed no promise of anything good or lovely. Her usual words, especially after she became ill, were, "Let me die, don't bother with me, it's not worth it!" She said that to me hundreds of times, and hundreds of times I refused to listen to her. If she didn't have the strength to get rid of the lice from her dress, I did it for her. I brought her water and made her wash. I forced her to swallow our miserable food. I implored her and I argued with her. I forced her to live.

9

Remaining Human

One evening we were lined up waiting for our portions of soup. Ten long lines wound behind the soup kettles. Suddenly, an upstairs window opened in a building opposite the kitchen. Our SS guards threw a bowl of gnawed bones onto the ground. What generous donors! Within seconds our lines disintegrated as twenty or thirty people ran to the scattered bones. Shoving each other aside, they fought over the leftover bones that were rolling in the dirt and snow. The rest of us watched in dismay, and some tried to stop those desperate ones who had gone out of their minds. It was too late. The SS stood grinning at the window and triumphantly enjoyed the view that was so painful to us. They sneered and laughed for they had succeeded in humiliating us. I thought about what we had become: nameless pariahs deprived of civil rights, famished, and without hope.

The emotional distress and the trials through which we passed did not have the same effect on all of us. Although we were living in the same situation, we did not react in the same way to our privations. Although we ate the same amount, we did not experience hunger in the same way. We did not control our feelings in the same way, and we did not share the same attitude to the sufferings of others. We did not keep our humanity in the same way.

We were from different regions: from all over Hungary, Northern Transylvania, and the sub-Carpathian area. Our backgrounds were also varied: some were from towns and some from the country, some were intellectuals, some labourers, farmers, and homemakers. Among us were also good-for-nothings, irresponsible people, and profiteers who had no concern for others, as well as many dull colourless people whose presence nobody noticed. At the same time many people were honest and well-meaning and gained top marks in the school of kindness and humanity. I have already mentioned Renée, our *Blockälteste*. Today all those who are still alive from the hundred women in our block, all those who survived the Holocaust, remember with gratitude her kindness, her fairness, and her honesty. Perhaps we should credit her for the fact that we in that block retained some control over our feelings and impulses.

Magda Roth was a small woman, about thirty-five years old. It was in the camp at Guttau that I first became aware of her presence among us. She was a labourer who had lost her family at Auschwitz and was all alone. She chose Olga Berger as her camp sister. Their relationship was not one of simple reciprocal dependency: Magda cared for Olga as for a daughter. In fact, she took everyone under her wing who needed protection. She helped the weak and distressed Irénke Goldmann. This poor woman was extremely near-sighted and needed strong glasses, but since her glasses were broken she had lost her balance. She also suffered from stiff, numb legs and still managed to drag herself to work. Magda often supported her the whole way. Magda would carry Irénke's hoe or heavy shovel on her shoulder as well as her own on the way to and from work. Irénke survived the war. She returned home and married our cousin, Harry Klärmann. However, she had contracted a fatal illness in the concentration camp, and she did not live long.

Magda Roth helped others besides Irénke. She was good at getting additional soup by lining up for it twice. Unlike others who used to swallow their food on the spot, Magda shared her additional soup with her protegées. One of her exploits qualifies as an act of heroism. I do not know whether she planned it or whether it was an inspiration of the moment, but one day she seized a bucket and went through the open door of the cellar to the vegetable stores. She filled the bucket with potatoes, greens, and fodder beets, and then marched confidently between the huts under the eyes of the SS guards and did not stop until she had reached Block 10. Here she cut the loot into small slices and went around all the huts looking for the sick until she had distributed every last piece. She did not expect any thanks. She just went on her way. In fact, she did not know most of those to whom she offered such rare delicacies. I myself think of her with gratitude, for in many respects it is due to her that I managed to bring Erzsi home.

Even in our destitution, we found ways of helping each other. While in the camp, Margit Goldstein discovered that she had a talent for massage. In the conditions in which we were living, with no access to medication or rest, massage eased our sufferings both psychologically as well as physically. Those who received massages felt it improved their health. A lot of people sought out Margit. She gave massages whether she was rewarded for them or not. If she gained an extra piece of bread by giving a massage, she always shared it with her friends.

One day, Babus Kemény took me to see Judit, who was engaged to a friend we had in common. Judit lived in Block 7, which was known as one of the most neglected and lice-ridden. Judit had lost a frightening amount of weight, and she had closed up inside herself. Even her eyebrows were teeming with lice. We discussed ways to help her, and came up with a single solution: we decided to remove her from her present environment, hoping that would lift her from her terrible apathy. We only saw one way to do this: to move her to our block. It seemed that this would be possible since a few days earlier one of our comrades had died of kidney disease. Our plan to move Judit over to us met resistance from our companions, but in the end we managed to convince Renée, our *Blockälteste*. She gave her consent with one condition: before bringing her, we had to delouse her. We had lice, too, but we prided ourselves on managing to control them to some extent. It was rumoured that Block 7 was ravaged by the *Volhinian* lice. Everyone was afraid of the interbreeding of lice. Millions were teeming in Judit's very short hair. Together with Babus, we washed her for three days in succession. We deloused her, washed her underclothes, and combed her hair until, in the end, she looked presentable. We were very satisfied. However, Judit rethought her situation and said that she would not move unless two friends from Cluj (Kolozsvár) could come with her. We understood her feeling of solidarity, and we thought that for good or ill they should remain together. We would have been ready to clean them up and move them too, but there were no more places in our block. So Judit stayed with the girls, but her decision had fatal consequences. She died three weeks later, followed by her friends. As soon as we stopped caring for her, she and her friends fell back into apathy from which they could not be shaken again.

Klári Friedmann was not living in our block, and it was only by chance that I got to know her. This slight, cultured, sad young woman was the privileged child of a wealthy family from Košice. She was modest and helpless. If she had been on her own in the camp, she would not have managed to evade death. She was fortunate that three of her cousins, whom Klári's father had supported financially, took her under their protection. As I mentioned before, they held key positions in the camp, the oldest being the *Lagerälteste*. As Klári had no leaning at all towards leadership, they did not give her a job, but instead they looked after her. The ambitious and assertive spirit of her cousins was foreign to Klári. During work, she once found herself near me, and I started talking to her. We discovered a lot of traits in common, and we became friends. From then on, she sought me out whenever she could. Living in the shadow of the most important leader, she often found out ahead of time what the SS were preparing. On such occasions, she sought me out to warn me. She was glad to be of help.

I have already mentioned F. Juliska from Nyiregyháza. A Christian, she had entered the ghetto of her own volition so that she could remain with her partner and their eighteen-year-old son. Of course at Auschwitz they too were separated from one another. I never heard a single word of complaint from Juliska. She only reviled the Hungarian fascists and the German Nazis. Otherwise, she used to tell us ten times a day how she had lived twenty wonderful years alongside her man and that her memories counted for more than anything else. We loved Juliska and we were sorry for her, perhaps even more than for ourselves. In the early days we tried to obtain privileges for her. Several of those who spoke better German tried to explain to the guards that Juliska was Aryan and was only a victim of circumstances. To our surprise, our efforts worked to her disadvantage. The SS guards only became more irritated with her: they hit, beat, and kicked the poor woman. Juliska endured it all with clenched teeth, but as often as she could, she took part in sabotage. She was a powerful, bold woman, ready to help her suffering comrades at any time. She often offered to watch the fire at night. Sometimes I used to wake at night, and dizzy with exhaustion, I would see her standing by the cast-iron stone with her back straight, watching over our dreams.

10

ILLNESS

*F*or long months we went on breaking and shovelling the hard earth. Just as we could not get used to the bites of the lice, so we could not accustom ourselves to the hard handles of the shovels. My palms were always covered in blisters and calluses. The frost was hard enough to crack stones, and my tortured hands developed a dry crust and turned blue and mauve. My ears froze worst of all. I envied the few girls who wore hats. I wondered if I could make a hood and even some gloves by sacrificing a piece of our blanket. I could not borrow a needle from anyone for such a big job, for needles were guarded as precious possessions. Only after waiting several days and exchanging two days' bread allowance did I manage to get hold of a needle of my very own. How rich I felt! I took sewing thread from Erzsi's red scarf, and I made two pairs of mittens and a hood so tight it stuck to my head. I even hemmed the edge of my hood with a red band. Many envied me because I was able to keep my head warm, and others smiled at my extravagance. Afterwards, I too wondered how I was able to squander my energy on a useless ornament. Yet now I realize that it was part of the struggle for survival.

One day, Erzsi pricked the middle finger of her left hand. The finger became infected and filled with pus. It grew worse and worse. Days passed. Erzsi stoically endured it, although her suffering increased. I watched her helplessly, filled with anxiety. At night, she howled with the pain. The doctor, whom I have already described, did not even try to help. She told Erzsi to be patient. Three weeks went by, and her whole arm was swollen, but the boil still did not come to a head and still did not burst. When I saw that two red stripes had begun to develop along her arm, I was overcome with horror. We all knew what that meant: blood poisoning. That would have been dangerous even in good conditions at home, but in the camp among all this filth and with no medication this condition was potentially fatal. We had to turn to the doctor again in the absence of any other solution. In the end she realized that Erzsi could not wait any longer, and she opened the abscess. But I shudder even today when I remember how she did it. She cut the skin around the middle of the infected finger and pulled it as if she were turning a glove inside out, with the skin, the nail, and the tip of the finger. She did all this without any anaesthetic. She even spoke harshly to Erzsi, saying,

"Stop whining, and don't be so sensitive. You are not at home now!" She tied the finger with a paper bandage, and without a single reassuring word she went on her way.

Towards evening, Erzsi's pain had become intolerable. I felt that if I went on looking at her without doing anything I too would go mad. I approached the doctor again, and I asked her to give me at least a small amount of a sedative or sleeping tablets. She refused. I could not go back empty-handed. As I stood there and racked my brain, I had an idea. I asked the kitchen for a pinch of salt and sugar, which I dissolved in a spoonful of water, and coloured with a drop of coffee. With trembling hands, afraid that I should lose a drop, I raised it to Erzsi's lips. Erzsi swallowed it as if it were a magic potion. Indeed it did have an amazing effect. She grew a little quieter, and exhausted by so much suffering, she fell asleep.

The immediate danger had passed, but Erzsi still felt unbearable pain. The rough and unfeeling manner in which the bandages were changed was additional torture. It was not only towards Erzsi that the doctor had this pitiless attitude; she was unfeeling in the face of any kind of suffering. After the war, at home, she was held accountable for her actions.

The danger of blood poisoning had passed, but in the absence of bandages, medication, and vitamins Erzsi's wound did not close up. It remained an exposed stump surrounded by flesh. Erzsi herself was terrified that somebody or something would touch it. She could not possibly have held a pickaxe or a shovel in her hand, or gone out with that wound in the cold. Fortunately by that time the SS had become more lenient. Until then, even *Häftlings* without shoes had had to stand in blizzards and terrible cold for the interminable roll calls. We had had to wait for hours until everyone had been counted. The only thing we could do to ease our plight was to take handfuls of hay from our sleeping places and put them under our feet. More and more women lost fingers and toes to frostbite, as they grew black, filled with pus, and finally dropped off. However ill we felt, as long as we were still alive, each one of us had to take part in the roll call. Until we were all accounted for, even the dead had to be present to make our numbers add up properly.

After a while, those who could not or did not want to go to work could remain behind. In so doing they lost their portion of bread and got only thin soup. The SS sold these portions of bread on the black market to peasants in the village. The soup and the bread were barely the minimum number of calories necessary for survival, and we had already lived for a long time on the resources of our own bodies. This new situation left us in a predicament. More and more of us shared our bread with a sister or a camp sister, with a daughter, a mother, or a friend.

The diminished bread supply led to disputes between Erzsi and me. Arguing that I was using more energy, Erzsi did not want to accept bread she had not worked for. I, on the other hand, would have given it all to her if it would have helped her gain a little strength.

Late one evening, to my great surprise, Klári Friedmann sought me out. She had just heard from her cousins that a commission was going to arrive the next day and a big selection was being prepared. She had come to warn us: Erzsi and all the others who were able to stand must go to work. In the meantime, the *Lagerälteste* got people moving as well.

Erzsi did not even want to consider going out the next day; she was too afraid for her hand. She was obstinate in her determination that she was going to stay behind even if she paid for it with her life. I argued with her until late in the night trying to convince her. In the morning I tried again, and in the end I managed to convince her to come.

During the day, I covered her and hid her so that the guards could not see that she was not shovelling. That day more than the usual number went out to work, but many were still left behind in the infirmary and in the *Zelt* who had sick status: the barefoot and the helpless.

When we got back from work, we learned what had happened to the sick. In the morning, they had been gathered together and shut into our block. The SS had shaved a stripe in each girl's short hair as a distinguishing mark. The door was locked, and a guard was put in front of it. They were not even able to go out to relieve themselves, so you can imagine the state in which we found the hut. Then they were loaded into a cart and sent to the railway station.

The loss of relatives and friends affected us deeply. It was an open secret that they would be taken to the crematoria at Auschwitz. We could not get used to such cruelty, and each of us mourned our loss privately.

When we came back from work the next day, we were tremendously surprised to find the mothers, sisters, and friends we had thought dead waiting for us at the entrance to the block. Trembling, they told us about the terror they had just gone through. After waiting a long time at the station for a train that had been ordered, they were mysteriously sent back to the camp. They did not know for certain what had happened. Some said that news had come that Auschwitz could not take them. The small group with its marked heads returned to the camp condemned, for a time, to live.

We speculated for hours on what had actually happened. Many people thought that the roads leading to Auschwitz might have been impassable because of the bombing or partisan action. Later, looking at the date, I wondered if it was more likely that it was just then that the *Sonderkommando* uprising took place in Auschwitz. It would have been then that crematorium III was blown up and crematorium IV had to be taken out of action.

So Erzsi was saved from the emotions accompanying a selection. As her finger still looked very bad, I did not even try to convince her to return to work. Instead I tried to push her to become more active within the camp. I wanted to see her more actively try to *organize* something, as many others did. I became more insistent after even I managed to obtain something. One day a number of carts filled with beetroots arrived in the camp, and I was among those who were picked to help unload them in the cellar stores. When no one could see me, I hid a big beetroot under my coat. I hoped this would improve our menu for a few days. I hid my treasure under Erzsi's head before setting out for work. How disappointed I was when I returned and could not find any trace of our beetroot. I even accused poor Erzsi for not knowing how to look after it. Perhaps it was still with my reproaches in her thoughts that the next day she tried to prove how efficient she was. On her way back to the block after having her bandage changed, she noticed that the door to the cellar was open. She immediately went down to the cellar and hid a few carrots under her coat. As she came out she walked right into the arms of an SS guard, who immediately noticed the bulge in her coat. He shook her fiercely and punched her several times. The carrots fell out and rolled in all directions. Erzsi came back without the carrots, happy that nothing worse had happened to her. That was her last attempt at *organizing* something in the camp and the last time that I urged her to try it. I accepted our fate. I gave up all hope of supplementing our food. After that, Erzsi withdrew further into herself and was tormented by new pains. Her right foot hurt her more and more and we did not know what caused it. The doctor could not be bothered with such trifles. Erzsi did not even want to get up any more. She lay down night and day without uttering a word. When I came back in the evenings I bent over her and when I felt her warm hands I rejoiced that she was still alive.

11

WINTER IN NORTHERN EUROPE

*B*y November, the earth was already frozen solid. Frost and cold winds from the North Pole
swept the flat landscape. We used the pickaxe more
than ever in our work, breaking the frozen earth and
wrenching heavy clods from the ground with growing difficulty. We suffered from cold and exhaustion,
but we could not rest as we continued to dig trenches
and tank traps.

The time came when not even pickaxes moved
the earth. We hoped that the work would stop at
this point, but it did not. *Wehrmacht* soldiers arrived
to dynamite the ground at identified places, and we
deepened their trenches with pickaxes and shovels and lifted out the broken earth with our hands.
Our slave drivers were joined by reinforcements of
Hitlerjugends, the Hitler Youth. Where one guard had
supervised thirty people, we now had twice as many

persecutors. They were always behind us, shouting incessantly. They lashed our backs from time to time with thin cane rods. It was harder to bear the cruelty of sixteen- and seventeen-year-olds than it was to obey the usual criminals. One day, near-sighted Irénke lost her balance, slipped, and fell. Before she could get up, a young Titan hit her back with his cane. Magda Roth could not keep quiet. She turned to face the boy and asked him:

"Hast du keine Mutter?" (Haven't you got a mother?)

We expected Magda's question to trouble him, but it did not. He had an answer ready: "You are not people. You are the last whores, thieves, and criminals." He spat out his answer with hatred in his eyes and foam at his mouth.

"Where did you get that from? Who told you that?" Magda demanded. "Do you know that only a few weeks ago these unfortunate creatures were mothers, carefree children, teachers, clerks, workers?"

Perhaps some of the boys realized on their own that propaganda had misled them, but this was not typical. They continued to use their canes, and we often heard their cruel laughter. Then they were mysteriously recalled. We were relieved because the SS had a different kind of merciless cruelty. These young people mistreated us blindly and with utter contempt.

Winter grew colder, bringing even stronger blizzards. The snow was a metre deep on the fields, and the temperature fell to −30°C. The winter of 1944 was an unusually hard one even for northern Poland. The dynamited ditches filled with snow. We were sent to clear them out and at great pains, to make them deeper. Soon the time came when everything seemed pointless. In the morning, we could see no trace of what we had done the day before. Not even the guards could manage to stay outside all day in the wind and the blizzards. This still did not bring respite for us. After roll call in the morning, we were forced out into the open field and left there until the evening.

Our guards retreated to shelter and left us on our own. We were abandoned in the open field, in the snow, the frost, and the strong wind. It was worse than work. We waited for time to pass in numb helplessness. At the beginning, all we did was stamp our feet on the spot. Then we began to form circles of eight to ten with our heads together so that we took in as little cold air as possible. For a while we moved our circle to the right and then to the left so as not to get dizzy. We were still careful not to touch anyone more lice-ridden than ourselves; we were afraid of the lice interbreeding. We stamped our feet on the spot or moved in a circle, hungry and thirsty. Frozen, we waited for evening so that we could get back to shelter. Some women still talked about food recipes. I avoided these as much as I could. It was enough for me to cope with the cold. I did not even crave special foods, such as cakes with nuts or cream. I would have liked to have my fill of dried bean soup and potato dumplings. Many laughed at me because they said I could no longer think of anything better. I longed for evening and the signal to leave. We were glad when we could line up in rows of five and set off. Our faces and hands were frozen, and our feet were numb. We could not even feel our numbness. During the long journey of several kilometres, the rhythmic marching made our blood flow again, and in the end this warmed us up a little.

During that terrible cold, our evening routine in the camp did not change. The evening baths grew rarer. Obtaining a few buckets of water had become a great ordeal. In groups of three or four, we went down to the river to get water. First, we made a hole in the ice with our pickaxes. We plunged our mess tins into the water and turned back. While we were returning to the camp, our hands froze to the handles of the tins. On the rough road, most of the water spilled onto our feet. After we had done our washing, we dried our clothes all night on the pipe of the iron stove. The lucky ones who had managed to *organize* potatoes cut them into thin pieces and baked them on the stove.

Looking for a simpler way of procuring water, we tried to melt snow in basins on the stove. I had always known that snow melts away to very little. I had read somewhere that one could obtain a litre of water from two hundred million snowflakes. I now had the opportunity to confirm this fact. How many journeys we had to make, and how many times we had to open the door, to obtain just one or two litres of water. We soon gave up the struggle. Instead of washing, we rubbed ourselves with snow.

It was already so cold that we could not go far from the block even to relieve ourselves, so we went near the block. This did not present any real danger at the time, but we worried that we might still be at Guttau when spring came.

It grew more and more difficult to cope with the severe winter; our energy and our moral strength were nearly gone. More and more of us, starting with those living on a reduced food ration, became discouraged and tired of the daily struggle to survive. Some did not wash for weeks. Some did not go out of the block. Some did not even go for their own soup but asked somebody else to do it, often in exchange for some service. They were willing to give up part of their soup, which increased their risk of perishing. Many fell into lethargy. The general atmosphere became much worse, especially after some cases of typhoid fever appeared. Now panic overcame even those who had previously trusted their own strength. That unusually hard winter, the deteriorating food, the loss of many friends, and the final blow of the danger of contagious disease devastated us all. The only thing that made us hold on was the sound of bombs exploding nearer and nearer. In the evening, we saw coloured flares shooting into the sky. We comforted ourselves with the thought that we were watching a signal sent by the partisans. One night, those who were sleeping near the doors thought they heard voices. Some thought they heard Yiddish. Were these hallucinations or real sounds? The voices promised a speedy liberation. In fact, a lucky few found a bit of bread and food in front of the door the next morning. We believed – we wanted to believe – that someone was thinking of us. Months later we learned that troops of partisans had indeed been in the neighbourhood.

Christmas arrived. Two sixteen-year-old girls from the sub-Carpathian region thought that because of the holiday the SS guards would be more lenient and that the inhabitants of the village would not refuse a small act of charity. In the evening, after we returned from work, they sneaked away from the camp grounds, crossed the road, and went in to the first house in the village. They did indeed receive a little sponge cake and other treats. They returned happy and perhaps too careless of the danger. The guards seized them and came up with a punishment to frighten the rest of us. The SS stripped the girls naked and made them sit cross-legged on the ground. They had to stay outside for three hours, sitting on the ice. We waited for them from afar, and our hearts went out to them as we wondered how long they could take it. Our hearts ached for them. Later, when the guards let them get up, they were stiff. Their comrades from Block 5 put them to bed, covered them with warm clothes, and gave them boiling soup. We were worried that there would be immediate consequences. I do not know if they contracted pneumonia, but certainly from a gynecological point of view they must have suffered all their lives.

Winter was at its height, and death was ravaging our numbers. By the second half of January there were so many dead that those who had been assigned to dig graves, for an extra portion of food, could no longer keep up. Frozen corpses piled up beside the block like wood.

Mourning touched our block too. Ancsa Hirsch, the healthiest and strongest woman amongst us, got typhoid fever and died unexpectedly within a few days. Ancsa had lived with her elder sister and mother in relatively good conditions. Aunty Hirsch, because she was older, worked in the kitchen. She had always managed to get hold of extra food for her girls, and she had brought buckets of warm water for bathing and washing. Ancsa was not embarrassed by her privileged situation and sometimes made hurtful comments to her companions, such as, "You will all rot here, but I will get through!" And yet it was Ancsa, the strongest and liveliest, the only one who continued menstruating until the end, who died.

"If that can happen, what hope is there for us?" we asked ourselves.

Poor Aunty Hirsch was beside herself with grief. At first she could not even accept the fact that her beloved daughter had died. When she realized that Ancsa could not be buried because not even a pickaxe could move the earth, we thought she would go out of her mind.

"Help me, girls," she implored. "I will dig the grave myself with my ten fingernails. I will not leave her unburied."

We felt Aunty Hirsch's grief deeply. We decided that, one way or another, we should try to help her, but we did not get around to it. The bombing intensified. The front approached rapidly. A feverish tension overcame everyone.

12

RETREAT

Wehrmacht soldiers appeared on the main road, their movements betraying their uneasiness. The explosions of bombs had drawn nearer, and we felt that in a few hours something important was going to happen. We had waited a long time for this moment. We had imagined liberation many times, but we did not know how it would happen. Uninformed as we were, we thought up possibilities, trying to guess what might happen to us.

In the morning we awoke to terrible yelling.

"Alle heraus, alle heraus! Los! Los!" was heard from every direction. Then something completely unusual happened: the SS burst into the block wielding rubber truncheons and drove everyone out, sick and healthy alike.

They did not take a roll call. They lined us up in rows of five, gave us shovels, and drove us into the field. Once there, they lined us up along the snow-filled trenches and commanded us to clear them out. The sun shone as we cheerfully shovelled the sparkling snow. We could hardly hide our delight.

"You won't fight in these trenches," we thought. The more frenzied the guards' yelling became, the more hopeful we became.

Thus passed that day and the next. We did not feel cold, hunger, or fatigue. A single thought preoccupied us all: the front was near, and we would all be liberated. For the first time, we took pleasure in our work. Hope warmed our hearts. We returned to the hut in high spirits.

I triumphantly shared the good news with Erzsi. For the first time in many weeks, I saw her apathetic gaze brighten. It lasted only a moment before she relapsed into indifference. I was afraid she thought this was just another of the little lies with which I had been deceiving her for a few weeks, but she was listening. Scraps of our companions' excited conversation started to reach her consciousness.

"There could be exchanges of gunfire that would endanger our lives."

"It would be better than perishing here on the hay, or starving to death, or catching typhoid fever."

Others saw things with greater clarity.

"This part of the front can't be defended. The trenches are unusable, and the road is open to the Russians."

"They've got no choice; they must retreat."

What interested us most of all was what might happen to us. Perhaps they would leave us here when they left, as they would certainly have more important things to worry about. In Riga, they had had time to make a selection, to empty the stores, even to take the last nail out of the walls. Here the situation was completely different. Half a year had passed since then, and now the SS were clearly in a rush.

"Perhaps we should hide?"

"If it were summer, we could hide in the woods."

"Let's be serious," came the response that jolted us back to reality. It was summer when we were in Riga and the Drina. What an opportunity! We could have thrown ourselves into the water then with our shirts on, but we did not. Where could we have gone with our short hair and our marked clothes? We did not know the language or the surroundings. We were just as isolated here.

Our circle closed in on itself. Helpless, we stared at each other. We were startled from our numbness when the door suddenly burst open. Three SS soldiers entered.

"Tomorrow morning at daybreak, we will start out," one of them said. "Only those who are perfectly healthy and have appropriate footwear should prepare for the journey. You will have a long way to go on foot, a very long way!"

They left us agitated and confused. Each tried to evaluate her own situation. Some definitely wanted to go but did not have shoes. Others would go but had sisters who were suffering from typhoid fever and they could not abandon them. Heated debates and negotiations started between those who wanted to go and those who wanted to stay behind. Erzsi, without a moment's consideration, decided to stay.

"I am so weak I can't even stand," she said with a fading voice.

"Well then we will stay; there is nothing to dispute," I said to calm her. "We will wait for the approach of the front."

Then Klári Friedmann, the well-informed, delicate, and frightened cousin of the *Lageralteste* sat down beside me and argued that Erzsi must be convinced that she could not stay. We had to make everybody realize that those who remained would be in danger of death.

During our camp life, we had survived many selections, and each time I had been ready to stay with Erzsi. Now, once again, perhaps for the last time, a decisive moment had arrived. I was deeply distressed that I would not live for the liberation in which I had believed so strongly. I had inspired many with my determination and taught many to believe in their own strength. It hurt me that I could do nothing for my own sister. I crouched next to Erzsi and reconciled myself to the thought of our inevitable end. I hugged her and whispered in her ear,

"It's okay. We'll stay."

She looked at me in fear, and in her eyes I saw the agitation taking place inside her. She seemed only then to realize that her death meant mine as well.

"You must go," she implored. "You have so much strength. You will endure it for sure."

"We have stayed together in spite of all the difficulties, and we are not going to be parted now. I'm not going to change that now," I said, putting my hand on hers.

It was then that my sister, who had seemed weary of life and indifferent to all that was happening around her, began to cry. In a faltering voice, she asked me to promise her that at daybreak I would set out on the journey.

On January 19, daybreak found us still debating. We had not talked as much for weeks as we did that night. In the morning, at the sound of the alarm, my sister stood up on her unsteady feet and, supported by my arm, made a few faltering steps. If I had seen her do this a few days earlier, I would have been overjoyed, but now I realized that I was asking the impossible of her. We stood embracing, realizing with astonishment that we were not alone in our tragedy.

We had to make haste. The strongest, those not held back by any sick ones, had already gone outside. It was then that Magda Roth came to my assistance. She took Erzsi by the arm and said to her firmly, "You must go and you can go! Teri will take one arm, and I will take the other. I promise I won't leave you until we get to Oradea."

Indeed, we did set off. Erzsi walked on as one hypnotized, as though her feet were not her own. We went out to the road, and I looked back one last time at the place of our suffering. My glance only lasted a fraction of a second before the stream of people carried me farther on, but what I saw was so painful that it was imprinted on my memory for my whole life. As we left, we waved goodbye to those who remained behind. Standing behind us I saw Kati Kajári, the strong, gentle, smart, and disciplined Kati with her broken and dejected camp sister Éva Vadas by her side. Éva had once been a radiant young woman; now, at twenty-three years old, she looked like her own mother. She reminded me of a witch from the stories of my childhood. Éva was skin and bone now, all edges and sharp nails. My schoolmate Éva Klein was there, too. She looked like she was in relatively good shape. She could have ventured on the journey, but her shoes were useless, and she had to stay with her sick sister. Böske Kálman also waved to us. She stayed behind because of Loli, who was in the infirmary with typhoid fever. Böske could not leave her. With them stood also Edith Hirschfeld and her younger sister and their aunt, clinging to one another.

We had no time for brooding. Magda Roth hurried us impatiently, saying that we should not wait for the order to leave. She told us to try to get to the beginning of the column because during the march we would certainly need to slow our pace, and we did not want to be left behind.

The SS lined us up in the usual rows of five, but they could not keep the order that had been strictly enforced on other occasions. We were not the only travelers: we were pushed off the road by fighting units coming from the opposite direction, heading for the front. Many civilians were fleeing their homes, especially those who had collaborated with the Germans, as well as others who were simply carried along by the flow of traffic. People were salvaging what they could in carts, wheelbarrows, and bundles. Villagers drove their animals in front of them with whips. It was chaos and we were constantly being pushed off the road. The refugees shrank away from us as if we were lepers. Indeed, we must have looked like escapees from a leper colony in our tattered and branded clothes and our blankets wrapped around our waists.

The frightening SS guards with the skulls on their uniforms still loomed over us, watching to ensure that we did not talk to anyone from the multitude of refugees. For hours on end, we marched away from the front, getting farther and farther from our chances of liberation. Erzsi, Magda, and I dragged ourselves slowly through the deep snow. We could not keep up and started falling behind. At last, the long-awaited order was heard: "Ruhe!" (Rest!). I was looking for somewhere to sit down when Magda Roth pointed out that we should move towards the front of the line. While the others were stretching out their tired feet, Magda and I dragged Erzsi towards the head of the column. We only stopped for as long as it took for Magda and Erzsi to change boots. We put Magda's big boots with the wooden soles on Erzsi's swollen feet, hoping this would help her to walk.

That day was unimaginable torture. We marched for thirty kilometres through deep snow. It is almost incredible that Erzsi managed the forced march after lying still for so long. At nightfall, we were crowded into a stable where we spent the night. Erzsi collapsed with exhaustion. With one final effort, she wanted to take her boots off, but we would not let her. I was afraid that we would not be able to get those big boots with the wooden soles back on her feet. Others also spent the night as they arrived, with their clothes and shoes on.

We continued our journey the next day. The lines had disintegrated. We stumbled along, hanging on to one another as best we could. Out of 1,000 women who had been in the camp initially, about 500 had started on this journey, about 150 had stayed behind in the camp, and the others had starved to death or had died of various illnesses. We crossed open fields and passed through woods and villages. In the afternoon, we arrived at the neat little town of Neumark (its Polish name is *Nowe Miasto*). The main square was buzzing with activity. Trucks were parked in front of the shops and were loaded with all kinds of goods. Everywhere was great haste and confusion. All we did was cross the town. In our misery, we found consolation in the fact that there must have been good reason for this great haste. It goes without saying that they gave us nothing to eat or drink. We quenched our thirst by eating snow. I was so completely exhausted and tortured by fear for Erzsi that I did not even feel hunger. I was obsessed by one thought: how much longer would she be able to go on?

We went another thirty kilometres on foot the next day. At dusk, we arrived at a manor house on a big farm. We had to climb narrow stairs to an attic used for hay storage where we were to spend the night. Once up there, Erzsi declared firmly that she could not go a step further. She asked me to take her boots off. I no longer opposed her, as I realized that I could not demand any more of her. I was already amazed, and even today am still amazed, that she was able to cover those sixty kilometres. To show my agreement, I took off her boots and mine and hid them under us in the hay. At that moment, we decided that the next morning we would not go anywhere but would bury ourselves in the hay, come what may.

I dozed fitfully that night. More often awake than asleep, I watched over our boots and gathered more hay so that we would have something to hide us. From time to time I glanced towards the attic door. Around daybreak I caught sight of the *Lagerälteste* in the doorway.

"Wir sind frei! Frauen, wir sind frei!" (We are free! Women, we are free!), she cried joyfully.

The front had been broken through with such astounding speed that the Germans only had time to save themselves by fleeing under the cover of the night.

"It's a good thing they didn't set fire to the attic with us in it," said Magda. They had not had time, and they might have been afraid to attract attention with such a big fire.

The most enterprising among us went straight down to the courtyard to look around. Erzsi did not move, and I stayed with her. The other ex-prisoners had already invaded the manor house before I finally decided to go down. We were the only ones in the main building and the other buildings. We gathered the courage to go farther. We went out the estate gate and knocked on the doors of neighbouring houses. All the doors were bolted. No one was there; everybody had taken flight and only the animals were left.

Once or twice during the day, a motorbike stopped in front of the manor house. Armed German officers were desperately looking for a telephone, but when they were convinced that it was not working they continued their flight. They did not pay us the slightest attention. We wandered around the whole day. When we lit a fire in the evening, two men appeared for a moment to warn us to put it out to avoid attracting the artillery's attention. This proved that the local population had hidden nearby; they did not dare show themselves.

We waited impatiently for both the morning and the Russian liberation army. The strongest among us ransacked the whole house looking for food. It seemed that the fleeing population had taken everything with them. Suddenly, I noticed that small fires had been lit here and there in the courtyard of the manor house. The fires were burning between bricks or stones, above which food was heating in pots from the kitchen. By the time we came to our senses, all the fowl had been taken. The alluring smells gave us no peace and spurred us into action. Olga, Magda's camp sister, had an idea: if the fowl were gone, why not kill a suckling pig? Reluctant, but urged on by hunger, we set to work on her plan. First, we needed a knife and a pot. As there was nothing left in the kitchen, we tried to find something outside the manor house. All the dwellings were locked. In the end I got into a kitchen through the window and found a cooking pot and a knife. The killing of the suckling pig came next. I never really liked being involved in this, but I could not claim any right to the meat and soup if I did not help out. I hated the sight of blood. I turned my head and caught hold of the pig's two back legs. I could feel its small warm body struggling in my hands. After that, I do not even know who cleaned it and how. By the time our pig made it into the pot, the others were already happily eating.

It was afternoon when the first column of Russian soldiers appeared. The Polish and Czech women and girls who understood their language threw themselves, crying, onto the soldiers' necks. The Russian soldiers looked at us in dismay. They were shocked by our rags, our clothing marked with the yellow star and red painted stripes, our short hair, and above all by our bodies of mere skin and bone and the starved look of our faces. We were the first Jewish *Häftlings* they had met. They stared at us in amazement and went on. One or two lingered for a few minutes. They realized that many of us were starving, so to help us they killed some beef cattle, cut them in two, and then went on their way. They tried to explain to us that it would be better for us to leave the manor as quickly as possible because there might be some big battles nearby. The Germans were still very near and might come back. They advised us to go back along the road by which we had come to get away from the front line. Many of us, especially those who had satisfied their hunger, were ready to leave. Among the first to leave were the Rosenberg sisters and the two Kemény girls, Erika and Margitka. They urged us to go with them. Because we were late starting our cooking, we tried to hold them back for a few hours, but they were extremely impatient. With words of encouragement, they went on their way. Those words still sound in my ears:

"Hurry up! Follow us. We will meet in Neumark station ... or in Oradea."

We, too, were overcome with excitement, and we regretted getting involved in cooking. We were afraid we would be late for the train. We snatched the half-cooked, tasteless meat out of the saucepan, swallowed a few mouthfuls of soup, and started out on the road by which we had arrived at the manor house two days before. When we rushed out, our hearts filled with terror. Before, we had neither the time nor the energy to look around us. Now, our attention was drawn to the torrent of Russian soldiers. They came in broken lines. They had motor vehicles. The soldiers looked astounded at our small groups. It was clear that they already knew who we were. From trucks, they handed us bread, cheese, and other food we had not seen for a long time. In a few minutes, our arms were full of food. We were sorry that we could not accept more, but we had nowhere to put it. We did not have so much as a pocket or a small cloth bag.

Unexpectedly, airplanes appeared overhead, reminding us that there was a war on. The soldiers got out of their vehicles and jumped into the ditches that extended along the embankment. We followed their example. We put the food next to us in the snow. Fortunately the planes went on their way without bombing us. The soldiers used this forced halt to take the badly wounded out of the trucks and stretch them out on the side of the road. The bandages on their heads and arms were soaked with blood. I did not have the strength to look to see if they were still alive. Had they taken them out so that medical orderlies could pick them up or because there was no point in taking them any farther?

Our path was flanked by burning houses. A windmill that we had admired when we arrived was now in flames, its burning wheel turning in the wind. I could not take my eyes off it. In the distance, I saw three windmills on fire, grinding the time with their wheels in flames.

It was getting dark when we arrived on the edge of Neumark. We knocked on the door of the first house. When we got inside we were overjoyed to meet the Rosenberg sisters and a few other girls we knew. With regret, they told us that German bombs had destroyed both the train tracks and the station.

The inhabitants of the house, an older woman and two younger women, received us with remarkable kindness. Lacking life experience and naive as we were, we did not understand the reason until the following day.

There were about twenty of us, perhaps more. Our hostesses prepared sleeping places for all of us, on beds, divans, and sacks of hay. Water was heated in a big pan on the stove, and we washed in turns. We had food in abundance. What more could we have wanted? When all was quiet around us, our hostesses shut the door behind them and disappeared. We were so happy that we forgot to ask them why they were leaving their own home, and they had given no explanation. We left the door unlocked so that the hostesses could return at any time.

The room was lit with a petrol lamp. We felt inexpressibly good in the warm semi-darkness. We rested in the stillness.

It must have been quite late when suddenly the door gave way and a Russian soldier entered. We were taken by surprise, but we were not frightened. Russian soldiers represented liberation for us. We were not wearing our marked clothing, and although our thin tortured bodies could not be seen under the blankets, our short hair betrayed our identity. One of us unexpectedly started to speak:

"Jidovski ... Lager ... Bolnoi." (Jews ... Concentration camp ... Sick.)

It seemed he understood. Suddenly, he took out his gun and fired into the lamp. In the darkness and terror that followed, he threw himself on the first girl in his path. Just as he was, with his coat on and his gun in his hand, he threw her down and pressed her to the ground.

It was a harrowing moment. Everyone tried to escape, hiding under beds, in cupboards or behind them. Many ran out into the freezing night and hid in the pigsty.

After that, we were troubled by conflicting thoughts. Could this be the liberation? How different it was from our expectations. Terror, horror, and confusion took hold of us. In this way, the night passed. No one spoke a word until dawn. In the morning, we looked at each other in dead silence.

We did not speak of what had happened, not then or since.

For years, all those who were liberated together and who returned home together met on the anniversary of our liberation to reminisce and to talk about different events surrounding our deportation. We talked about many things, but never about what happened on that night. We did not want to remember that.

13

Nowe Miasto

*A*t daybreak the next morning, we set out towards the centre of the town. A few days earlier, we had passed through this town with Germans beating us, but now no one was pushing and chasing us. Then, people had been feverishly packing: the army, the civilian population, and the Polish servants of the system were fleeing. Now, we saw a deserted and burned-out town. The front line had passed through Neumark. We were amazed. So this was what a town looked like after war. Burnt walls stood on their own, and burnt doors, smoke-covered windows and black empty window frames gaped at the passers-by. Everywhere were signs of a recent fire. On the streets, I caught sight of a few sad, exhausted people.

We stopped a Polish official wearing an armband with the national colours and asked for the right direction. He sent us to the town's command centre. We were pleased at this, for we thought that at last someone would look after us. We did not receive much encouragement from them. We learned that the fate of the liberated territories near the front was uncertain. For a time there was still a danger that the Germans could recapture them. The mere thought of this filled us with horror. We were also informed that many roads and the railways were damaged and would be unusable for a long time. Any undamaged roads were reserved for the movement of troops. For the time being we had no alternative but to stay. The town leaders were unable to take care of us, so we had to fend for ourselves. The only help they could offer us was a list of the addresses of abandoned houses in which we could settle. Disoriented, we stood in the street, in –20°C, in snow a metre deep, but free.

The first address we went to was a house with five rooms and electric central heating. We were delighted. We particularly admired the bathroom and well-equipped kitchen. The pantry and wardrobes, however, were empty. Apparently the occupants had held not only a good position but also had means of transport available when they left. We were on the point of taking over the house when one of our group reminded us,

"We will freeze and starve to death here. Who knows how long it will take before they get the electric heating working again?"

It was hard to leave such a beautiful, comfortable place, but in the end we moved on. Later, we regretted our lack of confidence, for only three days later the lights were on again in the city. We went back, but it was too late; somebody else had moved in.

The second address was a contrast with the first. It was a neglected house that had belonged to poor people. Situated on the first floor of an overcrowded rental apartment house, it was a simple flat with wooden floors and no bathroom. We had no choice but to move into it. In one of the rooms we found a big terracotta stove and in the kitchen an iron stove. Then we cleared the biggest room next to the kitchen and scrubbed the floor. This became our bedroom. There were twenty-one of us in the group. We all wanted to stay together, and we did so for several weeks.

I cannot explain, even today, how we bonded together. The nucleus of the group was made up of those from Oradea along with those we had befriended in the camp. These were people with deep feelings and strong nerves, capable of rising above hunger and pain without endless whining. Among us were those who in spite of their own suffering could still find the resources to help those who were more distressed than them. They were the ones who had remained human.

The older women, Margitka, Erika, and Babus, were tacitly accepted as our leaders. Erika Markovits, who later became the wife of Lajos Breiner, proved to be the most skillful among us. She was a powerful personality who could find an ingenious solution for anything. She became the group's main leader.

Margitka Goldstein, later Mrs. Erdös, continued to bring relief to our aching bones through her hand massages just as she had in the camp. We chose Erzsi Füredi as head cook, and we were not disappointed. She was a careful housekeeper, and despite our conditions, she cooked some incredible, simple and easily digestible healthy meals. Böske, Laci Blau's wife and the older of the Rosenberg sisters, could not forget the son who had been wrenched from her arms at Auschwitz. In addition to her community work, she anxiously watched over her younger sister Éva, the wife of József Halmi. Éva had just recovered from a serious illness on the eve of our deportation. The two Kemény sisters had strikingly different personalities. In spite of the crowded conditions in which we were living, we all got on very well. However, if disagreements occurred, the wise and well-balanced Babus filled the role of judge, while her younger sister Zsuzsi, who was always in high spirits, amused us with stories filled with sparkling humour. Magda Roth was also with us. She turned her love for her martyred little daughter to her camp sisters and those who were in greater distress than herself. I regarded her with special esteem and gratitude. Not then, not later, not even today can I forget that she gave my sister the strength to set out with us. In addition to these, we were joined by two girls from Debrecen, two from Cluj, and a few more whose names I can no longer remember.

We felt sorry for the two girls from Cluj. They had been surprised and unprepared when they fell victims to fascism. One was sixteen and the other eighteen, and both were sickly and unassuming. They fought their fate with difficulty, yet with tenacity. Their father was a Christian and their mother a Jew. As they told us later, their mother had died when they were about four and six years old, and their father sent them to a Catholic convent to be educated. They knew very little about their Jewish origins. While their father, a municipal employee, was at work one day, their landlady brought the gendarmes to get them. Without letting them tell their father or prepare themselves physically or emotionally, the gendarmes took the girls straight to the railway station and pushed them into a cattle car that was leaving for Auschwitz. They did not know anyone around them, nor in the camps where they arrived later. With only each other for support, they passed many lonely days. When they arrived in our barrack, we took them under our wing, which is how they came to be with us after liberation.

There was also a Czech girl. Today I am not certain if she was Czech or Slovak. We hoped that she would be of help in relations with the Polish locals as she spoke a Slavic language. We were bitterly disappointed. Whenever we asked her to help, no one could get more from her than "tak-tak" (yes-yes).

Although our group came together spontaneously, it coalesced very quickly. Each of us accepted the tasks that were imposed, without discussion or complaint, and we adapted to community life.

We split up into smaller groups. Each specialized in getting hold of at least one necessary article. Some organized a supply of wood and coal, while others obtained bread, meat, and spices. Some knew how to do anything, some cooked especially well, others washed, and still others did the cleaning.

The shops that had not been plundered or burned remained closed. Even if they had been open they would have been of no help since we had no zloty or any other kind of money. The only means we had of getting hold of food was rummaging through the cellars of burned-out houses. These food expeditions were sometimes successful and sometimes not. We often came home empty-handed even after many attempts, when quicker foragers had found things before we did. This way of getting supplies was always depressing, even though we knew we were not taking things from anybody. At least it was better than begging. The local inhabitants treated us with enmity from the beginning, and they refused to help us. We would have preferred that the authorities help us attend to our needs, but they refused our requests.

During our first days in the town, one of our group found a boarding school. This was a great discovery. We brought straw mattresses from there to cover the floor of the big room. After the wooden boards of the camp and sleeping on the floor so many times, we were very pleased with our new beds. We all stayed together in one room because we had grown accustomed to living together and we felt stronger together. In any case we had no means of heating more rooms. We spent our days in the kitchen where we made a fire for cooking. In the boarding school the girls had also found twenty cans, each containing twenty-five litres of a frozen substance. At first we thought it was ice cream, but when it melted we realized it was milk. We had not seen milk since we left home; we had not had it even in the ghetto. We were moved by the memories it evoked. We went to great trouble to carry all twenty cans to our new house, and we put them in one of the unheated rooms. For as long as we were in Nowe Miasto we would have a supply of milk.

Acquiring bread and meat was not a problem as the Russian soldiers gave us as much as we needed. Sometimes they gave us a whole bucket of soup that contained a lot of well-cooked meat. One of the Russian officers, who had secretly disclosed to Erika that he too was Jewish, once sent half a calf to our home. This made us happy, yet at the same time saddened us. I was glad of the meat that would feed us for a long time, and we could exchange some of it for sugar and fat. It saddened me to know that even in Russia, the cradle of socialism, an officer had to hide his Jewish origins.

We ate very carefully. It was rumoured that many people died in their eagerness to fill themselves. Too much food at once could prove fatal because of our empty stomachs. We tried not to eat too much fat. We preferred to eat small amounts several times a day. As we did not venture out after dark, and the only toilet was in the courtyard, we put a receptacle in the entrance. In the mornings, we took turns emptying it. We carried it down the open, icy stairs with great difficulty, but we had no choice. It was wartime, and lawlessness reigned. One never knew what to expect, what dangers were waiting. When evening came, we all gathered in the house. We locked the door with a key and a padlock and did not open it until morning, not even on the insistence of acquaintances. Sometimes one of the soldiers whom we had got to know brought us meat or soup. In front of the closed door they tried to explain that their unit was moving on. We did not reply, but in the morning we found things intended for us in front of our door. Another time, one of the soldiers sang us a serenade. He played the guitar delightfully for a long time in front of our door. We enjoyed listening to him from the darkness inside, but we did not make a sound.

Erzsi made an almost miraculous recovery. It was as if her leg and hand had never hurt her. She went about the streets cheerfully, and she was good at getting supplies. I, on the other hand, was very unskilled at this. I became passive, perhaps in a subconscious reaction to the fact that Erzsi no longer needed me to be strong. They soon gave up on my efforts to get supplies, and I helped two other girls with the housework.

Right at the beginning we acquired a big washtub. We always had water boiling in this, and we took turns washing and boiling our lice-ridden clothing. We became experts in the life cycle of the louse, which in its mature form dies in the wash but leaves persistent eggs. We began to follow their development and when they hatched we washed again in boiling water. To be very sure, we disinfected the clothing three times. This is how we finally rid ourselves of lice. One of my most torturous memories of life in the camps is the memory of louse bites, the stinging itch that only worsened whenever we finally got to rest and began to warm up. Now our nights were restful. At this time we began to look after our pus-filled wounds. Our hands and feet were covered in blisters, and the heavy work had reduced our palms to open sores. With no medication and bandages or vitamins in our food and because of the squalor in which we had lived, we had had no chance of healing. For several months I had had open wounds on my legs below my knees that would not close up. My thick cotton tights had stuck to those wounds each day. In the evening, I could only take them off by breaking open the wounds or soaking them with snow. Like the others, I sometimes used to put margarine paper on them. The greasy paper protected the wounds from my dirty stockings but at the same time stopped the healing process.

We wanted to get rid of our ridiculous, ragged old clothes, but we had no opportunity to do this. I said earlier that the Poles were hostile towards us. We might have found something to wear in the abandoned houses, but they had been locked up and we could only get into the cellars.

Three weeks passed, and we lived a relatively untroubled life: we had a roof over our heads, we had food to eat, and it was warm in our room. Yet we did not feel safe. The future still lacked certainty. We did not know when order would be restored or when we could set off for home. The question that worried us most was whether we still had any family left. We did not know the fate of the other camp detainees and we had no idea what might have happened to them. We did not even know anything about those we had just left in such an uncertain situation. What could have happened to them? Had they been exterminated? It was only after two or three years, when our former concentration camp comrades returned, that we began to learn of the horrors through which they had passed. Their story belongs here, so I will retell what Böske Kálmán told me at my request.

The Germans and their *Häftlings* began their retreat on January 19, 1945. On January 18, the day before, the doctor and three SS officers went through all the blocks and ordered all those with diarrhoea, who in her opinion could be suspected of having typhoid fever, to be moved into one block. Böske Kálmán's younger sister Loli had already had typhoid for four weeks and was in the infirmary. Böske did not feel well either, and also had diarrhoea, but she did not present herself since the conditions in the infirmary were dreadful. She hid that evening and that is how she managed to escape. Her friend Aranka Friedmann and her sister-in-law both offered to carry Loli in their arms so that she would not have to stay in the camp. She went to see her sister straight away but realized there was nothing she could do. Loli had a very high fever and had lost consciousness. She was lying with many others who were just as sick and with many more who were dead. Böske knew immediately that she could not accept such a sacrifice. Ella Róth and Sári Ungár (who were in relatively good shape but had only a few tufts of hay tied to their feet instead of shoes and therefore had to remain behind) helped Böske move Loli into Block 10 (our old block) because it was the cleanest block in the camp. They dragged the poor girl on a worn-out leather jacket, on the snow from the first block, the infirmary, to the last. Böske did not take her into their block, Block 6, because the conditions were dreadful there as the result of the irresponsible behaviour of *Lagerälteste* Lotte, a woman from Košice. After the war, she was tried for her inhumane behaviour and sentenced to ten years in prison. Her lack of conscience had caused the deaths of many of her campmates.

The next day, towards evening, three fully armed SS men drove everybody out of their blocks amid terrible shouting, starting with the infirmary. When she saw what was happening, Böske covered the unconscious Loli with hay gathered from the sleeping places around her. She and two other women from Lithuania who had aged prematurely because of their suffering hid in the depths of one of the bunks.

Ella Róth, Sári Ungár, and Anci Braun ran outside without thinking. Böske tried to keep them back, but she did not succeed. They probably thought that the sick would be taken after the group that started out in the morning, so they ran at the call of the SS. At a distance of twenty-five or thirty metres from the last block we had begun to dig a long trench a while earlier. At the time, the SS had told us that the trenches were to become latrines. The frosts had interrupted the work. The three SS men now drove the unfortunate, barefoot women, emaciated from illness and hunger, toward these trenches. Böske tried to follow events through a crack in the wall, but she could not see anything. All that reached her was the rattle of gunfire, then unearthly screams and moans. She did not know if minutes or hours passed. In such situations, each moment seems like an eternity. She waited in awful terror, horrified by the thought that the Germans might return. Suddenly the door opened. Ella Róth appeared with her head split open, Sári Ungár with her jaw smashed, and Anci Braun with her face so disfigured that she was unrecognizable. Shaken and afraid, they related the horrors they had just survived. Outside, in front of the trench that was now a communal grave, the SS men had fired several rounds, and when their ammunition was used up, they struck anyone who remained standing. In the meantime, it grew dark. Those who could still move dragged themselves to the block. Anci Braun lost her mind from the shock, and the others were no longer able to think clearly. They could grasp only one thing: they could not stay in the camp any longer. What else could happen before the Russians arrived? They knew from the noise of the explosions that they must be near. Böske wanted to take care of Loli at any price, but how? In the end, with a heavy heart, she had to leave her there. She covered her again with hay and bade her farewell. Loli, who until then had lain unconscious, seemed to understand what was happening around her, and she agreed with her eyes. At least so it seemed to Böske.

By the time they set out, it was already pitch dark and it was cold enough to freeze the blood in their veins. Their path took them past the trench of the dead. Trembling, they heard the death rattles of their comrades. There was no point in stopping, as they could not have helped them in the dark with only bare hands. They had to save themselves. So they went with heavy hearts, numb, stumbling along in the deep snow, defenceless. Sári Ungár and Aliz Blum collapsed many times because they had lost so much blood. They had no more strength, and they wanted to stay behind. Ella and Böske carried the two fallen women with a superhuman effort. If they had not been helped, they would certainly have frozen to death. After all their struggle, they finally found a haystack in a field, and they buried themselves in it. They spent that night and the next day hidden there. It was already day when Böske surveyed their surroundings from the haystack. She saw a house not far from them. Next to it was a cowshed covered with hay. After it got dark, they moved into the shed. They broke icicles off the roof and used them to quench their thirst and soothe their fever. The dogs of the house sensed their presence and suddenly began to bark wildly. The girls were frightened. They flattened themselves against the walls and kept quiet. The house's inhabitants came out at the barking of the dogs, but meeting only silence they went back to the house, locking the cowshed from the outside. The girls stayed hidden in the hay for a long time, until late one day hunger forced them to make a decision. Facing serious risk, Böske and Ella (the other two could not even move) got out through an opening in their hiding place, and wearing their branded rags, knocked at the door of the house. They met the most brutal refusal possible and were chased away without a scrap of bread or a glass of water. They went farther on. Their next attempt was more fortunate. They were invited into the house and treated to coffee with milk. Frightened, they asked the owners of the house if the SS men were still around. They took them to the window and showed them the tanks outside, pointing out the red stars on them. The Russians had been there for three days and the girls had not known. They stepped out into the street where they were surrounded by Russian soldiers. The Russians gave them chocolate, cheese, and money. They were standing, bewildered, with all this treasure in their arms, when a military field car stopped near them. The driver asked where he could take them. In Yiddish, Ella asked the driver, who was also Jewish, to go and look for the two girls in the stable and then to go back to the concentration camp. They picked up Sári and Aliz and placed them on a stretcher, and medical orderlies took care of them. They also found Loli alive. She had started to regain consciousness. The situation in the barrack was horrifying. The sight of helpless, exhausted, and shrivelled people, ulcerous with wounds, and the pitiful surroundings made a deep impression on the men, and the two officers started to cry openly.

On their return to the camp, Böske and the others learned that before the execution the three SS men had gone through the infirmary and three other blocks. They had injected the sick one by one, probably with poison. Later, they had returned to inspect its effect. For many, the injection had not been lethal. They bashed the women on the head with the butts of their guns, smashing their skulls. Lili Sharon, who was only twelve years old, hid herself under a dead body and escaped the injection but not the injuries. The SS broke many of her teeth. Gyöngyi Hert and Tova Braun were also among those who managed to survive. Today, they are all Israeli citizens.

Block 4, where sixty or seventy women were sick with typhoid fever, had been locked and surrounded with cans of petrol. It was clear that the SS meant to set fire to it, but for some reason they did not carry out this plan.

During those first days the Russian soldiers were not able to deal with the sick, but they left them a lot of food, mostly canned. This led to the death of many of the sick, as they rushed to satisfy their hunger. Perhaps it was not so much that they ate a great deal as that they were not cautious enough. Their tightened, dried up insides needed to get used to digesting gradually. Ilonka Lebovits, a lovely girl from Oradea, was one of the first to die from eating.

From the field of the dead, the Russians collected and buried eighty bodies. Among the survivors, nineteen remained invalids for the rest of their lives. Edit Hirschfeld, who had been a colleague of mine at the Jewish Gymnasium and who later became Mrs. Ausländer, was among them. Struck by the butt of a gun, she fell to the ground and could not get up again. Her wounded, bleeding feet froze to the ground in the snow. When the Russians found her, they had to use a pickaxe to free her. Both her legs had to be amputated below the knee. She spent months in the Deutscheilau hospital in Russia, where she received prosthetic legs. She was not able to return home until many years later. She had amazing energy and self-confidence. She worked and became an office administrator in the Jewish Hospital in Oradea. She got married and had a child, but a few years later she died of a kidney disease she had contracted when she had lain frozen.

Many staggering tragedies are linked to the field of the dead. As I mentioned earlier, Kati Kajári remained in the camp just to look after Éva Vadas. Éva escaped that night, while Kati was mortally wounded. A woman from Prague had remained behind because she was afraid to start out on the journey with her twelve-year-old daughter. They were shot. Both shots hit the mother, who had fallen over her daughter to protect her. The girl lay for hours under her mother's dead body, not daring to move until much later, when everything was quiet around her.

Now I must tell what happened to Böske. When the three SS murderers eventually left the camp, the survivors were visited by the partisans. It was then clear that the partisans were close by and that the rumours about them were not simply a fabrication of fantasy. The partisans gathered the survivors into two huts and brought them firewood and two petrol lamps so that they would not have to grope about in the dark. They also brought some food. The advancing Red Army appeared three days later. The Russian soldiers provided first aid to those who needed it and then went on. Those left in the camp had to provide better living conditions for themselves on their own. A Christian woman from Nyiregyháza, F. Juliska, who had entered the ghetto voluntarily, was among the survivors. Together with Ella Róth, who in spite of her smashed head was still one of the strongest, she set out to find a new shelter. They went to the barracks of the Hitler Youth, about three hundred metres away. They agreed that if they did not return, it meant that conditions were good.

It turned out that the Hitler Youth had fled even before the SS. Böske and then Magda Blau (who had spent the hellish night in the barrack for those suffering from typhus) had organized a sled from the courtyard of a peasant home. The owners did not like it, but they did not dare stand in their way as they were afraid that the Russians would support the ex-prisoners. They put Loli and Lili on the sled and set out uphill with them, to the house abandoned by the Hitler youth. It took great effort for them to drag their sick to the top of the hill and they succeeded only with incredible strain and numerous stops.

Inside, they found two big rooms with bunks and straw mattresses. They lit a fire in a small cast-iron stove and heated up water in a pot on the warm kitchen range. There was nothing they craved more than to clean up and to wash themselves.

After the situation at the front had quieted, they got to the hospital. With their recovery, the second part of their tragic story began. Rather than take them towards their home, the liberating forces took them deeper into Russia. Beyond Kujbisev they were attached to detention camps and forced to do heavy labour. Their trials read like a horror story. After repeated secret requests to the embassy and intervention from home, they were finally able to return to their country after many years.

24

THE ROAD TO WARSAW

*T*hat winter the temperature stayed around –20°C.
We lived from one day to the next, trying to get
food and keep ourselves warm and clean. We were
vegetating while we waited for the warmer weather
so we could set out for home. However, with time,
the people of the town recovered from their original
fright and realized that they had tolerated the presence of "foreign freeloaders" for too long. The commandant of the town sent a letter to all the "Jewish
houses" ordering us to leave the town in five days,
after which we would be expelled. They did not care
that an icy wind was blowing from northern Poland,
that the snow was deep, that there was no form of
transport, or that the front line was nearby; none of
this interested them at all. We sent a delegation to
the town authorities requesting that they postpone
our date of departure, but they held to their decision. We had no choice but to prepare for a journey

on foot, by a route on which we would find no means of transport until, in the best scenario, we arrived in Warsaw, 250 kilometres away.

While we began to make preparations, Erika, one of the older women and one of our leaders, spoke about the conditions of the journey to a Jewish Soviet officer. To our disappointment, he kept his Jewish identity secret, as did all the others we met. The officer agreed that our departure was risky in those troubled times, especially considering the lack of transport and food. He offered to take us by truck to a distant farm that had been abandoned by the Germans, where we could stay until the spring. However, we were still afraid of the unknown. After our bad experiences, we were very suspicious. How could we know if, sooner or later, we would not be chased from there too? We really had no choice but to start out on a journey with about five hundred other ex-*Häftlings* on February 13, 1945. We were still wearing the marked clothing we had been given months earlier in Stutthof, and the hard labour and constant wear had made them even more ragged. We had grown richer in some ways, though. We had sewn bread bags for our immediate needs on the journey. We still had blankets acquired from the Germans, and we had sewn hats and gloves from these. With enough provisions for two days in our bags, with our marked, ragged clothing and the torn thread-bare blankets, we set out on foot. Our direction was south. We were afraid of the great unknown. We did

not know the way or the country. We spoke neither
Polish nor Russian. We did not know the Polish people. The little contact we had had did not promise
much hospitality. We comforted ourselves with the
fact that in spite of all our problems, we were free
and so was the country we were heading for, where
we had spent our childhood and where we had grown
up. Our town of Oradea was free. We hoped, or deluded ourselves, that our loved ones were at home
waiting for us.

With mixed feelings we stumbled along the frozen, snow-covered main road. Once, a Russian military field car stopped next to us unexpectedly, and
a high-ranking officer got out and asked us who we
were. "Hungarians! Romanians!" many of us replied
at once and almost with one voice. He pointed to his
radio and told us with a face that radiated joy that
Buda had capitulated. It appeared to us at that moment, in our naiveté, that this meant the war would
end, the situation at the front would calm down, and
we would get home faster. After we had quieted down
a little, he took a closer look at us. It was not difficult
to surmise that we were deported Jews, as each of us
had either a big stripe in red oil paint on her back or
a star. We were very aware of this, but we had forgotten that we were still wearing our camp numbers
on our chests. The officer approached Erika and tore
hers off her coat. As if it were a signal from a magic
wand, each of us quickly put a hand to our breast,
and in an instant we were treading our registration

numbers underfoot in the snow and dirt. A few days later I wondered if we ought to have kept that dreadful humiliating label as a memento.

We only covered five kilometres in total on the first day. We arrived in a little village, where we presented ourselves to the local officials and asked for a room where we could spend the night. They split us up into small groups and assigned five or six girls and women to a house. The reception was not uniform. At some places, people let the ex-*Häftlings* into their houses and kitchens immediately. At others, the group was sent to pigsties or stables. Some were chased away, which happened to our group. We had to go back to the commandant for a new address. Night was well set in, and dogs were barking as we groped in the dark through deep snow using an unknown language to beg someone to open the door to us.

After such experiences, we could no longer freely enjoy the snowbound landscape bathed in sun and sparkling with light. Each day we worried where we would spend the night. Would we find somewhere to rest after the day's journey? Would someone take pity on us so that we could renew our strength for the next day's march?

Sometimes we were lucky. Today, I am still grateful to one family who took us in. They sat us down near their warm, lit iron stove and gave us a bucket of potatoes to clean. By the time those tasty potatoes were ready to eat, a piece of fried sausage, smelling wonderful, was sizzling on each of our plates. The kindness of those hosts brought tears of gratitude to our eyes. However, that was a rare occasion. More often we slept in cold pigsties and had to be content with leftovers of frozen, dubious-looking food that were rudely thrown to us. Even today I wonder how we coped with such a hostile, malevolent setting as the roads of northern Poland for three weeks.

Usually we went by foot. Sometimes an army truck would stop near us and the soldiers would call us to get in. When that happened, we easily covered ten to fifteen kilometres. We were so happy. Sometimes after we climbed up into the truck we realized it was going in the wrong direction and we lost precious kilometres. They were always in such a hurry that there was no point explaining where we were headed for, so we adopted another tactic. We asked where they were going, and we got on only if it was in the direction we were headed. Often something else happened: ten or twelve girls would climb on and the truck would start off. For fear of losing one another, we would jump from the moving truck. We were lucky that the snow was deep and no one was hurt.

For food, we only managed to eat when someone took pity on us. Usually that was about twice a day. We were lucky that we had been able to gain strength during the days we spent at Neumark, where we had been properly fed. We were able to cope now only because of that.

During this terribly difficult journey, uncertainty about shelter for the night was a constant stress. The memory of those days remains with me like a nightmare. Concern for my sister Erzsi added to my stress. Her pain had returned and with it her depression. She retreated into an even deeper silence. I do not know how she kept moving, how she dragged her feet along. We often had to slow down for her. One of the girls from Cluj, sixteen-year-old Ilonka, also became ill. We had no way of getting them to a doctor, and we did not know what was wrong with them. They were dying before our eyes. They did not complain, but it was more and more difficult for them to go on. Worried, we watched them closely, wondering how much longer they would be able to cope. Each day that ended safely went into the chapter of victories. From that long, seemingly unending journey, apart from that memorable supper, two incidents stand out for me.

On one of the days while we were still far away, I realized that we were approaching a bigger settlement, really a town, from the numerous church towers and the roofs of high buildings. We hoped that things would improve for us here. We went straight to the commandant and asked him to assign us a place where we could spend the night. We were greeted with astounding news: the town had been rearranged into a military centre and there was not a single civilian. They warned us that in our own interests we should leave as quickly as possible. Going out and taking a closer look around, we realized that there were only men in military uniforms in the street. We trembled, imagining what might have happened to us if we had stayed. We turned on our heels and set out straight away for the nearest village. In winter, especially in the North, it gets dark early, so we had to hurry. It was already pitch black by the time we arrived in the nearest village.

The other incident was friendlier but at the same time more painful. We were now only about twenty-five kilometres from Warsaw, which we hoped would be our salvation. When we asked for accommodation (I no longer remember the name of that small place) we were greeted with the surprising news that some Polish Jewish men had recently returned to the village. We got their address and went off to find them right away. We climbed up an open, frozen staircase at the back of a dilapidated building until we got to a very poor apartment. Four pale men with sunken eyes and as thin as skeletons were sitting in the light of a lamp in a poorly furnished room. They were the first liberated Jewish men we met. They had not been in concentration camps. They had survived the war years by hiding in dark corners and in the forests. They knew nothing about their families. They asked us lots of questions about where we had been, in which areas of the country, and in which camps we had met Polish Jews. Once again we were all sorry that we did not speak Yiddish and we could only understand each other through bits of German. We shared their poor supper. Not one of us felt like leaving to look for some place to sleep, so we spent the whole night squeezed next to one another for warmth on the wooden floor. They told us that a Jewish Council that would take care of us was already functioning in Warsaw. We went on our journey with new hope.

The winter cold had not yet finished. The roads were still covered with snow. Ilonka and Erzsi, our sick ones, were stumbling along with increasing difficulty. "This will be the last effort," we encouraged them. In spite of the fact that the majority would have liked to go more quickly, we all slowed our pace for the sick ones. Kindness had conquered: we had started out together, and we wanted to arrive together. In the meantime we were planning what we would do when we arrived.

"We must go to the Jewish Council first," was Erika's opinion. "We will rest there to our heart's content."

"We will have a feast," added Magda Roth.

"We should go and look for the embassy too," said Eva Halmi.

And I, the eternal optimist, wove the thread of the story even further. I started to describe the surprise of the staff at the Romanian Embassy.

"We'll probably be the first *Häftlings* they've ever seen in their lives. They will dress us up from head to toe."

This seemed likely because as far as we knew (and we may have been right), our camp had been the first to be liberated.

"They are sure to send us home by plane," we dreamed on. As far as I remember, we were not just trying to comfort Erzsi; we really believed it. The idea that we were going to go home by plane had taken shape in our minds while we were working at the airport in Riga.

That day we covered eighteen kilometres. Night was already falling when we entered the town. We were amazed to find that we had arrived in a town of ruins. The awful sight of stumps of burnt gateways and empty windows greeted us at every step. In whatever direction we looked, we saw only collapsed walls, staircases that were open or had been ripped out, and balconies hanging loosely, ready to fall. It was not hard to find the Jewish Council. Its headquarters were in two rooms, the first floor of a ruined house. A great number of people were moving through the offices. The administrators were very skilful. Two young people quickly assessed our situation and led us to a place where we could spend the night. We arrived in the ruins of what had been a Jewish temple. The walls were crumbling and the roof had collapsed. In spite of that, the space inside was completely filled with people, men and women together. Most of them were lying directly on the ground. Those who did not have a place were standing. The sight shocked us. The moment we stepped inside, we thought the structure would collapse any minute. Magda Roth, Olga, and a few others collapsed on the spot from exhaustion. The rest of us decided to return to the council and ask for a better shelter. They did not have anything better. By this time night had fallen and we stayed at the office and slept on the floor.

The next day we investigated the town more closely. It was Praga, a suburb of Warsaw. I had not imagined that bombing could have such destructive consequences. Most of the houses were now uninhabitable. Only one house in three or four could be partially used. People were living in these houses. Many had spent the six years of war here, and others had just returned from the front or from prisons or camps. They were looking for their families and were faced with the bitter reality of what remained of their former homes.

Our contact with the first big town was a great disappointment. Until then, we had thought of life at home as an island of tranquility, where we were impatiently awaited. Now we began to realize that our previous houses, which in fact were no longer ours, had perhaps been wiped off the face of the earth by bombs. We still knew nothing about our families. What was even harder was that we had still not met a single Jewish man who had been taken from Northern Transylvania. What had happened to them? From time to time, a painful thought struck me: what if our fathers and brothers had all perished as soon as they arrived at Auschwitz? I did not dare share my fears with anyone.

Although many people tried to persuade us against it, we decided to go into Warsaw the next day. We thought some representatives of the central authorities would be there. We walked for many kilometres before reaching the "town" on the other side of the Vistula. It was a dead town. It was a terrible sight: not a house was standing. All was in ruins. There were no open roofless rooms, no hanging balconies, no exposed and collapsed stairways, only shell holes, ruins and here and there the corner of a wall. We gazed about, bewildered. Not wanting to accept what we were seeing, we started out. We wandered for a long time in the deserted streets of ruins. The few Poles who stopped to talk to us spoke little French. Nobody wanted to speak German, and we did not speak Polish. All we understood was that the Germans had done this.

I heard the details of the Warsaw ghetto tragedy after I got back. I only learned about what really happened years later from Alexander Werth's book, *Russia's Great War 1941–1945*. He had been a Sunday Times and BBC correspondent.

In 1969 I retraced all the landmarks of my ordeal in Poland with my husband and my children Anna and Gábor. We also visited Warsaw. I knew that Warsaw had been rebuilt, yet my renewed acquaintance with the town shocked me as much on this occasion as it had the first time. This time, however, it was positive.

We went first to the old town, Staro Miesto. My first impression was a genuinely medieval atmosphere. We saw ancient narrow, colourful, many-storied houses, arched gateways, buildings with archways, narrow streets, niches with gothic windows and the walls of a medieval citadel. The houses of rich citizens, in Renaissance style and with superb frescos on the gables, stretched along the main square of the town. When we entered the houses from the courtyard and the staircases, we realized that all was not as it seemed. The faithful citizens of Warsaw had reconstructed the squares, the storefronts and the external facades of the streets. Using the original plans, photographs, and paintings, and at incredible material sacrifice, they had restored the face of the city. Inside the buildings we found comfortable homes and modern offices. The interior restoration of the churches was not done yet. Their beauty was surprising, with their whitewashed walls, icons, and modern statues of the Madonna.

We went to see the place where the Warsaw ghetto had been. Donka, a Polish Jew, had told me about the Warsaw ghetto during the first weeks of our life in camp. I learned from her that 360,000 Jews had been living in Warsaw when the SS units arrived. Immediately, the SS instituted a reign of terror in the Jewish quarters. They plundered, ransacked, and beat people who were already humiliated enough. They raped women and girls. They increased the number of inhabitants in the ghetto, crowding in ever more from new transports of Jews. In the end, in an area of a hundred hectares, half a million people were living in 100 apartment houses and 1,500 buildings. Forced labour, hunger, epidemics, and torture decimated their ranks.

Donka had been happy to leave the ghetto and be taken to a work camp.

Later, reading memoirs of survivors, I learned other details about the tragedy of the Warsaw ghetto. The story of the heroic uprising of virtually unarmed Jews against the German Nazis, who were attacking them with planes, grenades and flame throwers, warmed my heart. The Warsaw ghetto uprising lasted from April 19 to May 15, 1943. They managed to hold out by a superhuman effort.

Where the ghetto had been was a memorial plaque and three objects that reminded us of that heroic struggle: Nathan Rappaport's sculpture *Ghetto Heroes* and two sewer openings. The sewer openings were a symbol of the link with the underground world and the way in which the inhabitants of the ghetto secretly communicated with the outside world.

I was also preoccupied with the attitude of the Polish people. How did they relate to the tragedy of the Jews during the war? I visited the History Museum in Warsaw, which occupies one whole side of the main square of Staro Miesto. One wing of this enormous building had been dedicated to the years of the Second World War. Yet it was only with difficulty that I found exhibits that referred to what happened to the Jews. The total space offered to these events consisted of a single exhibition table. That attitude reminded me of the reception the Polish peasants had given us, the destitute *Häftlings*, in the winter of 1945.

Now I will go back to the winter of 1945. We were returning from the ruins of Warsaw when our attention was attracted to a group of women dressed in rags. They were accompanied by armed Russian soldiers. When we asked, they told us that they were girls from the German army who had been rounded up while they were trying to escape. They were dressed as *Häftlings* and had been trying to steal away unobserved. I became paralysed by fear that people could believe the same was true of us. It was true that when we set off from Nowe Miasto, the authorities in the town had made a *propuska*, a permit allowing free movement to our group of twenty-one people. In spite of that we were still afraid because as war conditions prevailed, absolutely anything was possible. We quickened our step. Helpful people guided us to a camp where liberated Jews were gathered. As far as we could tell from looking through the fence, former prisoners were living in good conditions here and everything seemed orderly. The occupants were dressed in clean clothing, well cared for, apparently calm and moved about untroubled behind the bars of the fence. We were glad that at least our situation too would be sorted out. As it turned out, that camp was full and they could not accommodate us.

Disappointed, we returned to Praga where we could not find any refuge other than the temple in ruins. (Months later I learned from Magda Roth that in the end the temple collapsed, burying hundreds of people. Magda broke her leg, ended up in hospital, and was only able to return home months later.)

We hurried toward the train station, where a new surprise awaited us. The station no longer existed, only a small building and railway lines on which empty carriages without engines were scattered. A sea of people had gathered on the platform: prisoners returning home, civilians from both the town and the country, people from the provinces who were carrying groceries in bags and baskets, and young people in military uniforms who were trying to find their way behind the front.

It was now the beginning of March. The thick layer of snow had not yet melted, and it was still very cold. In the small building, many people were crowded in the only room warmed by a cast-iron stove. It seemed impossible to get in. We spent two days and nights in the open. From time to time we could hear a shout: "The train is coming!" The crowd would start to move and the room would empty. When the news proved to be false, everybody trickled back to the heated room. Twice we managed to spend a short time inside, but at night we found ourselves outside. Some Italian soldiers who were also waiting for the train saved us from freezing to death because of the terrible night frost and cold. They pulled out the planks of the wooden fence and lit a fire between the rails. One side of us was warm with the flames of the fire and the other side was swept with a cold, cutting wind. However, by turning around and by stamping our feet on the spot to warm up, we survived those nights too. On the second day, the waiting continued with repeated false alarms. Finally a train going to Lublin arrived on another platform. A torrent of people started to move in an instant. It was then that our little group was split up. Each one ran in a different direction. Some made a detour around the train in front of us, others clambered over the stairs of the open carriages. Even more reached the other side by going underneath the carriages. I did the same thing. Dragging Erzsi after me, I took the shortest route. My blood froze when I thought that the train over our heads might start off. Slipping and dragging ourselves under the carriage, we reached our goal. For weeks on end we had dreamed of cutting short our sufferings with the help of some means of transport to get nearer to home, and here we were at last, with a puffing engine in front of us, with fifteen to twenty freight cars full of people. We were many and we stormed the train. Pushing Erzsi in front of me, I clambered up into the first car I came to. At that moment, I was not thinking about my comrades whom we had lost in the general chaos and tension. The only thing that mattered was to get on, and we had done it. We were almost stuck to the floor. Everyone was trying to find a place. There were so many baskets and bundles and bags. We ended up next to a heavy-set woman who found a place on Erzsi's foot and it was in vain that we begged her to free her foot; she did not move for the whole long journey. When we had arrived home, we looked up the distance between Warsaw and Lublin; it is about 250 kilometres. We traveled a night and a day with numerous stops, detours, and delays on dead rail tracks, and we arrived in Lublin at nightfall.

LUBLIN

*E*xhausted, we got off the train at Lublin. Erzsi's
face and hands were burning with fever and I
could hardly make her stand up. I had not even had
time to look around for our comrades when Babus
Kemény approached me and asked me to help her
carry the body of Ilonka, the girl from Cluj, out of
the train. She had died during the journey.

Many had died around me during those bitter
months, but all along I had shrunk from being very
close to death. Now there was no way I could avoid
it. With one arm, I seized Ilonka's feet (her body was
as light as a feather) and with the other I embraced
Erzsi. In this way, we made for the platform, where
we managed to meet up with the other members
of our little group. After a short discussion, we left
Ilonka's body on the platform with the intention
of burying her the next day. Her older sister spread
out her blanket on the ground; with half of it we

wrapped the poor wasted girl, who was still beautiful in death, and with the other half we covered her. We stood around her, speechless and shaken. It was hard to leave her alone. The next day, her sister confessed that the thought had crossed her mind to change her shoes with Ilonka's, who had been given the best pair because of her illnesses, but her conscience would not let her. We also knew what a great sacrifice it was to give up her blanket, which at the time was regarded as a treasure. We were certain that in a few minutes after we left she would be stripped naked. In spite of that, we felt that whatever happened, we owed respect to the dead.

In the meantime, some young people who spoke Yiddish approached us and told us to hurry towards the exit because in a few minutes all movement would be prohibited because of the curfew and we would not be able to get to a refuge. With a silent glance we bid farewell to Ilonka and set off. The thought that at last someone would care for us and we would not have to worry anymore about where we would spend the night made us happy. I felt that it was the final effort I would have to ask Erzsi to make. Ilonka's death had shaken us terribly. As with Erzsi, we did not know what illness she suffered from. I was very afraid that Erzsi would not be able to cope for much longer.

How far we went I really do not know. The journey seemed long to me. After dragging ourselves, staggering with every step, we arrived at Peretz House. The conditions here were completely different from those in the refugee camps we had seen around Warsaw. This was a spacious two-storied building with lots of rooms. Perhaps it had been a Jewish community center before the war. Other than the tables and chairs there was no furniture. People were lying or sitting on the bare floor. The rooms were heated, which gave us some consolation.

Erzsi collapsed in a corner, and we could not get another word out of her. I could not do anything for her that evening. The next day I learned that the shelter had a room for the sick, an infirmary, where she was accepted. At first, I found her a place on a bag of hay, but later she was given a real bed. Sadly, beds became free very often there, as the weary, sick people closed their eyes forever without anybody realizing it.

An older doctor, an Austrian Jew, examined Erzsi. I learnt later that she was only thirty-five years old. It was difficult to guess someone's age there. She diagnosed exhaustion. This was the most prevalent diagnosis, and even if it was not very exact it was certainly appropriate for those people who were wasting away. Women who were reduced to skin and bone lay still in their beds with dull eyes and blank stares. Often, we did not even notice when they died. Some disappeared from the ranks of the living without anybody even knowing their name. I remember that I berated God for allowing the unfortunate women to perish after liberation, after escaping from great dangers and so near to returning home.

I could not tear myself away from Erzsi, who was bedridden. I felt that as long as I was near her, she would not leave me. I did not go into the communal room to sleep but instead squeezed into one of the corners of the infirmary. While there, I was able to help some of the other sick people, with a kind word, a glass of water, or wiping the perspiration from a hot brow.

After I had to some extent sorted out Erzsi's situation, I started to inspect our new shelter. A great number of people were swarming through the rooms. Different Jewish men and women had flowed through here, coming from camps that had already been liberated: Hungarians, Germans, Romanians, Latvians and Poles. From then on, I finally began to meet liberated men as well as women, but I was upset to notice that men from Transylvania were still missing. Later I learned that most of our men had been taken from Auschwitz to German camps. Those in work detachments in the Ukraine were transferred to the Germans when they reached the area near Košice as they were retreating and were sent to Buchenwald, Dachau, Bergen-Belsen, Güntskirchen and other western camps. From talking to people, I began to build up a mental image of the enormous network of camps that covered the whole of Poland. The Nazis had gathered the Jews from occupied countries into sixteen "reserves" in Poland and then scattered the ones they allowed to live to all corners of the country. We probed one another with questions about where we had been and whom we had met. We were trying to trace our relatives because we did not know where they had been lost. Sadly, nobody had heard about my loved ones, but I did meet an old fellow-sufferer whom I had thought lost. One day new people arrived, and to my great joy I recognized Aunty Hirsch and her daughter Klári among them. In the last days of the camp Aunty Hirsch had lost her youngest child, Ancsa, the spoilt daughter, who had remained unburied because of the terrible frost and the unexpected retreat. Klári, who was also seriously ill, had been put into a cart by the SS guards during our retreat and had remained behind our group without any explanation. I thought at the time that Aunty Hirsch was going to lose her mind. Struggling inside herself, she kept up for a while with the group that was retreating. Then, after making a quick decision, she went back to look for Klári. We were convinced that she was going to certain death, but we could not do anything. So Aunty Hirsch had remained behind and we heard nothing more of her. We were sure that one of the SS guards had shot her or that she had died of hunger on the journey. However, that was not what happened at all.

Wandering from village to village, Aunty Hirsch had knocked on doors until she found Klári, who had been taken in and cared for by some kind people. These people did the same thing for Aunty Hirsch. Perhaps their fortune can be attributed to the fact that they came from an area where Slovakian was spoken and they could understand their benefactors. These people would not let them set off on their journey, even when their health improved, until the trains started moving again. In this way they were spared the long, tormenting, uncertain journey we undertook on foot.

In the throng of arrivals, I also met the girl from Budapest who had courageously come into the ghetto in Oradea of her own free will to save her cousin Ági Wilkesz. She had paid dearly for her kindness. She had passed through numerous camps but in the end had got away. It pained her that both Ági and Hédi had perished. She told me then that on that day when she had not been able to resolve the situation for which she had come, she went to the station in Oradea and took the first train for Budapest. She was so tired that she fell asleep immediately. During the night she was awakened unexpectedly and questioned, whereupon she gave her real name instead of the name on her false papers. They took her off the train and interned her, and from there she was sent to Auschwitz.

Nobody wanted to stay in Lublin for more than a few days. The Peretz House was considered to be a transit refuge, which explains why it was not fitted out. Our goal was to get home as quickly as possible. Home, home! The thought gave us wings. We did not know what the situation was at home or which of our loved ones would be there. We impatiently prepared to continue, but no one knew anything about the rest of the journey. Where was the border, and what awaited us there? None of those who had left had come back again, nor had they sent us any news. We only knew that we had to get hold of a document from the Jewish Council, the *propuska*, that confirmed that we were deportees and served as a permit for free travel to continue our journey. Our diminished group (a number of women had remained in Warsaw) went to the office. As had happened in Nowe Miasto, they wanted to give us a communal document. The members of our group conferred in whispers. In the end, Erika had the task of telling me that they could not wait until Erzsi was better. I knew that I had to stay behind. How painful that moment was; I had felt so safe in our little community. I asked for a separate document for Erzsi and myself. Gabi Révész from Debrecen reached a similar decision as she was also looking after her older sister who was ill.

After a few days' rest, the others did indeed set off. We felt the parting acutely. Frightened, I realized that I was staying behind in an entirely strange environment. They left me with the conviction that Erzsi would not survive and that it would be very difficult for me to find my own way home.

Indeed, difficult days followed. After a dreadful journey of six days by train and many hardships, they arrived home. They brought news of us to Oradea. At the same time, I started to adapt to the new conditions of life. At the time, I had no way of knowing that I would be compelled to spend five weeks in

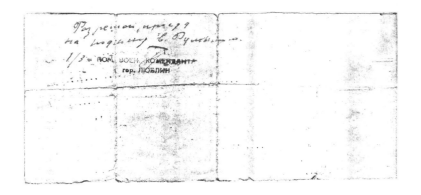

Lublin and that several difficult months of imposed "holiday" awaited me.

The stay in Lublin is one of my most painful memories. Since Ilonka's death, I had lived in constant fear. I felt that I could lose Erzsi at any moment, and I did not want to accept this thought. Erzsi had a temperature of 41°C and

The Red Cross in Lublin, Poland certifies that Romanian citizens Eliza and Tereza Klärmann are permitted to return home.

was barely conscious. Her lips were covered with a dry crust, and she had a lost, vacant look about her. In the camp, she had cut off my requests with a short "Let me die," but now she did not even make this effort. I was exasperated by the fact that she had become so indifferent and weary and that she did not even have the resources for this.

With difficulty, I forced her to swallow a few spoonfuls of food. This did not surprise me. The food, a litre of bean or lentil soup, was not at all suitable for a sick person. She really could not eat that kind of food. I realized that I had to try to obtain some lighter food that was at the same time rich in calories, but what kind of food and from where? Gabi Révész also wanted to help her sick sister and found the solution.

"We will beg!"

The next day we set off together to beg on the streets of Lublin. Even today I blush when I think of it. We were still wearing our concentration camp clothes, which had become even more threadbare with the passing of time. Our appearance would surely inspire pity. Even in those conditions, I was not able to lower myself to stretch out my hand for charity. Gabi assumed this task, while I babbled away in French about what made us resort to begging. We looked so pitiful that we were given some zloty. We were also helped by the fact that order had been restored in Lublin and a more peaceful way of life had begun to take shape after the war. We were so humiliated by our need to beg that as soon as we had collected the minimum necessary for a day, we left. Then, the real begging began, as I pleaded with Erzsi to swallow the food we had obtained at such pains: milk sweetened with a few drops of honey, an egg yolk mixed with sugar. I believed that feeding her scrupulously would keep her alive. Yet at the same time I was so wracked by remorse that I could not swallow a morsel of the food we had obtained by begging. I gave what was left to the fourteen- and fifteen-year-old girls who had been left on their own, particularly because their looks showed both hunger and disapproval at Erzsi's refusal to eat.

I no longer know how many days or weeks I went begging on the streets of Lublin. But I know that this situation troubled me so much that I could only walk with my eyes downcast. It is almost incredible how I managed to see nothing, absolutely nothing, of the town. I did not look at the monuments of the old town, the Renaissance or baroque palaces, the churches that had remained intact, the beautiful city hall building. When I returned years later with my family to remind myself of Lublin, I did not recognize a single building, but felt like I was there for the first time. Only the squeaking of the tram seemed familiar. However, I could not swear that at the time, the trams were already back in action. The Lublin in which I had stayed for five weeks in 1945 was completely unknown. I looked around without being able to reconcile myself to the idea that I could not remember anything from my past. At last we arrived at the train station; it was there on the platform that I recognized the place where we had left the body of poor Ilonka.

Gabi's sister soon recovered and they left. I could not continue to beg on my own. Yet I had to make sure Erzsi continued to have food. Meanwhile, I learned that an office had opened in Lublin to help Jewish refugees. I went there and related my problems to them. They must have seen many worse cases because my situation did not impress them. They let me leave without offering so much as a zloty. I set off for the house swallowing my bitter tears. A young woman roused me from my thoughts. She wanted to know the cause of my grief. She spoke French well and I told her about my sister's desperate situation. She wrote her father's address on a note and told me to look for him the next day. It was the address of the Red Cross. The next day I easily found the office of the young woman's father. He must have been waiting for me, because everything was very simple. He was only interested in who I was, and I said I was a Romanian refugee, thinking that if I told him I was Jewish, he would send me to the Jewish Office for assistance. He gave me three hundred zloty, which was a fortune for me and meant above all that I would not have to beg anymore. The door out was behind me. I had to turn round to go out. I was overcome with fear. I thought that if he saw the sign on the back of my coat, all would be lost. I had to turn around, and nothing happened. No one called me back. He must have known whom he was helping right from the beginning.

During those first days, I missed the friends who had gone back to Oradea terribly; after going through so much together, I felt very close to them. With the exception of Gabi, who had now also set off for home, I did not know anyone among the residents of the house. Waves of people were arriving all the time and then going on further. Except for those who were sick, only a single group remained: some ex-*Häftlings* who belonged to a Jewish community in Greece. Although Greece had been liberated from fascist domination in the second half of 1944, civil war broke out in 1945 as the result of internal tensions. Greek Jews had no way of knowing which side would win and how their return would be viewed. They did not dare set out for home.

I heard about the Greeks but I did not know them. Then a particular event made them the focus of general attention. The American Jewish Joint Distribution Committee, a charity, funded the provision of food for our shelter. We had no means of controlling the way in which help was administered, but we found that the quality of the food was getting progressively poorer. One day, the Greek boys took the kitchen by storm and discovered that the meat that had been kept from us had been cut up and sold at a café. The Greeks put the freshly cooked steaming meatballs on trays and distributed them among the sick people in the infirmary. It was then that I got to know Isaac and his friend Leon, who was barely eighteen. Following this incident, Isaac often sought me out, each time appearing with some small gift because, he said, he wanted to help my sick mother. Erzsi was only two years older than me, but she looked so worn that he thought she was my mother.

From information gathered from newspapers at home, I knew that the Italians, allies of Germany, had attacked Greece in 1940 and that in 1941 the Germans had invaded and occupied the country. However, I only learned recently what had happened to the Greek Jews afterwards. In Greece, 0.9 per cent of the total population, or 76,000 people were Jews, most of Spanish origin. As one of the biggest Sephardic communities in Europe, they were a strong community that faithfully kept up their traditions. Salonika had forty synagogues, and they had several newspapers in their own language, Ladino. By 1942, the men were enlisted in work detachments, where they also had to wear the yellow star. From there they were all deported. Jews from Salonika and Thrace were deported to Auschwitz in March 1943. Those from the islands followed. Isaac had been married. With eyes full of tears, he spoke about his wife and son who had been executed before his eyes. The Greeks spoke French like many nations on the Mediterranean Coast.

Weeks passed, and in time I made new friends at the infirmary. Manci Hegedüs was ill, and her sister-in-law Fira was looking after her. At the same time, they were looking after two young girls, Klári and Judit. When they saw how alone I was, they took me under their wing. It was good to have someone with whom I could share my thoughts. I only learned later, as events unfolded, how far their kindness and goodness went. At the request of a Polish Jewish couple, they had taken their two girls, Éva and Mita, into their care. The parents wanted to go to Palestine through Romania and Italy but did not dare take the journey with the whole family. They did not know what waited for them at the border, and it seemed safer for the children to travel together with ex-*Häftlings*.

Erzsi's state had not changed at all. Her fever was still over 40°C. She was skin and bone. After a while, new doctors arrived at Peretz House. I probed them too about what could possibly explain Erzsi's illness. One thought her feverish condition was due to a previous heart problem. That surprised me. I began to remember some acquaintances who had suffered in a similar way. I remembered the case of Ica Löwber, who at one time lived in the same house as us. She became so weak that she could not walk anymore. I had also known a boy who was so weak that he could only drag himself around the house on his knees until it was discovered that his tonsils were full of pus. In another case, an untreated tooth had caused the illness. In all these cases the illness was attributed to an abscess. After I had inquired of Erzsi whether perhaps her throat was sore, or a tooth ached, I felt her body all over, centimetre by centimetre. When

I reached the muscles of her right leg, Erzsi let out a shout. I examined it more closely. It was swollen to twice the size of her other leg. Until then, no one had noticed it because the exhausted doctors were only making routine examinations. They took their temperatures, listened to their hearts, prescribed some vitamins, gave fortifying injections and went on their way. I ran straight to the doctor with my new discovery. The doctor returned with a large syringe. He aspirated Erzsi's foot and the syringe filled with pus. Finally, we had a diagnosis. The doctors told us that Erzsi had to be operated on immediately but this could not be done in the infirmary. She had to go to the hospital. They took her the same day. In vain I begged them to let me go with her, as the fear of separation had taken root in me so deeply. The hospital, which was full to bursting, only admitted new patients in strictly limited numbers and only in very serious, urgent cases. I endured a few hours of tense waiting until they brought Erzsi back with an enormous bandage on her leg. They had made a long incision from the knee, almost to the ankle. By evening, her temperature had fallen to 37.2°C. By the morning she no longer had a fever.

Because I had been worried about Erzsi, I had not noticed that life in the shelter was becoming livelier. The news that the Russians would send us home by train spread like lightning. When this news reached me, I asked the doctor's advice if we could go too. His reply was categorical: after we had come this far, it would be awful to risk upsetting the recovery process with a journey about which we knew nothing. Having got over her fever, Erzsi became extremely active again. She watched the excited preparations of those around us and would not even listen to the suggestion that we should stay behind. In fact, none of the other ill people wanted to stay on their own in the big deserted building, among strangers, and that feeling only strengthened as our friends prepared for their journeys.

Meanwhile, the parents of the two young girls came to see us. They were getting the children ready for the journey with pillows, comforters and groceries. They were very worried. For four years they had lived by hiding in holes underground, in perpetual fear, to save their children from deportation and certain death. Now they were separating from them willingly. They planned to set out after our train had left and to meet us in Oradea. They did, in fact, arrive in Romania a few days later without problems and then waited impatiently and uncertainly for another four months, without any news of the children, until they finally arrived in Oradea with us.

They had another girl of seven. To avoid attracting attention to themselves, they had entrusted her to another woman. If someone became interested in who they were, they wanted to create the impression that they were abandoned orphans we had found on the road and whom we had taken into our care. No one expressed any interest about them. Still they were overwhelmed by fear. Even several months after the liberation of Lublin they did not believe in their unrestricted freedom. Even though Lublin had been liberated, the war was still on.

The children were incredibly well disciplined. They said a tearless, silent farewell to their parents. It was obvious from their faces and gestures that they had lived in fear all their lives, ready for any danger that might occur. A few days later, when we staged an apparently accidental meeting between the older girl and her two younger siblings, they met as though they had never seen each other before.

The great day arrived at last. A torrent of people swarmed into the street and set off for the station. The big house emptied. I remained alone with Erzsi and a few young girls who were not able to get up. They were all crying and begging me to do something so that we would not be left on our own. If we had known at the time what awaited us in the days that followed, we would not have struggled to leave. The problem was that our whole life had unfolded under the banner of uncertainty and chance. So many times, a single movement decided whether we were to stay together or separate, to remain alive or to die.

Begging those at the top, I managed to convince them to give us a small cart, and we set off in that to the station. In the enormous crowd, we managed to find our friends again. Months later, when I was back in Oradea, I found out that when the Jewish

Democratic League in Oradea learned from those who had returned home that many Oradeans were still in Lublin, they obtained a train and organized our return home. The train arrived three days after our departure. The organizers found Peretz House empty; it was only in the hospital that they found a few seriously ill people. They returned home disappointed, with empty carriages, while our ordeal continued.

At the station, we learned that our train was not on the track yet. We settled on the ground and waited. From the time that I had decided to set off on the journey, the thought plagued me that perhaps I was making a fatal mistake. As I was sitting there, a carriage appeared on the road with four elegant women in it. I was surprised to recognize one of the women. Wearing a trouser suit and with a suitcase in her hand was Zsuzsi Szmuk, my cousin from Sziget. It was not difficult to recognize her because she looked just the same as she did at home. I stared, completely baffled by this unusual apparition. Her surprise was even greater, when she discovered our lamentable situation. After a few minutes I learned how her situation had turned out so differently. She had come to Lublin with a smaller group five or six weeks earlier. There were only six of them. They had not even heard of Peretz House. They presented themselves to the Red Cross, who reserved a room for them at the hotel and gave them money and clothing. They offered to take Erzsi and I with their group, but they had no means of taking all of us. There were six of us, plus the two children. I could not and did not want to abandon those who had taken care of me through those difficult times.

16

CAMP LIFE IN CHERNIVTSI

*B*efore nightfall, the train was assembled and set off. Even the freight cars in which we rode did not darken our moods as we huddled on the floor, warming each other. We were overcome with joy, anticipating the moment when we would see our native country again; it was as if we could touch it with our hands.

My distress, however, did not let up. I told myself I was weak and irresponsible for giving in to Erzsi's wishes without considering all their consequences. Of course I was longing to get home to my family and share my thoughts with my loved ones, but all the while uncertainty plagued me. Questions crowded into my mind. How long would the journey last? When would we be able to change the dressing on Erzsi's leg? Would her fever return if she were not treated in time? Erzsi had been operated on only two days earlier. She had an enormous open cut on her leg under a dressing, from which blood and pus poured continuously. The jerking of the train made the dressing absorb the moisture faster. When the cotton wool and gauze were saturated and started to dry, they pressed on the wound, and her pain grew worse and worse. The situation appeared desperate when a solution presented unexpectedly itself. A group of Yugoslavian prisoners who were traveling in the last car of our train were accompanied by a medical team. This team went through all the cars and took note of the sick. When they got to us, they opened the bandages on Erzsi's leg and dressed them professionally with clean snow-white gauze. They repeated this every two days. In the end, the jerking of the train may actually have helped the healing process because by the end of our journey all the pus that had accumulated in the affected leg had worked its way out.

From the moment of our liberation, we had never felt so carefree as during this journey. All the Russians gave us to eat, though, was dry food and a kind of powder suitable for soup or porridge. Preparing this was easy because the train always stopped by the bank of a river. Campfires were lit within minutes of stopping, and some of the passengers mixed the dried soup with water. Others ran to the river to wash themselves. The only problem was that the conductor never indicated when the train was leaving. The engine would start to puff slowly and the train would begin to move, giving us little time to climb up into a carriage, even if it was not ours. I witnessed many amusing incidents. Once, a young woman was stark naked washing herself on the bank of the river when she saw that the train was setting off, so she ran after it just as she was, holding her clothes in her hands. She was glad when she was hauled up into one of the last carriages. Others ran to the train with kettles full of half-cooked food in their hands. Nothing could upset our joy, which increased with the arrival of spring. Green meadows, budding trees, the fresh green leaves, the chirping of the birds and the awakening of nature filled us all with joy. Even the presence of Russian soldiers accompanying the train did not bother us. They felt like traveling companions who were there to protect us.

At Lvov the cars transporting the Yugoslavians were disconnected, and they were redirected to Yugoslavia. We were sad to see them go. The next day the cars going to Czechoslovakia were detached. Even so, many remained.

After seven days in comfortless conditions but in good spirits, we arrived in Chernivtsi. We were received by the town commandant and by the local Jewish community. Only those who were traveling in the first carriages took part in the reception. We were asked to leave the train, but this order did not disturb us because we thought we had reached the border and would change trains for one that was going to Romania. Unfortunately, that was only in our dreams because the reality was very different. They lined us up and we set off towards town.

Our entry to the town did not remind me of the *Häftling* convoys and marches. We did not have to keep the strict rows of five. We were not led by the terrifying and inaccessible SS guards in their black uniforms adorned with death heads. A few relaxed, almost friendly Russian soldiers accompanied our lines. Yet we were led. We were being taken somewhere. Where? I had understood one thing: we were not continuing our journey. We became distrustful and agitated. Before reaching the town, we were led to an enormous, uninhabited building that we later learned was the Petru Rares military barrack. This building was completely filled with people in the days that followed. In addition to the Romanian, Hungarian and Greek Jewish deportees, there were Italian and Bulgarian Jews, as well as prisoners of war. There were Swabians of Romanian origin and Romanians who had left voluntarily with their families to work in Germany and who had later been taken as prisoners by the Russians. People were assigned rooms according to their countries of origin. I was not pleased to find myself under the same roof as my fellow countrymen who had been Nazi collaborators.

We now realized that we had arrived in a Russian camp that was surrounded by a fence. As with any military barracks, the rooms were enormous. Some of them could hold hundreds of people, with many-tiered bunk beds along the walls. Although the principle was similar, it was different from the German camps. Each person had her own place, as well as a space around it for personal things. Everything was clean and bright, spacious and airy. The hardest things to get used to were the Turkish toilets. It was the first time in my life I had seen something like that: just a hole in the cement floor and a place for the soles of boots.

We had food in abundance: bran soup three times a day, a second course prepared from tinned meat, seven hundred grams of bread per person, and a ration of tobacco. It was not the food we craved three months after liberation, but at least we were not starving, nor were we sent to work. After a few days I noticed that many people were having milk with bread and butter for breakfast and then other good things during the course of the day. The mystery was soon solved. We had noticed that surplus supplies of bread and tobacco could be cashed in at the fence. With rubles you could get anything. We also quickly realized that the camp was not guarded as strictly as we had imagined. More than that, when the soldier who was on guard could not see, or turned a blind eye, the wired fence could be lifted in places, and one could cross form one side to another.

I went to town with Fira, who spoke Russian well. We studied the situation first, and then we did some shopping in the market. It was a poor market, where demand was greater than supply. Bread in particular was in great demand, and we were able to replace our bran soup with food rich in calories.

Chernivtsi was not directly affected by the war. At least, we saw no signs of bombing where we were. There were, however, many derelict buildings. Wherever we looked, we saw grey disintegrating buildings, dark dirty windows and rusted drainpipes. The streets were dirty and full of rubbish, and the people were apathetic and poorly dressed. The shop windows were gaping and empty. The shopkeepers stood wearily in front of their empty shelves. It was a depressing sight. They were speculating on the black market. One could not buy salt or vinegar in the grocery store. Oil and sugar were rationed. Nonetheless, many things were available under the table, at prices inflated five or ten times. A shoemaker in a co-operative told Fira that his monthly salary was not enough to sustain him for three days. He made up his income working on the black market, right in his workshop. We reasoned that this was the fifth year of the war and Chernivtsi and the surrounding area were not the real Soviet Union but only a border area that had been under German occupation for a long time. What we were observing could not possibly be characteristic of the entire country.

May 9, 1945 arrived, the day the war ended. I went into town with Fira and the Greek boys. A military parade took place in the main square. A crowd had gathered around the troops, who had formed an orderly square. The flag was raised, the guard of honour marched past and a speech was made. Everything was done in an incredibly disciplined way. After the speech, we listened to the military fanfare. People listened until the end, without uttering a word and seemingly untouched, and then they dispersed. Isaac could not help remarking that in Greece, people would have sung and danced with joy.

I tried to rationalize the indifference of the inhabitants by the great losses of human life that had occurred. Almost every family was bereaved. During the war, many had disappeared or had been taken prisoner. The majority of the survivors were still far away. They had every reason to be in mourning.

We too could not rejoice unreservedly. Oradea had been liberated on October 12, 1944, and we were still far from home. We wanted to believe that there would be no obstacles to our return, but we did not dare hope. After so many disappointments we still could not make plans for the future. Nevertheless, the new situation galvanized nearly all of us. In the evening we went into town again to admire the lights that had been switched on after the long period of darkness. The windows of homes had been thrown wide open and the blackout cloths had been taken down. It was at that moment that we began to sense their feeling of liberation.

A few days later, also in the evening, we went to the theatre. We saw a Russian play, although I do not remember which one. Fira translated it into Hungarian for me and I explained it in French for our Greek companions. Of course, by the time we translated a part, the performance had moved on, so we did not understand much of the story. However, our whispers did succeed in annoying those nearby, and in the end, we had to leave the theatre.

The days and weeks passed, and slowly we adapted to the monotony of camp life. As the problem of our daily food supply had been resolved, we had plenty of time to become better acquainted with our new environment. Isaac and Leon, the two young Greeks, and my cousin, whom I had met in Lublin, often visited me. A relative whom I had not known until then found me. He was also named Klärmann. He had heard of Erzsi and me from someone in the camp, and he came looking for us. He showed us real warmth and brotherly love, both then and later. His visits were very helpful because he tried to inspire courage and a will to live in Erzsi. She had developed complications again. Although she was no longer in danger of dying, she had a thirty-centimetre long wound that penetrated to the bone and was not healing well. She was in pain. Because she had to protect the leg from injuries and from anyone touching it, she held it away from the board of the bunk bed, bent at a right angle from the knee. With time, the leg became fixed in this position. She could not stretch it even when she tried. By then, her injured leg had shortened. She could no longer walk. She was afraid that she would remain crippled, and if that happened, she did not want to go home. She did not want her fiancé to see her like that. Earlier, Józsi had not wanted to bind her to marriage for a similar reason, for fear of what would happen if he were "to be injured and returned home without an arm." And now Erzsi was repeating, "No one should marry me from pity." So Erzsi became silent, lying all day on her bunk, closed in on herself. Isaac came to see us often. He took her in his arms, carried her out into the sunshine and laid her down on a blanket on the grass. Meanwhile I looked up all the doctors I had heard of. Their contradictory advice baffled me. The Italian doctor advised me to do exercises with her all the time and to massage her leg. The Belgian doctor maintained that because the wound was not yet completely clean, any clot of pus entering the circulatory system could cause an embolism. The advice of another doctor was to sit little Mita on her knees and the knee joint would give way little by little because of the weight of the child. In the end, I listened to the doctor who advised us not to do anything. In his opinion, even if it took longer, the rigidity would disappear on its own.

These many meetings with doctors had one very positive outcome. A doctor from Sopron, Dr. Lebovits, had a look at Erzsi's leg, and we learned that he was a good friend of Józsi, Erzsi's fiancé. It was then that my sister heard of Józsi for the first time in months. This had a wonderful effect on her. She decided to heal. Now she wanted to get better.

A new event stirred our spirits. A large group that had been liberated three months earlier arrived from Auschwitz. They were no longer visibly in ill health.

They had been looked after for a while, and physically at least, they were on the road to recovery. We received the first truly authentic news about Auschwitz from them. The composition of the group itself was interesting. They were from different countries, including Hungary, Romania, Italy, Poland, Austria, and Holland, and there were men, women and children. That was the biggest surprise: children had survived Auschwitz. Until then, we had thought that the children had been among those first killed, along with the sick and the weak. Our surprise was even greater because we knew the parents of some of the children.

Rózsi Csengeri from Şimleul Silvaniei, the town of my birth, had her own twin girls and had taken two orphans into her care. Among those from Auschwitz were Mrs. Rosenthal from Oradea, the sister of a school friend, with two seven-year-old boys and a three-year-old girl. We soon learned the secret of the children's survival. The twins were kept in specially equipped barracks and were subjected to different painful and exhausting experiments. They had then become the lucky survivors. Many pairs of healthy twins had fallen victim to experiments carried out to investigate the anatomy of twins. After our return home, I read Dr. Miklós Nyiszli's book, *Auschwitz, a Doctor's Eyewitness Account* and learned that the great aim of the experiments was to increase the birth rate of the dominant Aryan race. They wanted to make German mothers bear as many twins as possible.

Those children who were interesting from a scientific point of view were kept in a camp with privileges, sometimes together with their mothers.

At the same time, we learned other peculiar things. This group arrived with another group of people with various deformities, including dwarves. In this group was a woman who had a nose similar to a horn growing out of her forehead. The poor woman tried to wrap up her head as much as possible to hide her deformity. Not even these people knew to what they owed their survival. Dr. Nyiszli's book gave me the answer to that too. The skeletons of disabled or deformed people who were killed violently were specially preserved and sent to the Kaiser Wilhelm Institute for Anthropology, Human Heredity, and Eugenics in Berlin/Dahlem. Their purpose was to provide material for propaganda to support the theory of Jewish racial degeneration. Like the twins, they were part of a group of selected victims. After meeting them, we realized that the hope of ever seeing our lost loved ones again was slim. Yet the desire to return home became stronger. Perhaps it was not so much for our lost home but rather to know for sure. We wanted to face reality. We had to know who was left. We knew that those who were still alive would go home.

From the other prisoner camps of Chernivtsi, those curious or interested in our fate often came to visit. Anton, a former Belgian soldier who had become a Russian prisoner, visited me many times.

One day he brought the surprising news that they were going to be taken home in a few days. He offered to take Erzsi and me with him.

"No, it's impossible, I want to go home," I replied immediately.

He started to describe how good our life would be if we went with him. Erzsi would immediately be admitted to a hospital where she would receive the very best care. His mother would look after me.

"Why do you want to burden yourself?" I asked him in the end.

"You could become my wife later, if it suited you.... And if not, once Erzsi was better, you could go home," was the simple answer.

This offer of marriage caught me so unprepared that if he had not had such a serious expression, I would have burst out laughing. Anton never courted me. He talked to me often about his war experiences, his work at home, and his widowed mother. He was very interested in Erzsi's state of health. I assumed he came because there was nothing better to do. I never thought for a moment that he saw me as a woman. I did not feel like a woman. My goodness, what I must have looked like, in my shapeless camp dress, with my short hair and missing my two front teeth! I had broken them in the camp at Dörbek when I had managed to *organize* a frozen beetroot and in my great hunger bit into it too quickly.

Anton did not force the issue, but he asked me to think about his proposal. He came back the next day, and when he saw that I was not changing my mind, he took a Saint Anthony medallion on a silver chain from his breast pocket.

"My mother gave it to me on the day I left for the front. It has given me luck. After four years I am going home healthy. It will watch over you from now on."

I protested. In the first place, he had not yet reached his home. Besides his mother would be disappointed if he returned without the medallion. He thrust the chain into my hand, together with a charm that was supposed to have miraculous powers. After he had given me his home address, he said farewell. I never saw him again.

Two months later, which seemed an eternity to us, another big group arrived. The Russians told us immediately that we would be going home, as there was not enough room for everybody. Among them were many from Oradea. They all wanted to send messages with us. They wanted to tell those at home that they were alive and hoped to get back sooner or later. They envied us.

"For you the hard part is over," they said. "Who knows how much longer they will keep us here?"

We did not have any packing to do. We got the bread bags and blankets ready, and in no time we stood lined up in the courtyard. Doubt seized many of us on the way to the station. Would they really take us home? Would we be victims of yet another deception? After a tense period of waiting we got into the cattle cars, highly agitated. We knew the geography of Romania. We hoped that the names of well-known towns would soon appear in Roman characters. We did not know if we were taking the route to the Siret River or to Vinnytsya. One thing was certain: we had to remain on this side of the Prut River. The train set off and soon crossed the Prut. It did not stop for a time that seemed interminable. We did not see a single station. Later we caught sight of town names written in Cyrillic letters and our fears increased. We had heard the names of these stations from our brothers who had been taken for labour service in the Ukraine. Now there was no doubt about it. We were not going towards Bucovina or Moldova but to somewhere farther inside the Soviet Union.

By a twist of fate, those who had been brought to take our place went home to Oradea two weeks later. I still do not know the reason. They brought news of us to our home, while we impatiently waited to see what turn of events our fate would take.

27

Isolated in Slutsk

When we realized the irreversible reality of the situation, panic broke out. Many of us had read *The Siberian Garrison* by Rodion Markovits, and we had a desolate image of Siberia in our minds.

"Just how many years of prison are awaiting us?" someone asked.

"Perhaps they are not taking us to Siberia, but to Birobidgean," suggested others who were better informed. A Jewish autonomous region had been set up in Russia in the 1930s.

"Or, even more likely, to Palestine...." said the unsuspecting. "Jews who have survived the disaster are being gathered there."

Our education at home had not given us much of a reference point to judge what this last alternative might have meant for us. In spite of that, if we could have chosen between these three possibilities, we would certainly have chosen Palestine, the future

Israel, even though it was still a British protectorate. No one asked us anything, and no one gave us any explanation. In our embittered state, and after so many trials, we were staggered by this turn of events. Regret and suspicion overcame us. Would we ever enjoy carefree days again, or were we destined only for forced labour from now on?

Until this point, our return home had seemed a close, palpable reality, and people felt that their behaviour had to correspond to the expectations and moral norms in which they had been educated. Now, the precepts of home had become so distant that many felt freed from family and social norms, patriarchal role models and customs.

While we were analyzing the possibilities in our mind, the train went on at express speed through the Ukrainian steppes. The images we caught sight of through the cracks of the half open doors and windows were depressing. We saw the marks of war: ruins, devastation, uncultivated land and decay.

After we had passed Minsk, near Slutsk, the train stopped in an open field and we descended. The sick and those who could not walk, including Erzsi, were boarded onto trucks. The rest of us set off by foot. My attempts to stay with Erzsi were useless; the Russians could not be persuaded. We had to cross a big field. Trenches transected our way, and it was an ordeal to cross them; I should have been used to them from Dörbek and Guttau. At one moment, I looked at my wrists and was surprised to note that the lucky medallion had disappeared. Although I had never been superstitious, I saw a sign of trouble in the loss of the charm. The voice of Anton echoed in my ears: "To give you luck from now on...." If the charm protected its bearer from misfortune, its loss could only have a contrary effect. What else could possibly happen to me? I could lose Erzsi. All the sick would be taken to another place. This, and similar thoughts, tortured me for the entire journey.

After this hard trip we finally arrived at our destination. We were to live in a big brick, multi-storeyed building, with bunk beds carved from planks and no other furniture. Erzsi had arrived ahead of us, together with the others who were sick. Slowly my anxiety began to subside

Gradually, we became acquainted with our new situation. Our group found its place on the second level of the building, on the top bunks. They told us that we were in Slutsk, quite some distance from any area of habitation, on the grounds of an enormous unused factory. The large buildings were hundreds of metres from each other. The Romanians, Hungarians, Greeks, and Italians were accommodated separately in these buildings. Each community had its own internal leader. Our *Nachialnik* was Ilus Rothschild, who later became Mrs. Jungreisz and was originally from Oradea.

We were dismayed by the Russians' arrangement to house us with those prisoners of Romanian origin who had gone to Germany of their own free will to work or for business. We objected in vain. The Russians made no distinction between those who were victims of the war and those who had profited from it. To them, the only thing that counted was that we came from the same country.

In Slutsk, we were completely isolated from the outside world. This had many unpleasant consequences. We did not know what was happening in the world. The war had ended, but we knew nothing about the destiny of each nation and where the borders of countries were now. To inform the masses, the Russians had put up notice boards in front of the buildings. Newspapers and pages from magazine with the more important news were posted here. Of course there was a delay of several weeks before their arrival or posting. For us, any news, any detail at all that we had been unaware of, was interesting. Thus we learned that Petru Groza's government had taken power, but we could not decipher the significance of this from between the lines. From the Hungarians' notice board, the Ludas Matyi humorous sketches offered a lot of information about the absurd aspects of the new society. Although the papers were only rarely changed, they were our first link with those at home and with the changes resulting from the war.

Another consequence of our isolation was that we had no buyers for our surplus bread. Our precious currency had been devalued. We no longer had anything to buy or anyone to buy it from. We had to give up milk and butter. As the days passed, we missed having a glass of milk in the mornings more and more. After hesitating for a long time, I went to take my share of the bran soup, which I had given up during our "life of plenty" in Chernivtsi. In the cold mornings, I ate the hot soup as if it were a delicacy. It bothered me to think that months after liberation, bran soup was still a treat. And there was still the uncertainty. What did the future hold for us? Weeks had passed and no one mentioned anything about going home. We were still afraid they would take us farther into the Soviet Union.

We were not treated badly. We had shelter over our heads and daily meals were assured, although our living conditions were modest. Most important, they did not put us to work. We were still very weak. Then there was a pleasant change in our lives. The Russians wanted to help us change our tattered appearance. As they were not able to give us civilian clothing, they distributed articles of their military uniform: shorts, pants and jackets. Erzsi was given a military skirt, as her leg was still not healed. I asked for trousers, which would make it easier to climb to my bunk. It was an incredible feeling to wear clean new clothes again. They also wanted to make our sleeping places more comfortable. We were given sacks made of grey cloth to fill with hay from the haystacks around the fields. Along with many others, I could not resist the temptation to cut up the cloth. In my mind's eye I saw my last beautiful blue wool dress. Modeled on this, I sewed a dress from the grey sack material. Without a sewing machine, just a needle in my hand, I worked painstakingly on the long seams for days on end. Seeing my efforts, my cousin offered me the lace from her underwear, and I used it to make neat little bows for the neck, cuffs and sleeves. Of course the dress of coarse grey cotton was only a pale reflection of my blue one, but it seemed very beautiful to me. It was the first dress I had really wanted for months. In the camp, I kept it for special occasions. When I returned home I put it away to save for its memories.

The days passed slowly. We were bored. The Italians somehow got hold of a soccer ball, and a competition started between the Italian towns: Turin against Rome, Genoa against Florence, etc. Later, the camps within the camp matched their forces. Many people gathered for the matches. The games helped to release tension.

Literary debates were also started at that time, to the general satisfaction of the Romanian and Hungarian intellectuals in the building. They were probably the initiative of József Gréda from Oradea, a literary translator who had been with us from Chernivtsi. This, however, was not enough to fill our free time. We went for long walks between the buildings. At first we visited a small circle of friends, but the relationships gradually deepened and extended to others. The Italian and Greek Jews visited the Hungarians and Romanians more and more frequently. Little adventures began, and great loves were born.

Although there were Greek Jewish women in the camp, the Greek men were more attracted to the Hungarian and Romanian women. I brought this up with my old acquaintance Isaac, who often visited us here too. He told me that the Greek girls in the camp were from the archipelago, while the men were of Spanish origin. At home these women were considered to belong to another caste, and that distance was maintained here. Although the men did not court the girls, they protected them and went out of their way to take care of them.

The Italian soldiers were well fed, well dressed, and attractive. Many serious friendships and love stories developed. I watched this phenomenon without understanding it. To me the Italians were just as fascist as the Germans. I did not understand how anyone could speak to them. On one occasion I found myself in an unpleasant situation. A couple stopped in front of me, and the girl, whom I knew well, wanted to present her companion to me. I blushed, and not knowing what to do, I quickly turned my back on them and walked off. The memory of their outstretched hands stayed with me for a long time. Later I was overwhelmed with shame for my stupid behavior, but I was convinced that I could not have done anything else. I tried to find some justification. Just as I did at other decisive moments, I turned to my father in my thoughts. What would he have done in my place? I could not find any consolation. I could not soothe my conscience.

A few days later, I met an Italian Jew. Although he had only spent two months in Auschwitz, he was in very bad shape and terminally ill. I learned from him that there were three different groups of people living in the Italian quarter, all on very good terms: the rank and file soldiers who had been taken prisoner by the Russians, former Italian partisans who had fought against the fascists, and Italian Jews who had been dragged to Auschwitz. My new friend told me something else: his Italian friends had hidden him for years, and he had only arrived to Auschwitz in December 1944. Then my wounded spirit began to awaken from the deep lethargy into which it had fallen. I had no right to generalize. There were still people with compassion. Nothing else should count.

One hot summer day after this incident, I went with a small group to the bank of a nearby river. We had just sat down when a violent wind started up, then thunder and lightning and torrential rain. We took flight and rushed off towards our barrack. A Romanian girl of about seven and her younger brother were running next to me. It was pouring rain and very windy, and the little girl was begging for someone to help her carry the little boy. Others must have heard her plea for help as well as me, but they were probably thinking, who was rushing to help children when our brothers and sisters were crying in pain and gasping for air in the gas chambers or when they were thrown in the fire? For a few minutes I fought with myself. What could this barefoot, unfortunate child in the rain do if the Nazis wanted to exterminate a percentage of humanity? What could two innocent children have to do with world politics? I could not endure the pleas of the little girl. I was not thinking of their parents any longer. I bent down, picked the little one up and took them home. I realized then for the first time that the return to our former community was not going to be easy. I would have to re-evaluate my feelings and my ideas. I became acutely aware of the destruction wrought in our injured and broken psyches.

I respected and very much loved Manci Hegedüs, Fira's sister-in-law. She watched over Mita and Éva, the two girls who had been entrusted to her, with very special care. She cared for them as if she were their mother. She taught them and looked after all their needs. The children developed well, and when their hair started to grow, we saw that the original colour had been black. From time to time, we cut their blond ringlets to even up their striped hair. Once, Éva asked to keep a blond tress for her Mother as a souvenir. Manci loved them so much that she would happily have adopted them permanently, but it was clear that their parents were waiting impatiently for them. We had already been living with the children for months when we noticed the outline of a solid object in Éva's comforter. We felt it more carefully. It was a cardboard booklet. Our first reaction was to open the comforter, but we did not want our curiosity to be interpreted as an intrusion.

Erzsi thought it could be a message left intentionally. Perhaps it was something about the children's adoption? After a long discussion, we opened the comforter. We were surprised to find a passport issued before the war in the name of the entire family, with visas for Palestine. These unfortunate people were prepared for their journey when Hitler's troops invaded Poland and confined the Jews in ghettoes and concentration camps. Now we understood the tension and the terror in which these people had lived in all their years of hiding. When I had met them in Lublin, they still could not believe that it was possible to leave Poland peacefully.

Erzsi's state had improved a great deal. The wound on her leg had not completely closed but was healing well. She did not dare to stand up because she could not have managed it, so she still needed to be helped. Her needs had to be met without her moving, and food had to be brought to her in bed. Isaac was a great help during those times. He carried her in his arms into the fresh air. At last the day came when, supported on his arm, Erzsi put her own feet down on the floor. Her knee was not yet straightened, but even if she needed help, she could walk when she needed to. The fact that she could walk and could now mange alone had a surprisingly strange effect on me. I became ill for no apparent reason. I did not have a cold. I did not have indigestion or any identifiable pain, but a great feeling of weakness overcame me. During our deportation, when I had a high fever, I had only missed a single day's work, and even on that day I had worked in the kitchen. I had never taken any notice of a cold or other trouble because I knew that whatever happened I had to remain strong. Now I was flat on my back.

During those days, the news spread again that they had decided to send us home at last. Isaac was now visiting me quite often, and when he saw that I was starting to recover, he made a courageous proposal. He knew my feelings well. I had never encouraged him and I even warned him as clearly as I could that neither he nor anyone else could arouse my interest. Now he asked me to pretend to the Soviet authorities that I was going to marry him. He hoped that this would enable him to join our group leaving for Romania.

Isaac presented me with a difficult dilemma. He had always been very good to me and to Erzsi. He deserved to be helped, but I did not want to commit myself even by a formality. However much I trusted him, I was still afraid that he might make demands later. In the end I rejected his request.

Nearly fifty years have passed since then. I still feel guilty today for my weakness then. I do not know the fate of the Greek group or what happened to Isaac. Civil war was raging in Greece at the time, so they could not return there. I never learned how long they remained in the Soviet Union. The fact that his return was postponed indefinitely still makes me feel guilty.

RETURN TO LIFE

*W*e packed quickly. At last we could throw away
the worn-out dresses the Germans had given
us. Besides the military clothing in which we traveled, our possessions had increased because of the
dress I had made out of sack material. We had also
kept our blankets and coats with us. We traveled to
the station in trucks and boarded the train in high
spirits. On the way, however, our spirits started to
fall. Our imaginations gathered speed faster than the
train, and we were already at home in our thoughts.
We were wondering what and who was waiting for
us there.

We no longer hoped to see my mother, my sister
Magda or little Anikó again. We had heard too much
about what had happened at Auschwitz to hold any
illusions about their survival. On the other hand, we
had great hopes that my father, who was strong and
had an iron will, might have survived the inferno.

It was at Chernivtsi that this conviction started to grow in me, when I met David Hönig, who was the same age as my father. Uncle Hönig had been a well-established merchant in Oradea and had sought us out as soon as he heard we were in the camp. After a short conversation, he asked us, "Do you realize what a special man your father is? I have never met a more honest man than him." Tears still come to my eyes when I think of that meeting. Then I thought if Uncle Hönig has survived, why should my father not endure it all, a healthy, robust man with such a strong personality?

Many were making plans about how they would live after their return home. I was not afraid. I felt strong enough. If it were necessary, I would be able to support the smaller family who would return home. I had a profession: dressmaking. I also had my baccalaureate in mathematics, which was rare at the time, particularly among women. Before the war I could have got a good administrative or secretarial position with these qualifications.

Our train stopped for the first time in Romania at Sighet. Seeing familiar places again provoked intense reactions. Many threw themselves to the ground. They kissed the earth so that the reality of the situation would sink in. We were really home! We stayed at Sighet for three hours. The Russian soldiers accompanying the train allowed people to go into the town. Many took advantage of this, particularly those from Sighet and the surrounding areas. Others went to look for relatives and friends. Erzsi went too, leaning on Fira's arm and hobbling to the central square. I stayed behind with Manci Hegedüs and the children. My cousin Zsuzsi Szmuk, who was originally from Sighet, went into town. She was shocked to find no one from her family. Her parents had been relatively young. Her two sisters had also perished. The crowd that returned from the town was smaller. The Russians then told us that our destination was Arad, where they had to hand over a group that numbered 1,550.

The train continued its journey towards Satu Mare. The news about our train reached Satu Mare before we did. An enormous crowd of people was waiting for us on the station platform. All the Jews who had returned home had come to the station. It was August now, and nearly all the survivors had already come back. Friends, relatives and sympathizers of the Jews had come too.

The convoy of Russian soldiers did not try to control the outpouring of emotion at this reunion. We all got off the train unhindered, but after the experience at Sighet, they had one condition: we were to leave our luggage on the train. They wanted to make sure we stayed on the train until Arad. I cannot begin to describe those exclamations of joy. Husbands met wives they thought they had lost, parents found their children, brothers met each other again, people found other relatives and friends.

I looked for and found acquaintances from Oradea. Inquiring what was known about Klärmann, one of them replied at once, "He is at home." I felt that father had survived, and tears of joy gushed down.

"But I was not talking about your father," stammered the person. "It's your brother, Duci, who has returned home."

I understood then what it is like for one eye to cry while the other is smiling. I was overwhelmed with joy to hear news of my brother. I rejoiced that he was alive, and yet the loss of my father caused me great sadness and pain. After endless months of worry, I now knew that I would never see him again.

I did not have much time to come to terms with my grief. My brother's brother-in-law, Gabi Schönberger, had heard of our arrival, and he had come to look for us. He insisted that we break our journey. He already knew much about my family. He told us that only Duci had returned. Olga, his older sister and Duci's wife, had died. His parents had not returned, and his other sister had also perished with her husband and children. Duci was currently in Bucharest, and he promised to contact him to come and collect us. He convinced us to stay. There was no hurry to get to Oradea now. I would have reached home with a heavy heart, as I now knew that nobody from the family was waiting for us.

We decided to stay, but nothing in the world was going to separate us from our luggage. When we had been banished from our home and had been deprived of our belongings, we had felt that we would never again be bound to possessions and material values. Yet now the prospect of another loss hurt us, and we felt that we could not be parted from our pitiful rags. Gabi tried in vain to convince us that they were of no use to us, but we did not listen. We were bound sentimentally to these objects, even though they had no value. When the Russian soldier turned his back to us, we got the luggage off the train and pushed it under the wheels to the other side of the train. We threw the luggage over the fence, and when we were sure that it was safe we left the train and walked out of the station empty-handed.

That first night was unforgettable: we were in a real home with family at last. We sat down to dinner for the first time in months, at a table covered with a white tablecloth. We had our first warm baths in a clean tub, and our first night sleeping in a bed with feather pillows and an eiderdown quilt. The next morning started well, too. The telephone rang, and it was for me. Karcsi Mózes from Oradea wanted to be the first to greet me on my return home. I was glad that he was alive, and I was happy that he was thinking of me. He gave me more good news. I learned that my friend Sári was alive and was at her sister's in Arad. Sari's sister survived the war in Arad, in Southern Transylvania, which had remained with Romania, from where the Jews were not deported.

Aunt Janka, my mother's sister, lived in Satu Mare. Although we had little hope of finding her alive, we set out to look for her. We were unsuccessful. We consoled ourselves with the hope that her children were still alive. We had loved Aunt Janka very much. Despite that she had been widowed, she let her children study and establish themselves far from her. With hard work they all did well. Three of them settled in Paris: Miklós became a doctor, Ella a pharmacist and Ilon a teacher. Sándor, the eldest, completed his engineering studies in Vienna, then took part in the resistance movement and left for Russia. They all survived the war, but I did not see them again until after the Iron Curtain was lifted.

As we had nothing left to do in Satu Mare, Erzsi and I impatiently awaited Duci's arrival. He came with the speed that traveling conditions at the time permitted. Trains ran rarely and slowly. Our eventual reunion was indescribable. We just looked at each other, unable to speak, suffocated by tears. After Duci's arrival, we set off despite Gabi's protests. The trains were so crowded that the only place we could find was on the train's outside ledge above the buffers.

My brother was ten years older than me. The year I was born, he left the family home. He studied at the German gymnasium in Brașov and then at the commercial academy in Vienna. We only saw each other during summer holidays. When he finally came back home, I was still a schoolgirl and he was a grown man. It would not have been surprising if he had treated me like a child, or if we had been unable to communicate because of our age difference, but it was not like that. We had a strong sibling bond and more than that, a friendship. Although I was the youngest in the family and he used to affectionately call me "shrimp," he always treated me as an equal and took me seriously. That day on the train, he went on holding my hand and Erzsi's hand. Suddenly he turned to me and like somebody who wants to give great joy said, "Teri, you can study at the university now. I am in a position to make it happen."

The proposition took me by surprise. My refusal would certainly have disappointed him. I felt very different from that blushing girl of fourteen who had once asked her father if she could continue her studies. I was even far removed from that girl of eighteen who had prepared with such tenacity to study abroad. So much had happened since then. At the moment the idea of studying did not appeal to me at all. In fact, it was completely alien to me.

We arrived in Oradea at night. It was still not long after the war. The country was still under Russian occupation. A state of emergency was still in force and it was forbidden to go out at night. We had to wait until dawn to enter the town. When the gate of the main hall opened at last, we were faced with the stark reality of the situation. Where were we to go?

We learned that strangers were living in our former apartment. Duci did not have high hopes about either our parents' home or his own. He was now alone, a bachelor. He waited for someone from the family to return. In time, he renewed his old business relationships and he began to travel a lot. Alone as he was, he did not want a home in Oradea. When he did come, he stayed with one or another of his comrades from his former labour service detachment. Finally he decided that we could go to the home of Zsiga Kenyeres, a close friend.

We set out with heavy hearts. Deportees were still arriving on the night trains. They were disorientated like us, perhaps even more baffled than we were. Representatives from the Jewish Democratic Alliance waited in front of the train station with a cart for those who were returning. Those who had no relatives or friends waiting for them were directed to the newly reopened Jewish Hospital. There, people who came back destitute or orphaned were looked after. We loaded our luggage on the cart and set off on foot behind it. It was impossible not to remember the route we had taken; we had entered the ghetto behind a similar cart. Both journeys were shattering. The two experiences were different, but both times we faced grief and pain. Then we had been plundered and stigmatized as we set off to the unknown. Now, although we were liberated, we felt much more bereft. We had lost our parents, our sister, a multitude of relatives and friends, and we had lost confidence. If the question of what was going to happen to us had tortured us before, now we were overwhelmed with worry about how we were going to go on living.

We separated from the group when we arrived at Zsiga's home. We were received with great love, as were all those who returned. Zsiga's sister prepared a bath, fed us and put us to bed. In the meantime, Zsiga hurried to get Karcsi Mózes, even though it was five in the morning. He woke him with the good news:

"Doctor, come quickly! Duci's sisters Teri and Erzsi have arrived!"

Karcsi came at once. I was in a borrowed night-gown, and I sat crouched behind Erzsi on the bed. For the first time I felt embarrassed that I had lost my two front teeth. Erzsi had begun to walk really well by now, but as she was still limping a little, she put off her meeting with Józsi until the next day. Her fears about this reunion were unjustified, and after she was convinced of this she made a full recovery. She quickly resumed her old identity.

During the war years, Józsi had worked at the local branch of the Foncière Insurance Company in Oradea. That was how he had met Erzsi. After the war, he could have returned to the head office in Budapest, but when he heard that Erzsi was somewhere in a camp in Russia, he decided to wait for her.

Erzsi's first goal was to get our old home back. Our apartment was next to the house in which Zsiga's family was living, at 1 Spiru Haret Street (Bocskai Street). When we went over we were greeted by an unfamiliar sight. The one-story building containing eight apartments had only one family and a caretaker living in it. This one family was living in our apartment. In the other apartments were a shoe factory, offices and half-empty stores. We learned later that of the previous inhabitants, the only ones who had returned were the widows of János Spitz and Sáji. Freiberger, the factory owner, had persuaded them to sell the rights to their apartments for a few pairs of shoes. He made us a similar offer, but Erzsi refused. She claimed her legal rights: the apartment must be returned. The building had enough living space because most of the offices and stores were half empty. After several weeks of requests, our home was to be returned to us when we met certain financial demands. To end the dispute, Duci paid it all. Thus, finally, after many disappointments, we repossessed what was truly ours.

We were at home, yet we did not feel at home. We found some of our furniture scattered throughout the apartment building, particularly the larger items that had been difficult to steal because of their weight. With these we furnished our home. The unpleasantness of our return home did not end here either. We had only the clothes we had brought back from our Russian captivity. We had no pillows, blankets, linens or tablecloths. Erzsi started to ask acquaintances for the things we had left for safekeeping.

The Kulcsár family received us with warmth and friendship. They had offered to help us when the news of our internment in the ghetto had spread. They sympathized sincerely with us at our losses and they cried for our parents. They had looked after our things with care and had kept them clean. We got everything back; nothing was missing. Out of gratitude, we wanted to leave some things with them, but they refused.

We also visited our old neighbour, Aunt Katz. I mentioned earlier that her sons had been spared from the ghetto only to be taken by force in the end. After this she was left on her own and moved from the house. She knew nothing about what had happened to her sons, and after losing them she lost the ground from under her feet and could not remember anything. In the end, she gave us the address of a young woman whom one of her sons had courted. She said she was sure we would find something at her place. The young woman acknowledged that she had received articles of clothing for safekeeping, but she said that she had buried them for fear of looting by the Russians and that most of them were ruined. We were already familiar with that story. Many people refused to give back things they had looked after saying that the Russians had plundered their homes.

As Erzsi and I were marriageable young women, our mother had been taking care of our trousseaus according to tradition. Part of this, along with poor Magda's things, had been left with the Kovacs family. We only recovered a part of this as the Kovacs family had given most of it to a goddaughter who had got married. When Erzsi went to get some of it back, the young woman greeted her with an angry outburst.

"They say many of you perished. In my opinion, too many came back. You should all have stayed where you were!"

When Erzsi told me about this, I was very glad I had not been there.

We were invited to many weddings during those weeks. The young people who had passed through the horrors of war and deportation were in a hurry to get married on their return home. One of the reasons for this phenomenon was that many young people found themselves left without any family and craved family life. I went to a few weddings myself. They all seemed depressing to me, for what kind of family celebrations could they be when the parents of the young couple were not present, nor were relatives and any older people? I was not able to rejoice with them. I could not relax and have fun. When I had dreamed of going home, I never thought of the trials I would have to pass through in those early days, or that each meeting would be one in which joy confronted pain. I caught sight of Paula Gelberger. I was glad that she had survived, but soon learned from her that she remained the sole survivor of her family. She had lost her three siblings, her brother-in-law and their children. Margitka Goldstein was also mourning the loss of twenty close relatives, including her parents and her husband. From her husband's family, fifteen people did not return.

Babus and Zsuzsi Kemény were mourning the loss of twenty close relatives. Karcsi was the sole survivor of his family. Izsak Mózes, his father, had been interned even before the establishment of the ghetto because of a false accusation. He had never returned from the Sárvár internment camp. No one ever saw his mother or his sisters Lilli and Magda again. He tried in vain to trace them. No one among the ex-deportees was able to offer any information, so he deduced that on the platform they had been sent to the left. His only aunt, his mother's elder sister, Irma, had survived in a way that was almost miraculous. She had been deported from Budapest when people were being driven on foot. They walked many hundreds of kilometres without food or water. They were well past Vienna when Irma and two friends slipped away and set out back to Budapest on foot. At sixty-two, she had achieved the impossible: she had escaped.

My family's fate was exceptional, as four out of five siblings were still alive. My sister Ibi was in America, and my brother Duci had survived. In the labour service, he was just as down and out as Erzsi. His return home was due to his comrades and to Karcsi, who was able to shake him periodically from his lethargy. Later, I often thought about the fact that Erzsi and I also had the good fortune that the men who were emotionally closest to us, and about whom we had worried through that time, returned. Listening to others, I realized that many were in a much worse situation than we were. They had ended up in camps near Vienna, Berlin, Dresden, and Hanover, yet most spoke about the horrors of Auschwitz. With few exceptions, nearly everyone had passed through there.

Zsuzsi Rauch spoke of how the senseless roll calls had worn her down, as had the overwhelming thirst, the selections and the emotions accompanying them, and especially the *Blocksperren* (the sealing up the blocks) ordered in such situations.

Lilli Blum spent three months in Auschwitz, before being sent to Frankfurt and then Ravensbrück. This is where the remnants of the labour detachments that survived the retreat of the Don River (an area close to Stalingrad where the Hungarian Army suffered great losses) ended up. In addition to the well-known measures, diabolical methods of extermination were also used at Ravensbrück. In the evening they would order a hot bath and then drive the naked, wet bathers outside and leave them there all night. Most were frozen stiff by morning. Those who survived this torture were machine-gunned.

My cousin, Manci Szmuk, had suffered severely in Auschwitz for two months. Like many others, she lost her parents upon arrival. About the fate of her twenty-two-year-old brother, Erwin whom they called Öcsike, she heard a year after the war from one of Erwin's friends. The friend received the news via the barbed-wire-fence network in Auschwitz that Erwin had been assigned to the *Sonderkommando* (special commando), which meant certain death. The *Sonderkommando* were a group of male inmates whose tasks included "assisting" those about to be murdered, and the disposal of the multitude of murdered Jewish people in crematoria and mass graves. Since the SS wanted to avoid witnesses of their horrible crimes, they also killed the members of the *Sonderkommando* at regular intervals. Manci, with a group of three hundred women, was taken to the Reichenbach camp, where the group was split up for work at the Telefunken and Haganuch enterprises. They manufactured parts for airplanes and submarines. In Auschwitz she met a cousin, Gizi, and they stayed together until January. Being together was a lifesaver. In January 1945, during the coldest days of winter, the Germans evacuated the whole camp on foot. Many died during the march. Manci became separated from Gizi and her group marched to Tratenau, where they worked on digging ditches. As the front approached, the prisoners were taken further west in open freight cars, under constant bombardment. They arrived to Kratzau in March, and were put to work again in factories. The French prisoners working alongside told them that they were working on the V-2 rocket, Germany's "miracle weapon." On May 8, 1945, one day before the end of the war, the Russians liberated them.

Sabina Rosenberg had spent eight months in the town of Bremen. She had worked in the Hanover area cleaning up rubble while the town was being bombed continuously. She had cleaned bricks and stones and put them in piles. They were always working in the street, out in the open. Sabina did not complain about the inhabitants of the town; on the contrary, she remembered with gratitude those who had at times given food to the women who were bent over on the ground. The SS guards, however, remained merciless beasts until the end.

I mentioned before that my friend Sári had also come back from the concentration camps. Of the four Feldheim girls, only Ági was selected on the first day. Sári, Rozsi, and Márta survived the selection. They were still together in Riga, where they had to clear forests, which was the hardest labour. From there they went to Stutthof. Sári had been right when she had advised us against joining their group when we had met at Stutthof. Later they were taken to Leipzig, where they worked in an airplane factory. The enormous hall was cold as an ice pit and the workers from the concentration camp did not have protective clothing. Márta had some good luck in that she ended up in the welding workshop, where it was not quite as freezing cold. Sári worked in the rivets section, and all day long she had to hold the ice-cold iron under the hands of a workman, without any protection, not even a glove. She had been unable to warm her frozen fingers. Soon after arriving home she got married and gave birth to a healthy boy. Sadly, she was not able to enjoy her happy family life for very long. The arthritic disease she developed in the camp worsened and contributed to her early death.

Rozsika Mózes from Șimleul Silvaniei, with whom I had shared a bench in first grade, told us about the ghetto in Șimleul Silvaniei and about our relatives there. This ghetto had been set up outside the town, in a brick factory that was out in the open. They had spent three or four weeks there in very crowded conditions and exposed to the elements. My father's two brothers had been taken from there with their families. Not one of them came back. After the trials she endured at Auschwitz, Rózsika was taken for a while to an underground armament factory near Breslau belonging to the Reinmetal-Krupp trust. There she worked in more favourable conditions but lived under the daily threat of bombing. From there she was moved to Mauthausen, near Vienna. When she thought she was almost home, they took her through Dresden to Buchenwald and then to Bergen-Belsen, forty kilometres from Hanover. Every time she started to talk about what had happened there her voice broke. It was impossible to describe what they had been through in those last weeks. They were given nothing to eat or drink. The people were as thin as skeletons, only skin and bone and covered with lice, when a typhus epidemic broke out. Death wrought havoc as fifty or sixty people died each day and remained unburied. In their efforts to restore order, the British soldiers needed gas masks and bulldozers to cart away the corpses.

Numerous tragedies and misfortunes were recounted. The former political prisoners Irma Berger, Ilus Schützenberger and Vilma Freundlich told me how they had arrived in an internment camp from a Budapest prison and then had gone directly to Bergen-Belsen. Besides the Jewish slave labourers, a huge number of Dutch, French and Spanish political prisoners were gathered in Mauthausen by the end of March. Later on many Russian prisoners of war arrived. Starvation took on such proportions that apparently there were even cases of cannibalism.

In addition to these terrible stories, we still had daily disappointments. For some reason I could not enjoy the present. When I had had to struggle for life itself, for survival, I had been confident and decisive, but now, at home, disappointment and grief overwhelmed me. I became sad and indifferent, and nothing in the outside world aroused my interest. If I had worked, if I had had responsibilities, perhaps I would have overcome my doubts more easily. I had wanted to find work immediately after our arrival but my brother felt that it was his responsibility to take care of us. Finally it was Karcsi who helped me to get through this emotional trauma, this psychological chaos. At this point I would like to point out the thoughtfulness of Karcsi's mother, who at the time of the deportation had thought to preserve the past through a few small valuables. She knew how much her son cherished his photograph album and his books, so she had asked her neighbours to take care of them. No one had touched their home until the end of the war. The neighbours, the family of Gergely Iszály and Aunt Muszka, were determined that their home should remain untouched and that no one should break in. One day a former faculty colleague of Karcsi's arrived and in spite of the neighbours' protests, forced the door of the house and took the books away. The carrier told us later where the books had been taken, and some of them were recovered. Karcsi then had the idea that I could sort out his library and catalogue the remaining books.

Karcsi was working in public health, and in his few free hours he gave consultations in his private office on Pavel Street. The library was in his office and I was able to work there all day. When I suggested to Erzsi that we should eat in a restaurant so that I would not have to spend time cooking, she would not hear of it. After all the garbage we had eaten for months, she wanted to eat homemade food at last. She generously took over all the housework.

I plunged into work. I did not just catalogue the books; reading started to give me pleasure again as well. Then suddenly, a change happened: I wanted to learn again. I wanted to go to university. I thought I could continue where I had been stopped at the age of eighteen. I registered at the Polytechnic (School of Engineering) in Bucharest but I soon realized that I had made a mistake. After my Bucharest experiment, it was Karcsi again who helped me to rediscover myself. "After so much suffering, don't be preoccupied with what would assure a paid job. I will stand by you, as will your brother. Allow yourself, for the first time in your life, to do things and to study what you really want to."

I registered at the university in Cluj to study art history and ethnography, with a minor in French. I know that at the time my choice elicited a few smiles. Some questioned my decision because art history was not taught in high school. The museum in Oradea only had an archaeology section, and it was always closed. None of that concerned me at the time. I was just glad to have found myself again. I could think clearly and logically again. I could study. I could love. I could be creative. There was one thing that I could not yet do, and that I did not want to do. I could not forget.

We Have No Right to Forget!

*A*s I share my memories, I feel that I should high-light certain things. Perhaps the reader will be surprised to learn that when I started to write down my memories, I did not know that they would become a book. It was not my intention to write about my intimate feelings and experiences. My sister Ibi had married Simon Preizler, and they had emigrated to America before the war. Destiny spared her the horrors of deportation, but perhaps she suffered as much as we did. She became ill because she could neither help us nor be with us. Later, she wanted to know everything that had happened to us. In response to her repeated requests, I began to write.

Before me, I have my notebook with the speckled cover. On October 20, 1945, a few weeks after our return home, I began to make notes of the events of the war. Even now, the uncertainty that had taken control of me is apparent from the first sentences:

Where shall I begin, when all this has neither beginning nor end. I feel like a leaf tossed high up by the wind. And after that, the wind carries it into the centre of the most powerful whirlwind and drops it. And now, when the storm has died down, I see with surprise that I am back where I started. I am at home, but I can no longer believe in the calm. I peer around in alarm; where is the new danger lying in wait? I recognize that the ground has been taken from under my feet. I feel that it will be hard to put roots down again.

At first I wrote in my journal every day, remembering and reliving events and trying to clarify what had happened. The wounds were still too fresh. I was not able to continue writing. I also did not feel that my sister was able to look cruel reality in the face. In my letters, I wrote our story in small doses, the way one gives bitter medicine. I watched how my brother-in-law, Magda's husband Lajos Fülöp, reacted to his enormous losses. He did not want to, and indeed could not accept reality. He did not believe what was written in letters and had come from America in the hope that it had all been a terrible mistake. When he learned everything, he burst into tears and collapsed.

We took on a new life of studying, work, and family. The birth of our children brought us joy but did not heal our wounds. The fire kept smouldering under the ashes. Mention of one small thing could cause a succession of irrepressible memories to come flooding to the surface. In 1956, in response to Ibi's request, Erzsi put on paper what had happened. She noted concisely and faithfully all that we had lived through. Under the title *Condemned to Life in the Shadow of Hell*, she put the typed pages between black covers and sent the little book off to our sister. Ibi told me later that since then, every Yom Kippur (the Day of Atonement), she reads the little book from the beginning to the end, remembering our dear parents and those loved ones who died.

I have deviated, however, from the story of how I came to write my memories. The years passed, our children grew up and had their own families. Our son Gábor became a doctor and settled in Israel, where he specialized in orthopedic and trauma surgery. Our daughter Anna, after finishing a degree in geography, got married in Canada and obtained a doctorate in urban planning. Both Anna and Gábor had children who during our visits asked a lot of questions about the family and the past.

Some years later we were visiting our daughter Anna in Canada. She asked me then to put everything onto tape. "I have three sons. I want to keep the memories for them in living words. By the time they grow up, they may not even want to believe what happened if they hear it from some foreign writer."

I was unable to put my memories on tape. The process was strange to me. So, acceding to the wishes of my family, I began to write again. I wrote, but I was only writing for my desk drawer. During the

Four years after my
return, with my
husband, daughter
Anna, and son Gábor.

years of communist dictatorship, I could not even
think of sending the manuscript abroad. In the end,
I got around the censorship by sending three or four
pages of text in my personal letters to Anna or my
sisters. In that way the first hundred pages of typed
text were drawn up, and the children were given
copies, so that each family got a copy. In the sum-

My sister Erzsi with her
husband József Révész.

Family photo
taken on the Bar
Mitzvah of Oren,
one of my Canadian
grandchildren.

mer of 1992, Anna had a Bar Mitzvah celebration in
Ottawa for their second son, Oren, who was thirteen
and had reached the age of majority by Jewish law.
We all gathered together as we had at the golden wedding anniversary of my maternal grandparents. Once
again the consequences of the Holocaust were apparent. We, the grandparents, were the oldest present.
The older generation was missing. Of course, we had
talked about the tragic events of the past. This time,
my children demanded that on my return home I
complete my memoirs.

I set to work. With time I became aware that
it was not only the memory of relatives, friends,

acquaintances, and innocent companions in suffering who had been killed, that made me write. And it was not only to make people remember and to feel the inconceivable horror. It was also to point out the threat of this danger recurring. Young people today, who grew up in a democracy, think just as we did before the war, "That kind of thing could never happen here. It's impossible." They do not know what extreme xenophobia can lead to, how hatred for people and misconceived nationalism know no bounds. I would like to cry out to the whole world, "We will not forget! We have no right to forget!"

We few survivors have no right to forget. The victims should not disappear through the trap door of history. They remain in the minds of the masses only for as long as we remain vigilant in reigniting the eternal flame of their memory. We owe this to our children, their children and the generations to come, especially to the Jews of the Diaspora.

From the moment that I realized these things, writing became a duty. Then, one day, an old and good acquaintance of mine, Imre Fábián, the writer, journalist and chief editor of the publishing company *Literator*, looked me up. For three or four decades he had followed my work in ethnographic research and as a museum curator. He wanted to know what I was doing now. My memoirs captured his interest immediately. After reading a few chapters, he offered his help in publishing it. I am indebted to him for this and am very grateful. From then on, the completion of the book was hastened by Imre Fábián's wish to offer the few survivors and those close to them this piece of writing dedicated to the memory of the Holocaust, on the very day of its commemoration in 1993.

EPILOGUE

The biggest ghetto in the northern part of Transylvania was in Oradea. This was no coincidence as Oradea had been home to a large and vibrant Jewish community before Hitler's rise and the Second World War. In 1944, 25 to 30 per cent of the city's ninety thousand inhabitants were Jewish. While not always accepted, in the course of the years and particularly at the turn of the nineteenth and twentieth centuries, Jews went through great social and cultural development. The Jewish population of Oradea comprised a large number of intellectuals – doctors, lawyers, professors and writers. There were also numerous engineers, distinguished artists, architects, renowned merchants, and artisans who left their imprints on the city's daily life, culture, and architectural profile. Since the turn of the century the Jewish population had contributed a great deal to the renewal of the city's economic and spiritual life. Perhaps this awareness made the town's Jews loyal, and perhaps this was the reason why every Jew thought that the town would refuse to abandon them. That did not happen. In 1944, the Jewish population was deported by the Hungarian fascists while the people of Oradea did not put up any organized resistance.

However, a few beautiful individual manifestations of solidarity were seen, such as secretly feeding hidden Jews, obtaining false papers, and helping in illegal border crossings. First I will mention the names of those who were given the title of Righteous Gentile and whose names are recorded in the Yad Vashem Museum in Jerusalem: Kálmán Appan, Mrs. Appan (born Mária Pataki), Rozália Farkas, Rozália Antal and Julianna Szakadathi. In addition, the following people helped in rescue operations: Sándor Pap, Mária Szabó, József Szücs, Martin Tibulak and Péter Csurka, a former gendarme officer and the son of Mrs. Appan from her first marriage.

I particularly want to honour the memory of Dr. Maxim Virgil, professor at the Greek Catholic Theological Institute, and of Gheorghe Mangra, curator of the institute, who later served as an ordained priest and helped young people who were in hiding. I also honour the memory of Dr. Lajos Szabó the Calvinist pastor, and of Dr. János Ópalotai, the Roman Catholic chaplain who predated baptismal certificates of those living in mixed marriages to prove that they had become Christians. I remember with gratitude Dr. Marina Mihai, who was the Romanian Consul in Oradea at that time, and Dr. Ion Isaiu, her deputy. They were informed about the terrible situation in the ghetto of Oradea by Dr. Miksa Kupfer.

Through official communication they forwarded the news to the Swiss Red Cross. The Consulate's chauffeur, who with the help of other diplomats assisted several escapes, also deserves recognition.

Of the Jews who survived deportations, few returned to Oradea, perhaps two thousand souls. A small, new and young community formed, growing within years to perhaps one-fifth the size it had once been. Many survivors, myself included, wanted to reclaim the wasted years almost at once. I immersed myself in work. I went to university, got married, gave birth to two children. My husband, Dr. Károly Mózes, a young medical doctor, was already much appreciated in the city. Our frame of mind was identical, he supported my efforts and we lived in blissful agreement.

I had not quite finished my university studies when I took a job as a librarian and archivist at the Oradea Historical and Archeological Museum. Unfortunately, due to state policy, one's place of employment was not the choice of the individual, and I worked there only for a short period of time. They transferred me to the Folk Art School, where I taught History of Art and Aesthetics. I took on this position with pleasure, but in a few years I had to change my place of work once again. The authorities put me in charge of Arts and Culture at the local newspaper, and later I became director at a cultural centre.

A few years later I had the opportunity to return to work again for the museum. In time, the state as-

The Oradea Holocaust
Memorial in the
courtyard of the
Orthodox Synagogue.
Photo credit: Lempert
Family Foundation.

signed a new site for the museum, the three-story baroque palace of the former Roman Catholic bishopric. The Ethnographic and Folk Art Department I directed was organized on the top floor. Within a short period of time my group had to collect from the rural villages those ethnic artefacts that were still available, prepare a plan and set up a new permanent exhibit. I finally found the niche I had always wished for. We often set out to survey the region, the villages. We were living during a period when farmers were leaving their villages en masse to relocate in cities. The village population was changing its ethnic clothing for city attire, and industrial goods were flooding the villages. We had to work extremely quickly to save the now doomed folk values so carefully preserved through many generations. After a great deal of hard work we were successful in assembling an enormous collection of ethnographic material and creating a modern, elegant, permanent exhibit.

I retired twenty-five years ago. The permanent exhibit I organized for the Oradea museum lives on unchanged. I feel that I accomplished something lasting during my lifetime. In the course of my active working years and after retirement, I published several books on ethnic art and many scientific essays. In recognition of my work, I received several awards and prizes, among them the Athenaeum and the Ethnos awards in 1994.

During my retirement I often thought of the spiritual legacy and culture created and left behind by generations of Jewish people. I felt it should not go to waste and decided to write about the times I had lived through in Oradea and about the life of the Oradean Jews. First I wrote my memoirs under the title *Bevérzett kötáblák*, published later in English under the title *Staying Human through the Holocaust* and, two years later, the history of the Oradean Jews in the book *Váradi zsidók (The Jews of Oradea)*. Both volumes were soon translated into and published in Romanian as well.

My husband, Dr. Károly Mózes, a specialist in internal medicine and infectious diseases, worked as a Department Head of the Oradea Hospital of Contagious Diseases until the age of eighty-three. His name is credited with the establishment in 1947 in Oradea of the Institute for Medical Technicians, which he directed for two decades. He wrote and published several medical books, among them *Tehnica ingrijirii bolnavului* (Techniques in Caring for the Sick), which reached eight editions. For his widespread and sustained humanitarian activities he was awarded in 2003 the title of Honorary Citizen of the City of Oradea.

When *Staying Human through the Holocaust* was first published in Hungarian fifty years after the Holocaust, it took the city by surprise. The first people who read the book were the typesetters of the printing house, which was still using the old typesetting method. They had been reading with great interest the stories, which were totally unknown to

Photo taken at the festivities where my husband Dr. Károly Mózes was awarded the title of Honorary Citizen of the City of Oradea

them, and were impatiently waiting for updates from the publisher. Held at the Fine Arts Exhibition Hall, the book-signing event was attended by four hundred people. In Oradea I was well known within the framework of my professional activities. People were now realizing with surprise that the fragile woman living a quiet life among them had been a former deportee, a survivor. Many, mostly young people, had no knowledge about the historical circumstances of those faraway times, and now they came face to face with the tragedy the Jewish population had gone through on one side, and what the attitude of the local people towards those shocking events had been on the other.

I also received a great number of letters from acquaintances and from people I didn't know until then, from the furthest points of the world, including Australia, Sweden, Great Britain, Germany, France, United States, and Venezuela. Many individuals looked me up and I made several new friends. To give a better picture of this, I am quoting below from some of the letters I received. This is what Mrs. Károly Elekes, a retired teacher in Oradea, said in her letter:

"I was so shocked by the true, horrific yet objective and hatred free writing of a survivor, that I can not hold back my thoughts of sympathy and that is why I'm writing you. We were living witnesses to this event at the time, we knew and felt that something inhuman was going on, but no one ever fully believed that so much suffering, mourning, such satanical cruelty was to be endured."

"I am a professor at the University of Szeged, specialized in History of Hungarian Literature," wrote in his letter Mihaly Ilia from Hungary, whom I had not known before.

"I would like to tell you that I was impressed and stirred up by your book. I must comment on it ... It impressed me that after so much suffering you are writing about your life without any hatred. I know that in return, we must not forget the atrocities, since today we find many, both here and there, who want to deny this shame, which is not only the shame of the butchers, but that of all who did not raise their voice against it, did not help, want to keep quiet about it and reverse what happened. Your book is a great and authentic argument in the hands of all those who know what happened and don't want to forget, for fear that the horrors may be brought upon us again."

György Klein, a retired journalist in Bucharest, expressed similar thoughts.

"I was touched by the calm objectivity of your book," he wrote. "Perhaps the nearly fifty years which elapsed contributed also to the composed view you were able to take in examining those re-lived events. It is a difficult task to write in a humane fashion about an inhuman era. This fact constitutes perhaps the greatest value of your book."

Radu Reizel, a retired actor in Tel Aviv, declared:

"You spoke also for those who could no longer speak for themselves, who fell to the ground and could never get up; for those who returned from the inferno of Auschwitz, as well as for the ones who haven't been there and can thus find out about what took place there."

Former camp companions expressed their thanks to me for putting on paper what they were unable to relate to their loved ones. In her letter Mrs. József Halmi, from Montreal wrote: "Now, when I relive once again through the printed word the horrors we suffered together ... I want to thank you for myself, my daughter Kati, as well as the younger generation of my family for having written this book, which will preserve the memory of the unbelievably sad tragedy of the Holocaust even for us."

Susana Geroe, a teacher from San Diego, California wrote in the same spirit.

"I'd like to thank you Aunt Teri for having recorded in writing with such meticulousness that painful and difficult era in which our parents' generation lived. It helps us second-generation survivors a great deal to know exactly how those shockingly insane events happened. They are also part of our past and upbringing."

I could continue quoting from letters, but I'll stop here. I'd like to mention, however, one more development directly related to the book's publication.

In the book I recounted of the tragic event which took place in the Guttau (Gutowo) camp after the able-bodied inmates were forced to march in retreat before the advancing Russian Army. The three SS soldiers left in the camp organized a pogrom among the gravely sick, defenceless, wrecked, unclad inmates who remained there. They murdered 150 miserable *Häftlings*. Among those murdered was Kati Kajári, a young woman from Oradea.

Kati Kajári's two brothers survived the Holocaust. Les Keller settled in New York, while his twin brother Gabriel Keller lived in Paris. After learning from my book that their sister lost her life in Gutowo, they decided to find the town where that terrible act took place. They traveled to Poland, went to the town of Gutowo and they were astonished to learn that there had been no camp in the vicinity, nor had anyone heard of mass murder. They immediately thought there was a misunderstanding, as it had been known for a fact that one thousand women had suffered in that camp. The brothers came to see me personally for a more specific description of the place. I pointed out to them that there was a river on the outskirts of our camp, from where we used to bring in water. Armed with this new information, they went back to Poland, where they learned that there were three towns with similar names. They were finally able to determine with help from local authorities where the former camp stood. They searched for and found a survivor, Stanislaw Rueinski, who was a seventeen-year-old witness of those shattering events. They spoke at length to Mr. Rueinski; they found out from him that his parents, Wanda and Julian, had been helping those in need with vegetables, potatoes and water, whenever a possibility presented itself. He knew about six pregnant women who gave birth in the camp under great secrecy. Although they provided the babies with clothing, given the circumstances the little ones died. He further had knowledge of the three SS soldiers who injected the gravely ill women with phenol and, when that didn't bring about the desired outcome, carried out the horrific bloodbath. They chased out the women into an open area and fired at them until their ammunition lasted. Afterwards, they crushed the unfortunate victims with their rifle butts.

People from among the town's residents buried the bloody victims of the tragedy in a mass grave in the local schoolyard. They placed a commemorative black stone column above the grave with the inscription "In Memory of Murdered Jewish Women from Austria, Czechoslovakia, Holland, Yugoslavia, Poland, Romania, Hungary and the Soviet Union – Victims of the Gutowo Branch of Concentration Camp of Stutthof."

The monument, which the brothers found in excellent condition, is cared for by the students of Rumenica's school, a town located about half a mile from Gutowo. I think with gratitude of the town's people, who keep alive the flame of memory. They acknowledged that on All Saints Day they light a memorial candle in remembrance of the victims.

I am also grateful to the Keller brothers for the many, many pictures they took of that place of suffering and the monument – pictures they brought to me, which I can now include here in this edition of the book.

I am sure that my memoirs have both small and large omissions, and for these I apologize. I am recalling events that happened half a century ago. The passage of time has erased from my memory a few names I wished to mention. I was already branded with the yellow star when someone whose name I do not remember greeted me and walked with me on the main street. Similarly, I do not remember the name of the person who offered to smuggle me out

Memorial raised by the community of Gutowo in the memory of women murdered by the Nazis there. Photo: Les Keller.

of the ghetto, and who without any reward saved some of our belongings.

With the help of acquaintances I have tried to identify as many names as possible, but I might have made mistakes with the first names. Finally, I admit that I changed the name of my former begging partner of Lublin. I have no way of knowing whether she would acknowledge today something she did in a desperate and hopeless situation.

I hurt. Revisiting these memories for the English translation hurts me very much. However, it gives me a sense of reassurance and hope to know that by making the book available in English to a wider readership, I can help to ensure that the senseless deaths of those innocent victims won't be forgotten and the light of memory will stay alive.

Teréz Mózes, October 2004